The Black Americans

A History in Their Own Words
1619–1983

THE
BLACK
AMERICANS

A History in Their
Own Words
1619-1983

EDITED BY

Milton Meltzer

Thomas Y. Crowell

New York

Library of Congress Cataloging in Publication Data
Meltzer, Milton, 1915–
   The Black Americans.

   Summary: A history of Black people in the United
States, as told through letters, speeches, articles,
eyewitness accounts, and other documents.
   1. Afro-Americans—History—Sources—Juvenile
literature.   2. United States—Race relations—Sources—
Juvenile literature.   [1. Afro-Americans—History—
sources.   2. Race relations—Sources]   I. Title.
E185.B55 1984   973'.0496   83-46160
ISBN 0-690-04419-4
ISBN 0-690-04418-6 (lib. bdg.)

Designed by Constance Fogler
4 5 6 7 8 9 10

Contents

Foreword

This book is for readers who want to know about the experience of Black Americans and to understand the significance
of their history for our country and our times.

In these pages the people who helped shape history tell their
stories in their own words. This is how the world looked to
them. They speak through their letters, diaries, journals, autobiographies, speeches, resolutions, newspapers, pamphlets,
testimony before courts and in legislative hearings. In these
primary sources black men, women, and children reveal what
they thought and felt, what they did, what they achieved. They
help us see why things are the way they are. And why there is
still much to be done to make this a truly free and equal society.

This history was originally published in three volumes under
the title *In Their Own Words*. It has been revised and updated
for a one-volume edition. While a few documents have been
omitted, new ones have been added to bring the story into the
1980's. Here are the personal accounts of slaves and free Blacks,
of abolitionists, of soldiers in the Civil War, from the great
years of Reconstruction when Blacks voted and held office and
made the laws, and the long dark decades that followed the
overthrow of Reconstruction.

Then come reports of the mass migration from the cotton
fields of the South to the big cities of the North and West, and
the deep changes in black life it brought about. Testimony
follows on the black people's role in a war-torn world, their
achievements in the Harlem Renaissance, the trials of the Great
Depression, the hope offered by the New Deal and the pow-

erful surge of unionism, the rise of the freedom movement in the fifties and sixties, and now, in the eighties, the renewal of black politics that may power major social change in America.

There is a note to introduce each voice. It identifies the speaker and sets the experience in its historic moment. Some of the documents are given in full, but many have been shortened without changing their meaning. Paragraphing and punctuation have been modernized for the sake of easier reading. The source is given at the end of each document. The index will help the reader to locate people, events, and topics.

The Black Americans

A History in Their Own Words 1619-1983

I Saw a Slave Ship

A Dutch warship brought the first cargo of twenty Blacks to Virginia in 1619. Millions of other Blacks were torn from their African homes and carried to the New World before the slave trade was ended. The Africans brought here against their will were not born slaves. In their homelands they were free farmers and herdsmen, craftsmen skilled in pottery and weaving, wood-carving, and ironworking. They were traders and hunters, musicians and dancers, poets and sculptors. Some were princes and warriors, rulers of kingdoms large and small.

In Africa their cultures were rich and varied, as different from one another as were the African peoples themselves. Their colors, their languages, their food, their clothing differed in a range as great as the difference in size between the pygmies and the giant Watusi of Africa.

They came in chains, brought by men who chose to use slaves because they would bring greater profits than the masters could get from their own labor, or from other types of labor.

The Blacks were no better fitted physically to do the hard labor of the agricultural South than were the whites. Nor were

Blacks better fitted psychologically to live in slavery. In the past, it must be remembered, long before America was colonized, whites of many countries had been forced to submit to slavery. With the same variety of brains and emotions, the same range of ability and personality, Blacks could find slavery no more a blessing than could whites.

As traffic with the New World increased, and the demand for slave labor swelled, the buying and selling of Africans gave way to piracy and kidnapping.

Americans did not neglect the profits of the trade. By 1645 a Yankee sea captain was sailing the Rainbowe *out of Boston on the first American voyage for slaves. Down to the War for Independence the slave trade was vital to New England's merchants.*

An early victim of slave trading was Gustavus Vassa. He was born in Benin, in what is now Nigeria, in 1745. At the age of eleven he was kidnapped from his family and sold into slavery. Later he was sold again to traders and chained on a slave ship bound for America. He was sold to a Virginia planter, and then to a British naval officer, and finally to a Philadelphia merchant who gave him the chance to buy his freedom. As a ship's steward he traveled widely. He also worked to bring an end to the slave trade. In 1791 he wrote his autobiography. It contains a passage describing the voyage of the slave ship that carried him to America.

THE FIRST OBJECT which saluted my eyes when I arrived on the coast was the sea, and a slave ship, which was then riding at anchor, and waiting for its cargo. These filled me with astonishment, which was soon connected with terror, when I was carried on board. I was immediately handled, and tossed up to see if I were sound, by some of the crew; and I was now persuaded that I had gotten into a world of bad spirits, and that they were going to kill me. Their complexions too differing so much from ours, their long hair, and the language they spoke (which was very different from any I had ever heard), united to confirm me in this belief.

Indeed, such were the horrors of my views and fears at the moment, that, if ten thousand worlds had been my own, I would have freely parted with them all to have exchanged my condition with that of the meanest slave in my own country. When I looked round the ship too and saw a large furnace or copper boiling, and a multitude of black people of every description chained together, every one of their countenances expressing dejection and sorrow, I no longer doubted of my fate; and, quite overpowered with horror and anguish, I fell motionless on the deck and fainted.

When I recovered a little, I found some black people about me, who I believed were some of those who had brought me on board, and had been receiving their pay; they talked to me in order to cheer me, but all in vain. I asked them if I were not to be eaten by those white men with horrible looks, red faces, and long hair. They told me I was not: and one of the crew brought me a small portion of spirituous liquor in a wine glass; but being afraid of him, I would not take it out of his hand. One of the blacks therefore took it from him and gave it to me, and I took a little down my palate, which, instead of reviving me, as they thought it would, threw me into the greatest consternation at the strange feeling it produced, having never tasted any such liquor before.

Soon after this, the blacks who brought me on board went off, and left me abandoned to despair. I now saw myself deprived of all chance of returning to my native country, or even the least glimpse of hope of gaining the shore, which I now considered as friendly; and I even wished for my former slavery in preference to my present situation, which was filled with horrors of every kind, still heightened by my ignorance of what I was to undergo.

I was not long suffered to indulge my grief; I was soon put

down under the decks, and there I received such a salutation in my nostrils as I had never experienced in my life: so that with the loathsomeness of the stench and crying together, I became so sick and low that I was not able to eat, nor had I the least desire to taste anything.

I now wished for the last friend, death, to relieve me; but soon, to my grief, two of the white men offered me eatables; and, on my refusing to eat, one of them held me fast by the hands, and laid me across, I think, the windlass, and tied my feet, while the other flogged me severely.

I had never experienced anything of this kind before; and although, not being used to the water, I naturally feared that element the first time I saw it, yet nevertheless, could I have got over the nettings, I would have jumped over the side, but I could not; and, besides, the crew used to watch us very closely who were not chained down to the decks, lest we should leap into the water: and I have seen some of these poor African prisoners most severely cut for attempting to do so, and hourly whipped for not eating. This indeed was often the case with myself.

In a little time after, amongst the poor chained men, I found some of my own nation, which in a small degree gave ease to my mind. I inquired of these what was to be done with us? They gave me to understand we were to be carried to these white people's country to work for them. I then was a little revived, and thought, if it were no worse than working, my situation was not so desperate.

But still I feared I should be put to death, the white people looked and acted, as I thought, in so savage a manner; for I had never seen among any people such instances of brutal cruelty; and this not only shewn towards us blacks, but also to some of the whites themselves.

One white man in particular I saw, when we were permitted to be on deck, flogged so unmercifully with a large rope near the foremast, that he died in consequence of it; and they tossed him over the side as they would have done a brute. This made me fear these people the more; and I expected nothing less than to be treated in the same manner.

I could not help expressing my fears and apprehensions to some of my countrymen: I asked them if these people had no country, but lived in this hollow place (the ship)? They told me they did not, but came from a distant one.

"Then," said I, "how comes it in all our country we 'never heard of them!' " They told me because they lived so very far off. I then asked where were their women? Had they any like themselves? I was told they had: "And why," said I, "do we not see them?" They answered, because they were left behind.

I asked how the vessel could go? They told me they could not tell; but that there were cloth put upon the masts by the help of the ropes I saw, and then the vessel went on; and the white men had some spell or magic they put in the water when they liked in order to stop the vessel. I was exceedingly amazed at this account, and really thought they were spirits. I therefore wished much to be from amongst them, for I expected they would sacrifice me: but my wishes were vain; for we were so quartered that it was impossible for any of us to make our escape.

While we stayed on the coast I was mostly on deck; and one day, to my great astonishment, I saw one of these vessels coming in with the sails up. As soon as the whites saw it, they gave a great shout, at which we were amazed; and the more so as the vessel appeared larger by approaching nearer. At last she came to an anchor in my sight and when the anchor was let go I and my countrymen who saw it were lost in astonishment to observe the vessel stop; and were now convinced it was done by magic.

Soon after this the other ship got her boats out, and they came on board of us, and the people of both ships seemed very glad to see each other. Several of the strangers also shook hands with us, black people, and made motions with their hands, signifying I suppose, we were to go to their country; but we did not understand them.

At last, when the ship we were in had got in all her cargo, they made ready with many fearful noises, and we were all put under deck, so that we could not see how they managed the vessel.

But this disappointment was the least of my sorrow. The stench of the hold while we were on the coast was so intolerably loathsome that it was dangerous to remain there for any time, and some of us had been permitted to stay on the deck for the fresh air; but now that the whole ship's cargo were confined together, it became absolutely pestilential.

The closeness of the place, and the heat of the climate, added to the number in the ship, which was so crowded that each had scarcely room to turn himself, almost suffocated us. This produced copious perspirations, so that the air soon became unfit for respiration, from a variety of loathsome smells, and brought on a sickness among the slaves, of which many died, thus falling victims to the improvident avarice, as I may call it, of their purchasers.

This wretched situation was again aggravated by the galling of the chains, now become insupportable; and the filth of the necessary tubs, into which the children often fell, and were almost suffocated. The shrieks of the women, and the groans of the dying, rendered the whole a scene of horror almost inconceivable.

Happily perhaps for myself I was soon reduced so low here that it was thought necessary to keep me almost always on deck; and from my extreme youth I was not put in fetters. In this situation I expected every hour to share the fate of my companions, some of whom were almost daily brought upon deck at the point of death, which I began to hope would soon put an end to my miseries. Often did I think many of the inhabitants of the deep much more happy than myself. I envied them the freedom they enjoyed, and as often wished I could change my condition for theirs.

Every circumstance I met with served only to render my state more painful, and heightened my apprehensions, and my opinion of the cruelty of the whites. One day they had taken a number of fishes; and when they had killed and satisfied themselves with as many as they thought fit, to our astonishment who were on the deck, rather than give any of them to us to eat, as we expected, they tossed the remaining fish into the sea again, although we begged and prayed for some as well as we could, but in vain. Some of my countrymen, being pressed by hunger, took an opportunity, when they thought no one saw them, of trying to get a little privately; but they were discovered, and the attempt procured them some very severe floggings.

One day, when we had a smooth sea and moderate wind, two of my wearied countrymen who were chained together (I was near them at the time), preferring death to such a life of misery, somehow made through the nettings and jumped into the sea: immediately another quite dejected fellow, who on account of his illness was suffered to be out of irons, also followed their example; and I believe many more would very soon have done the same if they had not been prevented by the ship's crew who were instantly alarmed.

Those of us that were the most active were in a moment put down under the deck, and there was such a noise and confusion amongst the people of the ship as I never heard before, to stop her, and get the boat out to go after the slaves. However two of the wretches were drowned, but they got the other, and afterwards flogged him unmercifully for thus attempting to prefer death to slavery.

In this manner we continued to undergo more hardships than

I can now relate, hardships which are inseparable from this accursed trade. Many a time we were near suffocation from the want of fresh air, which we were often without for whole days together. This, and the stench of the necessary tubs, carried off many.

During our passage I first saw flying fishes, which surprised me very much: they used frequently to fly across the ship, and many of them fell on the deck. I also now first saw the use of the quadrant; I had often with astonishment seen the mariners make observations with it, and I could not think what it meant. They at last took notice of my surprise: and one of them, willing to increase it, as well as to gratify my curiosity, made me one day look through it. The clouds appeared to me to be land, which disappeared as they passed along. This heightened my wonder; and I was now more persuaded than ever that I was in another world, and that every thing about me was magic.

At last we came in sight of the island of Barbadoes, at which the whites on board gave a great shout, and made many signs of joy to us. We did not know what to think of this; but as the vessel drew nearer we plainly saw the harbour, and other ships of different kinds and sizes; and we soon anchored amongst them off Bridge-Town.

Many merchants and planters now came on board, though it was in the evening. They put us in separate parcels, and examined us attentively. They also made us jump, and pointed to the land, signifying we were to go there. We thought by this we should be eaten by these ugly men, as they appeared to us; and, when soon after we were all put down under the deck again, there was much dread and trembling.

From *The Interesting Narrative of the Life of Olaudah Equiano, or Gustavus Vassa the African. Written by Himself, 1791.*

Freedom's Journal

FREEDOM'S JOURNAL.

" RIGHTEOUSNESS EXALTETH A NATION."

CORNISH & RUSSWURM. Editors & Proprietors

NEW-YORK, FRIDAY, MARCH 23, 1827.

[VOL. I. No. 2.

MEMOIRS OF CAPT. PAUL CUFFEE.

At this time, being about twenty years of age; he thought himself sufficiently skilled to enter into business on his own account. He laid before his brother David, a plan for opening a commercial intercourse with the state of Connecticut. His brother was pleased with the prospect, they built an open boat and proceeded to sea. Here for the first time his brother found himself exposed to the perils of the ocean, and the horrors of a predatory warfare which was carried on by the Refugees. They had not travelled many leagues before

so well skilled in figures, that he was able to solve all the rules of arithmetical calculation. He then applied himself to navigation, in which by the assistance of a friend he made a rapid progress, and found himself able to engage in nautical and commercial undertakings of great extent.

To be Continued.

From the Christian Spectator.

PEOPLE OF COLOUR.

The many recent movements in behalf of the children of Africa, give strong indications

slaves of one another. V. 42. Comp. Exod. xxi. 16. with Deut. xxiv. 7. See Neh. v. 5, 8. Neither has Christianity interfered in this respect to abolish slavery. Paul has given directions for the mutual deportment of masters and servants, or slaves, as they were in those days."

" By mentioning three several times the slave's subjection to Christ, the apostle mitigated the evils of slavery; for he shewed that both the command and the obedience were limited by the law of Christ."—*M Knight.*

Our own laws recognise involuntary servi-

mighty has established between man and Brute, is so completely removed that not a trace of it shall remain, the march of ameloration in the condition of the blacks will be slow indeed."

Eph. v. 2. 1 Cor. vi. 21, 22.

(To be Continued.

FROM ZION'S HERALD.

A FRAGMENT.

In one of those delightful autumnal ev-

Antislavery newspapers began in 1821, when the white editor Benjamin Lundy launched his Genius of Universal Emancipation *with six subscribers. It was even harder to start the first black newspaper,* Freedom's Journal. *It was founded in New York in March 1827 by John B. Russwurm and Samuel E. Cornish. Young Russwurm had just graduated from Bowdoin with the first college degree given a Black in the United States. When he sailed for Liberia in 1829 to become the new republic's superintendent of education, the Reverend Mr. Cornish carried on as editor.*

In their first editorial, the editors struck out at prejudice and slavery.

WE WISH TO plead our own cause. Too long have others spoken for us. Too long has the publick been deceived by misrepresentations, in things which concern us dearly. . . .

The civil rights of a people being of the greatest value, it shall ever be our duty to vindicate our brethren, when oppressed; to lay the case before the publick. We shall also urge upon our brethren (who are qualified by the laws of the different states), the expediency of using their elective franchise; and of making an independent use of the same. We wish them not to become the tools of party. . . .

It is our earnest wish to make our Journal a medium of intercourse between our brethren in the different states of this great confederacy: that through its columns an expression of our sentiments, on many interesting subjects which concern us, may be offered to the publick: that plans which apparently are beneficial may be candidly discussed and properly weighed; if worth, receive our cordial approbation; if not, our marked disapprobation.

Useful knowledge of every kind, and everything that relates to Africa, shall find a ready admission into our columns; and as that vast continent becomes daily more known, we trust that many things will come to light, proving that the natives of it are neither so ignorant nor stupid as they have generally been supposed to be. . . .

We would not be unmindful of our brethren who are still in the iron fetters of bondage. They are our kindred by all the ties of nature. . . .

From the press and the pulpit we have suffered much by being incorrectly represented. . . .

Our vices and our degradation are ever arrayed against us, but our virtues are passed by unnoticed. And what is still more lamentable, our friends, to whom we concede all the principles of humanity and religion, from these very causes seem to have fallen into the current of popular feeling and are imperceptibly floating on the stream—actually living in the practice of prejudice, while they abjure it in theory, and feel it not in their hearts.

Is it not very desirable that such should know more of our

actual condition; and of our efforts and feelings, that in forming or advocating plans for our amelioration, they may do it more understandingly? In the spirit of candor and humility we intend by a simple representation of facts to lay our case before the public, with a view to arrest the progress of prejudice, and to shield ourselves against the consequent evils. We wish to conciliate all and to irritate none, yet we must be firm and unwavering in our principles, and persevering in our efforts.

If ignorance, poverty and degradation have hitherto been our unhappy lot; has the Eternal decree gone forth, that our race alone are to remain in this state, while knowledge and civilization are shedding their enlivening rays over the rest of the human family? . . .

The interesting fact that there are five hundred thousand free persons of colour, one half of whom might peruse, and the whole be benefitted by the publication of the Journal; that no publication, as yet, has been devoted exclusively to their improvement—that many selections from approved standard authors, which are within the reach of few, may occasionally be made—and more important still, that this large body of our citizens have no public channel—all serve to prove the real necessity, at present, for the appearance of the *Freedom's Journal.*

From *Freedom's Journal*, March 16, 1827.

Walker's Appeal

David Walker didn't have to be told that if a slave struck his master it meant death. Freeborn in North Carolina, but the son of a slave father, he knew slavery—what the South called the "peculiar institution"—firsthand. His hatred of slavery drove him to Boston, where he sold old clothes and subscriptions to Freedom's Journal. *He burned to deliver his own message to the slaves, and in 1829 he published his pamphlet,* Walker's Appeal. *It was a harsh outcry against the injustices done the Black, and an open call to rise up in arms and overthrow slavery. In a year it ran through three editions, terrifying the slaveholders. Georgia offered $10,000 for Walker taken alive and $1,000 for him dead. State after state in the South made it a crime to circulate the* Appeal, *and a crime to teach Blacks to read. Suddenly, Walker disappeared; some said murdered. But the* Appeal *went on, slashing like a sword at ignorance and docility.*

MY BELOVED BRETHREN: The Indians of North and of South America—the Greeks—the Irish, subjected under the king of Great Britain—the Jews, that ancient people of the Lord—the inhabitants of the islands of the sea—in fine, all the inhabitants of the earth (except however, the sons of Africa), are called *men*, and of course are, and ought to be free. But we (coloured people), and our children are *brutes!!* and of course are, and *ought to be* SLAVES to the American people and their children forever!! to dig their mines and work their farms; and thus go on enriching them, from one generation to another with our *blood* and our *tears!!!!* . . .

They think because they hold us in their infernal chains of slavery, that we wish to be white, or of their color—but they are dreadfully deceived—we wish to be just as it pleased our Creator to have made us, and no avaricious and unmerciful wretches have any business to make slaves of, or hold us in slavery. How would they like for us to make slaves of, and hold them in cruel slavery, and murder them as they do us? . . .

Fear not the number and education of our *enemies*, against whom we shall have to contend for our lawful right; guaranteed to us by our Makers; for why should we be afraid, when God is, and will continue (if we continue humble), to be on our side?

The man who would not fight under our Lord and Master Jesus Christ, in the glorious and heavenly cause of freedom and of God—to be delivered from the most wretched, abject and servile slavery, that ever a people was afflicted with since the foundation of the world, to the present day—ought to be kept with all of his children or family, in slavery, or in chains, to be butchered by his *cruel enemies*. . . .

If you commence, make sure work—do not trifle, for they will not trifle with you—they want us for their slaves, and think nothing of murdering us in order to subject us to that wretched condition—therefore, if there is an *attempt* made by us, kill or be killed. Now, I ask you, had you not rather be killed than to be a slave to a tyrant, who takes the life of your mother, wife, and dear little children? Look upon your mother, wife, and children, and answer God Almighty; and believe this, that it is no more harm for you to kill a man, who is trying to kill you, than it is for you to take a drink of water when thirsty; in fact, the man who will stand still and let another murder him, is worse than an infidel, and, if he has common sense, ought not to be pitied. . . .

Remember Americans, that we must and shall be free and enlightened as you are, will you wait until we shall, under God, obtain our liberty by the crushing arm of power? Will it not be dreadful for you? I speak Americans for your good. We must and shall be free I say, in spite of you. You may do your best to keep us in wretchedness and misery, to enrich you and your children, but God will deliver us from under you. And wo, wo, will be to you if we have to obtain our freedom by fighting. Throw away your fears and prejudices then, and enlighten us and treat us like men, and we will like you more than we do now hate you, and tell us no more about colonization, for America is as much our country, as it is yours.

Treat us like men, and there is no danger but we will all live in peace and happiness together. For we are not like you, hard hearted, unmerciful, and unforgiving. What a happy country this will be, if the whites will listen. What nation under heaven will be able to do any thing with us, unless God gives us up into its hand?

But Americans, I declare to you, while you keep us and our children in bondage, and treat us like brutes, to make us support you and your families, we cannot be your friends. You do not look for it, do you? Treat us then like men, and we will be your friends. And there is not a doubt in my mind, but that the whole of the past will be sunk into oblivion, and we yet, under God, will become a united and happy people. The whites may say it is impossible, but remember that nothing is impossible with God.

From *Walker's Appeal, in Four Articles: Together with a Preamble, to the Colored Citizens of the World, but in particular, and very expressly, to those of the United States of America, written in Boston, State of Massachusetts, September 28, 1829.*

Nat Turner's Revolt

In 1831, a year after David Walker vanished, the Virginia slave *Nat Turner,* as if in reponse to Walker's Appeal, *led seventy Blacks in a revolt that slaughtered fifty-seven men, women, and children in rural Southampton County. Troops rushed in to put down the uprising and killed over one hundred Blacks—the innocent as well as the insurrectionists—in a savage massacre. Wild rumors and alarms swept through the South. The apparition of slave revolt made sleep uneasy.*

But it was not the first time. Rebellions began in the seventeenth century, aboard the first slave ships bound for the American colonies. As slaves continued to fight for their freedom, the bondage laws were made harsher and harsher. Gabriel Prosser's large-scale plot to attack Richmond with a thousand men in 1800 was betrayed at the last moment and the slave preacher and his followers hanged. Another plot, led by the free Black Denmark Vesey, was exposed in Charleston in 1822 and Vesey and thirty-six others executed.

Nat Turner was educated and a preacher. He believed God had chosen him to deliver his people from bondage. As he lay in prison, waiting to go to the gallows, he made this statement about his life and his mission.

I WAS THIRTY-ONE years of age the second of October last, and born the property of Benjamin Turner, of this county. In my childhood a circumstance occurred which made an indelible impression on my mind, and laid the groundwork of that enthusiasm which has terminated so fatally to many, both white and black, and for which I am about to atone at the gallows. It is here necessary to relate this circumstance. Trifling as it may seem, it was the commencement of that belief which has grown with time; and even now, sir, in this dungeon, helpless and forsaken as I am, I cannot divest myself of.

Being at play with other children, when three or four years old, I was telling them something, which my mother, overhearing, said it had happened before I was born. I stuck to my story, however, and related some things which went, in her opinion, to confirm it. Others being called on, were greatly astonished, knowing that these things had happened, and caused them to say, in my hearing, I surely would be a prophet, as the Lord had shown me things that had happened before my birth. And my mother and grandmother strengthened me in this my first impression, saying, in my presence, I was intended for some great purpose, which they had always thought from certain marks on my head and breast. . . .

On the 12th of May, 1828, I heard a loud noise in the heavens, and the Spirit instantly appeared to me and said the Serpent was loosened, and Christ had laid down the yoke he had borne for the sins of men, and that I should take it on and fight against the Serpent, for the time was fast approaching when the first should be last and the last should be first.

Question: "Do you not find yourself mistaken now?"

Answer: "Was not Christ crucified?"

And by signs in the heavens that it would make known to me when I should commence the great work, and until the first sign appeared I should conceal it from the knowledge of men; and on the appearance of the sign (the eclipse of the sun, last February), I should arise and prepare myself, and slay my enemies with their own weapons.

And immediately on the sign appearing in the heavens, the seal was removed from my lips, and I communicated the great work laid out for me to do, to four in whom I had the greatest confidence (Henry, Hark, Nelson, and Sam). It was intended by us to have begun the work of death on the 4th of July last. Many were the plans formed and rejected by us, and it affected my mind to such a degree that I fell sick, and the time passed without our coming to any determination how to commence— still forming new schemes and rejecting them, when the sign appeared again, which determined me not to wait longer.

Since the commencement of 1830 I had been living with Mr. Joseph Travis, who was to me a kind master, and placed the greatest confidence in me; in fact, I had no cause to complain of his treatment to me. On Saturday evening, the 20th of August, it was agreed between Henry, Hark, and myself, to prepare a dinner the next day for the men we expected, and then to concert a plan, as we had not yet determined on any. Hark, on the following morning, brought a pig, and Henry brandy; and being joined by Sam, Nelson, Will, and Jack, they prepared in the woods a dinner, where, about three o'clock I joined them. . . .

I saluted them on coming up, and asked Will how came he

there. He answered, his life was worth no more than others, and his liberty as dear to him. I asked him if he thought to obtain it. He said he would, or lose his life. This was enough to put him in full confidence. Jack, I knew, was only a tool in the hands of Hark. It was quickly agreed we should commence at home (Mr. J. Travis') on that night; and until we had armed and equipped ourselves, and gathered sufficient force, neither age nor sex was to be spared—which was invariably adhered to. We remained at the feast until about two hours in the night, when we went to the house and found Austin. . . .

I took my station in the rear, and, as it was my object to carry terror and devastation wherever we went, I placed fifteen or twenty of the best armed and most to be relied on in front, who generally approached the houses as fast as their horses could run. This was for two purposes—to prevent their escape, and strike terror to the inhabitants; on this account I never got to the houses, after leaving Mrs. Whitehead's, until the murders were committed, except in one case. I sometimes got in sight in time to see the work of death completed; viewed the mangled bodies as they lay, in silent satisfaction, and immediately started in quest of other victims.

Having murdered Mrs. Waller and ten children, we started for Mr. Wm. Williams'—having killed him and two little boys that were there; while engaged in this, Mrs. Williams fled and got some distance from the house, but she was pursued, overtaken, and compelled to get up behind one of the company, who brought her back, and after showing her the mangled body of her lifeless husband, she was told to get down and lay by his side, where she was shot dead.

The white men pursued and fired on us several times. Hark had his horse shot under him, and I caught another for him as it was running by me; five or six of my men were wounded, but none left on the field. Finding myself defeated here, I instantly determined to go through a private way, and cross the Nottoway River at the Cypress Bridge, three miles below Jerusalem, and attack that place in the rear, as I expected they would look for me on the other road, and I had a great desire to get there to procure arms and ammunition. After going a short distance in this private way, accompanied by about twenty men, I overtook two or three, who told me the others were dispersed in every direction.

On this, I gave up all hope for the present; and on Thursday night, after having supplied myself with provisions from Mr. Travis', I scratched a hole under a pile of fence-rails in a field, where I concealed myself for six weeks, never leaving my hiding-place but for a few minutes in the dead of the night to get water, which was very near. Thinking by this time I could venture out, I began to go about in the night, and eavesdrop the houses in the neighborhood; pursuing this course for about a fortnight, and gathering little or no intelligence, afraid of speaking to any human being, and returning every morning to my cave before the dawn of the day.

I know not how long I might have led this life, if accident had not betrayed me. A dog in the neighborhood passing by my hiding-place one night while I was out, was attracted by some meat I had in my cave, and crawled in and stole it, and was coming out just as I returned. A few nights after, two Negroes having started to go hunting with the same dog, and passed that way, the dog came again to the place, and having just gone out to walk about, discovered me and barked; on which, thinking myself discovered, I spoke to them to beg concealment. On making myself known, they fled from me. Knowing then they would betray me, I immediately left my hiding-place, and was pursued almost incessantly, until I was taken, a fortnight afterwards, by Mr. Benjamin Phipps, in a little hole I had dug out with my sword, for the purpose of concealment, under the top of a fallen tree.

During the time I was pursued, I had many hair-breadth

escapes, which your time will not permit you to relate. I am here loaded with chains, and willing to suffer the fate that awaits me.

From *The Confessions of Nat Turner, the leader of the late insurrection in Southampton, Va.*, edited by Thomas R. Gray, 1831.

Picking Cotton

The purpose of slavery was to provide the labor that could bring profits to the master. Most Southern farmers had small holdings and few or no slaves. The wealthy slaveholders, who ruled the South's economy and politics, owned huge plantations with hundreds and thousands of slaves. Whether the estate was large or small, an efficient owner made money out of his slaves. Down to the Civil War it was more profitable for the planter to keep his workers in bondage than to use free labor.

*Defenders of slavery claimed the bondsmen cheerfully ac-
cepted their condition. But how did the slave look at the year-
round routine of growing cotton? One record of what it was like
in Louisiana was left by the ex-slave Solomon Northup. Northup, born free, was kidnapped in Washington and enslaved for
twelve years in Louisiana. His story, taken down by a Northerner
in the year of his rescue, 1853, sold 27,000 copies in two years.*

THE GROUND IS prepared by throwing up beds or ridges,
with the plough—back-furrowing, it is called. Oxen and mules,
the latter almost exclusively, are used in ploughing. The women
as frequently as the men perform this labor, feeding, currying,
and taking care of their teams, and in all respects doing the
field and stable work, precisely as do the ploughboys of the
North.

The beds, or ridges, are six feet wide, that is, from water
furrow to water furrow. A plough drawn by one mule is then
run along the top of the ridge or center of the bed, making the
drill, into which a girl usually drops the seed, which she carries
in a bag hung round her neck. Behind her comes a mule and
harrow, covering up the seed, so that two mules, three slaves,
a plough and harrow, are employed in planting a row of cotton.

This is done in the months of March and April. Corn is
planted in February. When there are no cold rains, the cotton
usually makes its appearance in a week. In the course of eight
or ten days afterwards the first hoeing is commenced. This is
performed in part, also, by the aid of the plough and mule.
The plough passes as near as possible to the cotton on both
sides, throwing the furrow from it. Slaves follow with their
hoes, cutting up the grass and cotton, leaving hills two feet and
a half apart. This is called scraping cotton.

In two weeks more commences the second hoeing. This time
the furrow is thrown towards the cotton. Only one stalk, the
largest, is now left standing in each hill. In another fortnight

it is hoed the third time, throwing the furrow towards the cotton in the same manner as before, and killing all the grass between the rows.

About the first of July, when it is a foot high or thereabouts, it is hoed the fourth and last time. Now the whole space between the rows is ploughed, leaving a deep water furrow in the center. During all these hoeings the overseer or driver follows the slaves on horseback with a whip, such as has been described. The fastest hoer takes the lead row. He is usually about a rod in advance of his companions. If one of them passes him, he is whipped. If one falls behind or is a moment idle, he is whipped. In fact, the lash is flying from morning until night, the whole day long. The hoeing season thus continues from April until July, a field having no sooner been finished once, than it is commenced again.

In the latter part of August begins the cotton picking season. At this time each slave is presented with a sack. A strap is fastened to it, which goes over the neck, holding the mouth of the sack breast high, while the bottom reaches nearly to the ground. Each one is also presented with a large basket that will hold about two barrels. This is to put the cotton in when the sack is filled. The baskets are carried to the field and placed at the beginning of the rows.

When a new hand, one unaccustomed to the business, is sent for the first time into the field, he is whipped up smartly, and made for that day to pick as fast as he can possibly. At night it is weighed, so that his capability in cotton picking is known. He must bring in the same weight each night following. If it falls short, it is considered evidence that he has been laggard, and a greater or less number of lashes is the penalty.

An ordinary day's work is two hundred pounds. A slave who is accustomed to picking is punished if he or she brings in a less quantity than that. There is a great difference among them as regards this kind of labor. Some of them seem to have a natural knack, or quickness, which enables them to pick with great celerity, and with both hands, while others, with whatever practice or industry, are utterly unable to come up to the ordinary standard. Such hands are taken from the cotton field and employed in other business. . . .

The hands are required to be in the cotton field as soon as it is light in the morning, and, with the exception of ten or fifteen minutes, which is given them at noon to swallow their allowance of cold bacon, they are not permitted to be a moment idle until it is too dark to see and when the moon is full they often times labor till the middle of the night. They do not dare to stop even at dinner time, nor return to the quarters, however late it be, until the order to halt is given by the driver.

The day's work over in the field, the baskets are "toted," or in other words, carried to the gin-house, where the cotton is weighed. No matter how fatigued and weary he may be—no matter how much he longs for sleep and rest—a slave never approaches the gin-house with his basket of cotton but with fear. If it falls short in weight—if he has not performed the full task appointed him, he knows that he must suffer. And if he has exceeded it by ten or twenty pounds, in all probability his master will measure the next day's task accordingly.

So, whether he has too little or too much, his approach to the gin-house is always with fear and trembling. Most frequently they have too little, and therefore it is they are not anxious to leave the field. After weighing, follow the whippings; and then the baskets are carried to the cotton house, and their contents stored away like hay, all hands being sent in to tramp it down. If the cotton is not dry, instead of taking it to the gin-house at once, it is laid upon platforms, two feet high, and some three times as wide, covered with boards or plank, with narrow walks running between them.

This done, the labor of the day is not yet ended, by any means. Each one must then attend to his respective chores.

One feeds the mules, another the swine—another cuts the wood, and so forth; besides, the packing is all done by candle light. Finally, at a late hour, they reach the quarters, sleepy and overcome with the long day's toil. Then a fire must be kindled in the cabin, the corn ground in a small hand-mill, and supper, and dinner for the next day in the field, prepared. All that is allowed them is corn and bacon, which is given out at the corncrib and smoke-house every Sunday morning. Each one receives, as his weekly allowance, three and a half pounds of bacon, and corn enough to make a peck of meal. That is all—no tea, coffee, sugar, and with the exception of a very scanty sprinkling now and then, no salt. . . .

The softest couches in the world are not to be found in the log mansion of the slave. The one whereon I reclined, year after year, was a plank twelve inches wide and ten feet long. My pillow was a stick of wood. The bedding was a coarse blanket, and not a rag or shred beside. Moss might be used, were it not that it directly breeds a swarm of fleas.

The cabin is constructed of logs, without floor or window. The latter is altogether unnecessary, the crevices between the logs admitting sufficient light. In stormy weather the rain drives through them, rendering it comfortless and extremely dis- agreeable. The rude door hangs on great wooden hinges. In one end is constructed an awkward fire-place.

An hour before day light the horn is blown. Then the slaves arouse, prepare their breakfast, fill a gourd with water, in an- other deposit their dinner of cold bacon and corn cake, and hurry to the field again. It is an offence invariably followed by a flogging, to be found at the quarters after daybreak. Then the fears and labors of another day begin; and until its close there is no such thing as rest. He fears he will be caught lagging through the day; he fears to approach the gin-house with his basket-load of cotton at night; he fears, when he lies down, that he will oversleep himself in the morning. Such is a true, faithful, unexaggerated picture and description of the slave's daily life, during the time of cotton-picking, on the shores of Bayou Boeuf.

From *Twelve Years a Slave*, by Solomon Northup, 1853.

Slavery Days

In the middle 1930's fieldworkers of the Federal Writers' Project were assigned to travel through the Southern states to gather the life histories of ex-slaves. The former slaves were now seventy-five to over one hundred years old. A set of simple instructions and questions helped get them to recall and talk freely about the time of slavery. Dozens of subjects were covered by the questions. The recollections and father-to-son traditions jotted down

by the interviewers proved a folk history of slavery—"history from the bottom up"—that adds evidence to such slave narratives as Northup's, recorded during the abolitionist period.

In what follows you hear the voices of the ex-slaves of one state, Virginia, as they talk about several aspects of their lives in slavery.

MY MA WAS COOK, an' I used to clean house. I liked dustin' part best 'cause I could git my hands on de books and pictures dat ole Marse had spread out all over his readin' room. Ole Missus used to watch me mos' times to see dat I didn't open no books. Sometimes she would close up all de books an' put 'em on de shelf so's I couldn't see 'em, but Marse never liked her messin' wid his things. Dere was one book dat I was crazy about . . . didn't know nothin' of what it was 'bout, but it had a lot of pictures, Injuns and Kings and Queens wid reefs [wreaths] on dey heads. Used to fly to dat book and hold it lookin' at de pictures whilst I dusted wid de other hand.

One day while in de readin' room I heard a step comin' fum de kitchen. 'Fore I could move, de door open an' someone came in. Thought sure it was Missus, but it was Marsa. He looked at me an' saw what I was doin,' but he never said nothin.' I closed de book up an' put it back in place. Was scared fo' many a day dat I was gonna git a hidin,' but guess he never tole Missus after all.

Hired Out

I recollect how Miss Sarah Anne hired out a bunch of her slaves to de railroad dat dey was buildin' thew de woods. Dey hires slaves in one place an' use dem to cut down de timber and saw it up into ties. Den dey hire hundreds of 'em in de next place. Well, when de railroad come to Pamplin, dey hired all de slaves, an' Miss Sarah Anne's too. An' chile, you orter hear dem slaves singin' when dey go to work in de mornin'. Dey all start a-comin' from all d'rections wid dey ax on dey shoulder, an' de mist an' fog be hangin' over de pines, an' de sun jus' breakin' 'cross de fields. Den de slaves start to sing:

> *A col' frosty mo'nin'*
> *De niggers feelin' good*
> *Take yo' ax upon you' shoulder*
> *Nigger, talk to de wood.*

An' de woods jus' a-ringin' wid dis song. Hundreds of dem jus' a-singin' to beat de ban'. Dey be paired up to a tree, an' dey mark de blows by de song. Fus' one chop, den his partner, an' when dey sing TALK dey all chop togedder; an' purty soon dey get de tree ready for to fall an' dey yell "Hi" an' de slaves all scramble out de way quick 'cause you can't tell what way a pine tree gonna fall. An' sometime dey sing it like dis:

> *Dis time tomorrer night*
> *Where will I be?*
> *I'll be gone, gone, gone*
> *Down to Tennessee.*

De slaves sing dis sorrowful, 'cause some of 'em know dey gonna be beat or whipped, or sol' away. Course Miss Sarah Anne ain't sol' none, but ole man Derby what had hundreds wud sell some of his'n ev'y time ole slave trader come 'round. No matter what a slave's hire bring, ole slave trader could beat de price.

Food and Clothing

Now you see, dar was good marsas an' bad marsas. Marsas what was good saw dat slaves lived decent an' got plenty to eat. Marsas what was mean an' skinflinty throw 'em scraps like dey feed a dog an' don' care what kind of shack dey live in. Warn't no law sayin' dey got to treat slaves decent. . . .

Hoe-cakes was made of meal. You mix a cup of meal wid water an' pat it into small cakes. Greast it if you got grease— dat keep it from stickin.' Den you rake out de ashes an' stick it on de hoe into de bottom of de fire an' cover it up. Let it cook 'bout five minutes, den take it out, rub de ashes off an' pick out de splinters. Wash it off wid warm water an' eat it fo' it cools. Don't taste like nothin' if you let it get cold. . . .

De women folks would spin de cotton, card it and weave it. Den dey could cut it an' sew it. Had to turn everything dey made over to marsa—warn't 'lowed to take nothin' fo' yo'self. Couldn't spin nuf clothes for ev'body. All dat didn't git home-spun got guano bags.

In Sickness and Death

Anytime a slave got sick or had de misery, ole Marsa Tom would give him a dram of whiskey. Sometimes I'd go to Marsa Tom an' say, "Marsa, I done got a terr'ble cole f'om someplace. Don't spec I gonna be able to work today." Marsa laugh an' say, "Come on, you black rascal. Nothin' wrong wid you. All you want is a drink of whiskey." Den he give it to me. An' sometime I go back to him de second or third time, an' tell him de same thing. Sometime he remember he already give it to me an' sometime he don't. All depend on how much Marsa Tom done took hisself. . . .

Mother always said you got to feed sickness 'cause it's in de blood. Said dat rubbin' was bad, 'cause it jus' rub de pain inside. Mother had a tea fo' ev'y which complaint, even one she used to give fo' child birth. . . .

Dr. Dick taught papa all dey was to be knowed 'bout de medicine business. Was one slave woman dat even Dr. Dick gave up fo' daid. Papa give her some special roots. I ain't gonna tell you what. An' de nex' day de woman could swaller and eat. Papa taught me all de roots. Dere's de master weed, an' de Peter's roots, and May Apple, an' Sweet William, an' plenty mo'. You got to know how to fix 'em, dough. . . .

Now on our place when a slave die, ole overseer would go to de saw mill an' git a twelve inch board, shape it wid a point head and foot, an' dig a grave to fit it. Slaves tie de body to de board dressed in all de puhson's clothes 'cause wouldn't no one ever wear 'em. Whoever wear a dead man's clothes gonna die hisself real soon, dey used to say. John Jasper would go from place to place preachin' funerals fo' slaves. Sometimes dem slaves been daid an' buried a year or mo'. Den one Sunday ole Jasper would preach one big sermon over dem all.

Getting Married

Didn't have to ask Marsa or nothin.' Just go to Ant Sue an' tell her you want to git mated. She tell us to think 'bout it hard fo' two days, 'cause marryin' was sacred in de eyes of Jesus. Arter two days Mose an' I went back an' say we done thought 'bout it an' still want to git married. Den she called all de slaves arter tasks to pray fo' de union dat God was gonna make. Pray we stay together an' have lots of chillun an' none of 'em git sol' 'way from de parents. Den she lay a broomstick 'cross de sill of de house we gonna live in an' jine our hands together. Fo' we step over it she ast us once mo' if we was sho' we wanted to git married. 'Course we say yes. Den she say, "In de eyes of Jesus step into Holy land of mat-de-money." When we step 'cross de broomstick, we was married. Was bad luck to tech de broomstick. Fo'ks always stepped high 'cause dey didn't want no spell cast on 'em—Ant Sue used to say whichever one teched de stick was gonna die fust. . . .

*

When you married, you had to jump over a broom three times. Dat was de license. If master seen two slaves together too much he would tell 'em dey was married. Hit didn't make no difference if you wanted to or not; he would put you in de same cabin an' make you live together. . . .

Marsa used to sometimes pick our wives fo' us. If he didn't have on his place enough women for the men, he would wait on de side of de road till a big wagon loaded with slaves come by. Den Marsa would stop de ole nigger-trader and buy you a woman. Wasn't no use tryin' to pick one, cause Marsa wasn't gonna pay but so much for her. All he wanted was a young healthy one who looked like she could have children, whether she was purty or ugly as sin. Den he would lead you an' de woman over to one of de cabins and stan' you on de porch. He wouldn't go in. No Sir. He'd stan' right dere at de do' an' open de Bible to de first thing he come to an' read somepin real fast out of it. Den he close up de Bible an' finish up wid dis verse:

> *Dat you' wife*
> *Dat you' husban'*
> *I'se you' marsa*
> *She you' missus*
> *You married.*

The Funniest Things

Charlie could make up songs 'bout de funnies' things. One day Charlie saw ole Marsa comin' home wid a keg of whiskey on his ole mule. Cuttin' 'cross de plowed field, de ole mule slipped an' Marsa come tumblin' off. Marsa didn't know Charlie saw him, an' Charlie didn't say nothin'. But soon arter a visitor come an' Marsa called Charlie to de house to show off what he knew. Marsa say, "Come here, Charlie, an' sing some rhymes fo' Mr. Henson." "Don't know no new ones, Marsa," Charlie answered. "Come on, you black rascal, give me a rhyme fo' my company—one he ain't heard." So Charlie say, "All right, Marsa, I give you a new one effen you promise not to whup me." Marsa promised, an' den Charlie sung de rhyme he done made up in his haid 'bout Marsa:

> *Jackass rared*
> *Jackass pitch*
> *Throwed ole Marsa in de ditch.*

Well, Marsa got mad as a hornet, but he didn't whup Charlie, not dat time anyway. An' chile, don' you know us used to set de flo' to dat dere song? Mind you, never would sing it when Marsa was roun', but when he wasn't we'd swing all roun' de cabin singin' 'bout how old Marsa fell off de mule's back. Charlie had a bunch of verses:

> *Jackass stamped*
> *Jackass neighed*
> *Throwed ole Marsa on his haid.*

Don' recoll' all dat smart slave made up. But ev'ybody sho' bus' dey sides laughin' when Charlie sung de las' verse:

> *Jackass stamped*
> *Jackass hupped*
> *Marsa hear you slave,*
> *   you sho' git whupped.*

Runaways

I heard a rap—bump! bump! on my do'. I answered a-hollerin! Den someone whispered, "Hush! Don' say nothin', but let me in!" I let her in. Lawd, dat 'oman was all out of bref an' a-beggin'—"Kin I stay here tonight?" I tole her she could, so dar de 'oman done sleep right dar behin' me in my bed all night. I knowed she had runned away, an' I was gonna do my part to he'p her 'long. I took an' heared de hosses an' talkin' in de woods. Dogs jes' a-barkin'. I peeped out de winder an' saw dem white folks go by. I didn't move, I was so scared dey was gonna come in de cabin an' search fo' dat po' 'oman. Nex' mornin' she stole out from dar, an' I ain't never seen her no mo'. . . .

We was workin' on de road one day, an' two fellows named Body an' Ned Coleman slipped off an' ev'y day would sleep in leaves an' hin' trees, an' durin' de night dey would travel. Dey was tryin' to make it to Ohio where you was free. Dey traveled on an' on, night after night. One night dey stopped at a place an' asked for some food an' tol' what dey was doin', an' de people tol' dem dey was 'bout one night's journey from de line. De nex' day dey went to sleep in a wooded place, an' after a while dey heard a noise, an' it was two Newfoundland dogs dat was grazin' de cattle. Dey ran, but de dogs caught dem, an' dey was sent back to de railroad. When dey come back to de railroad de boss beat dem. De boss sent fo' de master to come an' git dem. Dey tole me how near dey was to de line when dem dogs caught dem. Body died soon after. I spec' it was from de whippin'.

Patrollers

In dese meetin's ole Jim Bennett, de preacher, didn't know a letter in a book, but he sho' could preach. Dar wasn't no Bible in dem days 'cept what de white folks had, an' dey wan't gwine let no slave see hit even if he could read.

Old Jim would keep a knot of lightwood handy, an' he'd stick hit close to de fire to draw de pitch out it. When de patterollers come to de door 'twas already hot, you see. Preacher would run to de fireplace, git him a light an' take dat torch an' wave hit back an' fo'th so dat de pitch an' fire would be flyin' ev'y which a way in dese patterollers' faces. Out de doors de slaves would go; dar was a mighty scramble an' scuffle in de dark, an' de slaves would scatter in all directions. You see, patterollers was mostly after de preacher 'cause he was de leader o' de meetin'. Was a terrible lashin' comin' to him dat got caught. . . .

But there was ways of beating the patterollers. De best way was to head 'em off. I 'member once when we was gonna have a meetin' down in de woods near de river. Well, dey made me de lookout boy, an' when de paddyrollers come down de lane past de church—you see dey was 'spectin dat de niggers gonna hold a meetin' dat night—well, sir, dey tell me to step out f'm de woods an' let 'em see me. Well, I does, an' de paddyrollers dat was on horse back come a-chasin' arter me, jus' a-gallopin' down de lane to beat de band. Well I was jus' ahead of 'em, an' when they got almost up wid me I jus' ducked into de woods. Course de paddyrollers couldn't stop so quick an' kep' on 'roun' de ben', an' den dere came a screamin' an' cryin' dat make you think dat hell done bust loose. Dem old paddyrollers done rid plumb into a great line of grape vines dat de slaves had stretched 'cross de path. An' dese vines tripped up de horses an' throwed de ole paddyrollers off in de bushes. An' some done landed mighty hard, cause dey was a-limpin' roun' an' cussin' an' callin' fo' de slaves to come an' help dem, but dem slaves got plenty o' sense. Dey lay in de bushes an' hole dere sides a-laughin', but ain't none o' 'em gonna risk bein' seen. All right dat night, but de nex' mornin' gonna come. Help de white man den but in de mornin' he done forgot all 'bout how you help him. All he know is dat you was out. So after ole paddyrollers go on limpin' back to de town, we go on to de woods an' hold our meetin'.

Arter dat, ole paddyrollers got wise an' used to tie dey horses an' come creepin' thew de woods on foot, tell dey fin' whar dis meetin' was gwine on. Den dey would rush in an' start whippin' an' beatin' de slaves unmerciful. All dis was done to keep you f'om servin' God an' do you know some o' dem devils was mean an' sinful 'nough to say, "If I ketch you here servin' God, I'll beat you. You ain't got no time to serve God. We bought you to serve us."

From *The Negro in Virginia*, sponsored by The Hampton Institute, 1940.

The ABC's

One of the most brilliant Americans of the nineteenth century started life as a slave on a Maryland plantation. Frederick Douglass never knew his father and saw his mother only a few times before her death. Until he was eight he lived a hungry, cold, and ragged life. Then he was sent to Baltimore to work first as a servant and later as a shipyard laborer. Slaves were forbidden education, but the boy managed to learn to read and write. And with knowledge came the power to win freedom and a great place in his country's history. In 1838, at the age of twenty-one, he fled slavery. In the years ahead his growth was spectacular. As lecturer, editor, writer, organizer, diplomat, he earned the leadership of the black people in their struggle to emancipate themselves. The story of how Douglass learned his ABC's is part of his book Narrative of the Life of Frederick Douglass, *published in 1845. It is a superb autobiography, and was immediately popular here and in Europe.*

VERY SOON AFTER I went to live with Mr. and Mrs. Auld, she very kindly commenced to teach me the A, B, C. After I had learned this, she assisted me in learning to spell words of three or four letters. Just at this point of my progress, Mr. Auld found out what was going on, and at once forbade Mrs.

Auld to instruct me further, telling her, among other things, that it was unlawful, as well as unsafe, to teach a slave to read.

To use his own words, further, he said, "If you give a nigger an inch, he will take an ell. A nigger should know nothing but to obey his master—to do as he is told to do. Learning would spoil the best nigger in the world. Now," said he, "if you teach that nigger how to read, there would be no keeping him. It would forever unfit him to be a slave. He would at once become unmanageable, and of no value to his master. As to himself, it could do him no good, but a great deal of harm. It would make him discontented and unhappy."

These words sank deep into my heart, stirred up sentiments within that lay slumbering, and called into existence an entirely new train of thought. It was a new and special revelation, explaining dark and mysterious things, with which my youthful understanding had struggled, but struggled in vain. I now understood what had been to me a most perplexing difficulty— to wit, the white man's power to enslave the black man. It was a grand achievement, and I prized it highly.

Though conscious of the difficulty of learning without a teacher, I set out with high hope, and a fixed purpose, at whatever cost of trouble, to learn how to read. The very decided manner with which he spoke, and strove to impress his wife with the evil consequences of giving me instruction, served to convince me that he was deeply sensible of the truths he was uttering. It gave me the best assurance that I might rely with the utmost confidence on the results which, he said, would flow from teaching me to read.

What he most dreaded, that I most desired. What he most loved, that I most hated. That which to him was a great evil, to be carefully shunned, was to me a great good, to be diligently sought; and the argument which he so warmly urged, against my learning to read, only served to inspire me with a desire and determination to learn.

In learning to read, I owe almost as much to the bitter opposition of my master, as to the kindly aid of my mistress. I acknowledge the benefit of both. . . .

My mistress was, as I have said, a kind and tender-hearted woman; and in the simplicity of her soul she commenced, when I first went to live with her, to treat me as she supposed one human being ought to treat another. . . . Slavery proved as injurious to her as it did to me. . . . Under its influence, the tender heart became stone, and the lamblike disposition gave way to one of tigerlike fierceness.

The first step in her downward course was in her ceasing to instruct me. She now commenced to practice her husband's precepts. She finally became even more violent in her opposition than her husband himself. She was not satisfied with simply doing as well as he had commanded; she seemed anxious to do better. Nothing seemed to make her more angry than to see me with a newspaper. She seemed to think that here lay the danger. I have had her rush at me with a face made all up of fury, and snatch from me a newspaper, in a manner that fully revealed her apprehension. She was an apt woman; and a little experience soon demonstrated, to her satisfaction, that education and slavery were incompatible with each other.

From this time I was most narrowly watched. If I was in a separate room any considerable length of time, I was sure to be suspected of having a book, and was at once called to give an account of myself. All this, however, was too late. The first step had been taken. Mistress, in teaching me the alphabet, had given me the inch, and no precaution could prevent me from taking the ell.

The plan which I adopted, and the one by which I was most successful, was that of making friends of all the little white boys whom I met in the street. As many of these as I could, I converted into teachers. With their kindly aid, obtained at different times in different places, I finally succeeded in learning to read. When I was sent on errands, I always took my book with me, and by doing one part of my errand quickly, I found time to get a lesson before my return. I used also to carry bread with me, enough of which was always in the house, and to which I was always welcome; for I was much better off in this regard than many of the poor white children in our neighborhood. This bread I used to bestow upon the hungry little urchins, who, in return, would give me that more valuable bread of knowledge. . . .

I was now about twelve years old, and the thought of being a slave for life began to bear heavily upon my heart. Just about this time, I got hold of a book entitled *The Columbian Orator.* Every opportunity I got, I used to read this book. Among much of other interesting matter, I found in it a dialogue between a master and his slave. The slave was represented as having run away from his master three times. The dialogue represented the conversation which took place between them, when the slave was retaken the third time.

In this dialogue, the whole argument in behalf of slavery was brought forward by the master, all of which was disposed of by the slave. The slave was made to say some very smart as well as impressive things in reply to his master—things which had the desired though unexpected effect; for the conversation resulted in the voluntary emancipation of the slave on the part of the master. . . .

The idea as to how I might learn to write was suggested to me by being in Durgin and Bailey's shipyard, and frequently seeing the ship carpenters, after hewing, and getting a piece of timber ready for use, write on the timber the name of that part of the ship for which it was intended.

When a piece of timber was intended for the larboard side, it would be marked thus—"L." When a piece was for the starboard side forward, it would be marked thus—"S.F." For larboard aft, it would be marked thus—"L.A." For starboard aft, it would be marked thus—"S.A." I soon learned the names of these letters, and for what they were intended when placed upon a piece of timber in the shipyard. I immediately commenced copying them, and in a short time was able to make the four letters named.

After that, when I met with any boy who I knew could write, I would tell him I could write as well as he. The next word would be, "I don't believe you. Let me see you try it." I would then make the letters which I had been so fortunate as to learn, and ask him to beat that. In this way I got a good many lessons in writing, which it is quite possible I should never have gotten in any other way.

During this time, my copy-book was the board fence, brick wall, and pavement; my pen and ink was a lump of chalk. With these, I learned mainly how to write. I then commenced and continued copying the Italics on *Webster's Spelling Book*, until I could make them all without looking on the book. By this time, my little Master Thomas had gone to school, and learned how to write, and had written over a number of copy-books. These had been brought home, and shown to some of our near neighbors, and then laid aside. My mistress used to go to class meeting at the Wilk Street meeting-house every Monday afternoon, and leave me to take care of the house. When left thus, I used to spend the time in writing in the spaces left in Master Thomas's copy-book, copying what he had written. I continued to do this until I could write a hand very similar to that of Master Thomas.

Thus, after a long, tedious effort for years, I finally succeeded in learning how to write.

From *Narrative of the Life of Frederick Douglass*, 1845.

Why Am I a Slave?

Frederick Douglass

"I didn't know I was a slave until I found out I couldn't do the things I wanted." That was how an old ex-slave put it when he was asked how it felt to be in bondage in childhood. Not having anything to say about the use of your own time and labor was probably what made you feel worst. That was lack of freedom. Of course slaveholders commonly claimed their slaves were cheerful and peaceful, content with their condition. And slaves— humble and smiling in front of their masters—would be mad to proclaim their wishes to be free, knowing the penalties for showing disloyalty.

There are not many records of how the slave really felt. In

*his autobiography Frederick Douglass tells how he first came to
question slavery, when he was still a child.*

WHY AM I A SLAVE? Why are some people slaves, and
others masters? Was there ever a time when this was not so?
How did the relation commence?

These were the perplexing questions which began now to
claim my thoughts, and to exercise the weak powers of my
mind, for I was still but a child, and knew less than children
of the same age in the free states. As my questions concerning
these things were only put to children a little older, and little
better informed than myself, I was not rapid in reaching a solid
footing. By some means I learned from these inquiries, that
"God, up in the sky," made everybody; and that he made white
people to be masters and mistresses, and black people to be
slaves.

This did not satisfy me, nor lessen my interest in the subject.
I was told, too, that God was good, and that He knew what
was best for me, and best for everybody. This was less satis-
factory than the first statement; because it came, point blank,
against all my notions of goodness. It was not good to let old
master cut the flesh off Esther, and make her cry so. Besides,
how did people know that God made black people to be slaves?
Did they go up in the sky and learn it? or, did He come down
and tell them so. All was dark here.

It was some relief to my hard notions of the goodness of
God, that, although he made white men to be slaveholders, he
did not make them to be bad slaveholders, and that, in due
time, he would punish the bad slaveholders; that he would,
when they died, send them to the bad place, where they would
be "burnt up." Nevertheless, I could not reconcile the relations
of slavery with my crude notions of goodness.

Then, too, I found that there were puzzling exceptions to

this theory of slavery on both sides, and in the middle. I knew of blacks who were not slaves; I knew of whites who were not slaveholders; and I knew of persons who were nearly white, who were slaves. Color, therefore, was a very unsatisfactory basis for slavery.

Once, however, engaged in the inquiry, I was not very long in finding out the true solution of the matter. It was not color, but crime, not God, but man, that afforded the true explanation of the existence of slavery; nor was I long in finding out another important truth, viz: what man can make, man can unmake.

The appalling darkness faded away, and I was master of the subject. There were slaves here, direct from Guinea; and there were many who could say that their fathers and mothers were stolen from Africa—forced from their homes, and compelled to serve as slaves. This, to me, was knowledge; but it was a kind of knowledge which filled me with a burning hatred of slavery, increased my suffering, and left me without the means of breaking away from my bondage. Yet it was knowledge quite worth possessing.

I could not have been more than seven or eight years old, when I began to make this subject my study. It was with me in the woods and fields; along the shore of the river, and wherever my boyish wanderings led me; and although I was, at that time, quite ignorant of the existence of the free states, I distinctly remember being, even then, most strongly impressed with the idea of being a free man some day. This cheering assurance was an inborn dream of my human nature—a constant menace to slavery—and one which all the powers of slavery were unable to silence or extinguish.

From *Narrative of the Life of Frederick Douglass*, 1845.

A Kidnapping

As the Northern states one by one prohibited slavery, the number of free Blacks grew. Some were born free, some freed themselves by running away, some were given freedom by their masters, some bought their freedom. One tenth of the million Blacks in the United States in 1800 were free. By the Civil War, there were about five hundred thousand free Blacks, half living in the South and half in the North. They knew only marginal freedom. From the time of the American Revolution that margin had shrunk until it was sometimes hard to tell the difference between slave and freeman. It was easy for whites to claim a Black was a slave; the law gave the Black poor chance to defend himself. Kidnapping a free Black and forcing him into slavery was a common practice. New Yorkers organized a Vigilance Committee to resist kidnappers. In July 1836 David Ruggles, black bookseller and

*abolitionist who headed the committee, described a kidnapping
in this letter to the newspapers.*

IT IS TOO BAD to be told, much less to be endured!—
On Saturday, 23d instant, about 12 o'clock, Mr. George Jones,
a respectable free colored man, was arrested at 21 Broadway,
by certain police officers, upon the pretext of his having "committed assault and battery." Mr. Jones, being conscious that
no such charge could be sustained against him, refused to go
with the officers. His employers, placing high confidence in his
integrity, advised him to go and answer to the charge, promising
that any assistance should be afforded to satisfy the end of
justice. He proceeded with the officers, accompanied with a
gentleman who would have stood his bail—he was locked up
in Bridewell—his friend was told that "when he was wanted
he could be sent for."

Between the hours of 1 and 2 o'clock, Mr. Jones was carried
before the Hon. Richard Riker, Recorder of the City of New
York. In the absence of his friends, and in the presence of
several notorious kidnappers, who preferred and by oath sustained that he was a runaway slave, poor Jones (having no one
to utter a word in his behalf, but a boy, in the absence of
numerous friends who could have borne testimony to his freedom), was by the Recorder pronounced to be a SLAVE!

In less than three hours after his arrest, he was bound in
chains, dragged through the streets, like beast to the shambles!
My depressed countrymen, we are all liable; your wives and
children are at the mercy of merciless kidnappers. We have no
protection in law, because the legislators withhold justice. We
must no longer depend on the interposition of Manumission
or Anti-Slavery Societies, in the hope of peaceable and just
protection; where such outrages are committed, peace and justice cannot dwell. While we are subject to be thus inhumanly

practised upon, no man is safe; we must look to our own safety
and protection from kidnappers, remembering that "self-
defence is the first law of nature."

Let a meeting be called—let every man who has sympathy
in his heart to feel when bleeding humanity is thus stabbed
afresh, attend the meeting; let a remedy be prescribed to protect us from slavery. Whenever necessity requires, let that remedy be applied. Come what, any thing is better than slavery.

From *The Liberator*, August 6, 1836.

A Slave Sale

*What was slavery like as a way of living? By the 1830's, ex-
slaves, freed or runaway, were beginning to tell their stories in
print. Many of these tales were very widely read. Their fasci-
nating details and dramatic adventures carried a powerful anti-
slavery message. The narrative of Josiah Henson so impressed
Harriet Beecher Stowe that when she wrote her novel* Uncle
Tom's Cabin, *Henson was the model for her hero.*

*Solomon Northup, a free Black of New York, was kidnapped
in Washington in 1841 and forced into slavery on a cotton plantation near the Red River in Louisiana. Freed in 1853, his story
of slavery was recorded in* Twelve Years a Slave. *From it is
drawn this vivid picture of a slave sale.*

IN THE FIRST PLACE we were required to wash thoroughly, and those with beards to shave. We were then furnished
with a new suit each, cheap, but clean. The men had hat, coat,
shirt, pants and shoes; the women frocks of calico, and hand-

kerchief to bind about their heads. We were now conducted into a large room in the front part of the building to which the yard was attached, in order to be properly trained, before the admission of customers. The men were arranged on one side of the room, the women at the other. The tallest was placed at the head of the row, then the next tallest and so on in the order of their respective heights. Emily was at the foot of the line of women. Freeman [owner of the slave pen] charged us to remember our places; exhorted us to appear smart and lively,— sometimes threatening, and again, holding out various inducements. During the day he exercised us in the art of "looking smart," and of moving to our places with exact precision.

After being fed, in the afternoon, we were again paraded and made to dance. Bob, a colored boy, who had some time belonged to Freeman, played on the violin. Standing near him, I made bold to inquire if he could play the "Virginia Reel." He answered he could not, and asked me if I could play. Replying in the affirmative, he handed me the violin. I struck up a tune, and finished it. Freeman ordered me to continue playing, and seemed well pleased, telling Bob that I far excelled him—a remark that seemed to grieve my musical companion very much.

Next day many customers called to examine Freeman's "new lot." The latter gentleman was very loquacious, dwelling at much length upon our several good points and qualities. He would make us hold up our heads, walk briskly back and forth, while customers would feel of our hands and arms and bodies, turn us about, ask us what we could do, make us open our mouths and show our teeth, precisely as a jockey examines a horse which he is about to barter for or purchase. Sometimes a man or woman was taken back to the small house in the yard, stripped, and inspected more minutely. Scars upon a slave's back were considered evidence of a rebellious or unruly spirit, and hurt his sale.

An old gentleman, who said he wanted a coachman, appeared to take a fancy to me. . . . I learned he was a resident in the city. I very much desired that he would buy me, because I conceived it would not be difficult to make my escape from New Orleans on some northern vessel. Freeman asked him fifteen hundred dollars for me. The old gentleman insisted it was too much as times were very hard. Freeman, however, declared that I was sound of health, of a good constitution, and intelligent. He made it a point to enlarge upon my musical attainments. The old gentleman argued quite adroitly that there was nothing extraordinary about the Negro, and finally, to my regret, went out, saying he would call again.

During the day, however, a number of sales were made. David and Caroline were purchased together by a Natchez planter. They left us, grinning broadly, and in a most happy state of mind, caused by the fact of their not being separated. Sethe was sold to a planter of Baton Rouge, her eyes flashing with anger as she was led away.

The same man also purchased Randall. The little fellow was made to jump, and run across the floor, and perform many other feats, exhibiting his activity and condition. All the time the trade was going on, Eliza was crying aloud, and wringing her hands. She besought the man not to buy him, unless he also bought herself and Emily. She promised, in that case, to be the most faithful slave that ever lived. The man answered that he could not afford it, and then Eliza burst into a paroxysm of grief, weeping plaintively. Freeman turned round to her, savagely, with his whip in his uplifted hand, ordering her to stop her noise, or he would flog her. He would not have such work—such snivelling; and unless she ceased that minute, he would take her to the yard and give her a hundred lashes. Yes, he would take the nonsense out of her pretty quick—if he didn't might he be d——d. Eliza shrunk before him, and tried to wipe away her tears, but it was all in vain. She wanted to be with her children, she said, the little time she had to live.

All the frowns and threats of Freeman could not wholly silence the afflicted mother. She kept on begging and beseeching them, most piteously, not to separate the three. Over and over again she told them how she loved her boy. A great many times she repeated her former promises—how very faithful and obedient she would be; how hard she would labor day and night, to the last moment of her life; if he would only buy them all together. But it was of no avail; the man could not afford it. The bargain was agreed upon, and Randall must go alone. Then Eliza ran to him; embraced him passionately; kissed him again and again; told him to remember her—all the while her tears falling in the boy's face like rain.

Freeman damned her, calling her a blubbering, bawling wench, and ordered her to go to her place, and behave herself, and be somebody. He swore he wouldn't stand such stuff but a little longer. He would soon give her something to cry about, if she was not mighty careful, and that she might depend upon.

The planter from Baton Rouge, with his new purchase, was ready to depart.

"Don't cry, mama. I will be a good boy. Don't cry," said Randall, looking back, as they passed out of the door.

What has become of the lad, God knows. It was a mournful scene indeed. I would have cried myself if I had dared.

From *Twelve Years a Slave*, by Solomon Northup, 1853.

Christmas on the Plantation

Working "from day clean to first dark" under the overseer or his drivers was the usual routine for the slave. It was natural for him to give as little as possible of his unpaid toil, and equally natural for the slaveholder to try to get as much as he could out of his bondsmen.

Most masters let their slaves rest and relax on Sundays, and some gave half of Saturdays, too. Special holidays were few— Good Friday, Independence Day, Christmas. To celebrate the last, there were often two or three days, with gifts and feasts and passes to visit. The ex-slave Solomon Northup left this record of Christmas on a Louisiana plantation in 1841.

THE ONLY RESPITE from constant labor the slave has through the whole year, is during the Christmas holidays. Epps allowed us three—others allow four, five and six days, according to the measure of their generosity. It is the only time to which they look forward with any interest or pleasure. They are glad when night comes, not only because it brings them a few hours repose, but because it brings them one day nearer Christmas. It is hailed with equal delight by the old and the young; even Uncle Abram ceases to glorify Andrew Jackson, and Patsy forgets her many sorrows, amid the general hilarity of the holidays. It is the time of feasting, and frolicking, and fiddling—the carnival season with the children of bondage. They are the only days when they are allowed a little restricted liberty, and heartily indeed do they enjoy it.

It is custom for one planter to give a "Christmas supper," inviting the slaves from neighboring plantations to join his own on the occasion; for instance, one year it is given by Epps, the next by Marshall, the next by Hawkins, and so on. Usually from three to five hundred are assembled, coming together on foot, in carts, on horseback, on mules, riding double and triple, sometimes a boy and girl, an old woman. Uncle Abram astride a mule, with Aunt Phebe and Patsy behind him, trotting towards a Christmas supper, would be no uncommon sight on Bayou Boeuf.

Then, too, "of all days i' the year," they array themselves in their best attire. The cotton coat has been washed clean, the stump of a tallow candle has been applied to their shoes, and if so fortunate as to possess a rimless or a crownless hat, it is placed jauntily on the head. They are welcome with equal cordiality, however, if they come bare-headed and bare-footed to the feast. As a general thing, the women wear handkerchiefs tied about their heads, but if chance has thrown in their way a fiery red ribbon, or a cast-off bonnet of their mistress' grandmother, it is sure to be worn on such occasion. Red—the deep blood red—is decidedly the favorite color among the enslaved damsels of my acquaintance. If a red ribbon does not encircle the neck, you will be certain to find all the hair of their woolly heads tied up with red strings of one sort or another.

The table is spread in the open air, and loaded with varieties of meat and piles of vegetables. Bacon and corn meal at such times are dispensed with. Sometimes the cooking is performed in the kitchen on the plantation, at others in the shade of wide branching trees. In the latter case, a ditch is dug in the ground, and wood is laid in and burned until it is filled with glowing coals, over which chickens, ducks, turkeys, pigs, and not unfrequently the entire body of a wild ox, are roasted. They are furnished also with flour, of which biscuits are made, and often with peach and other preserves, with tarts, and every manner and description of pies, except the mince, that being an article of pastry as yet unknown among them. Only the slave who has lived all the years on his scanty allowance of meal and bacon, can appreciate such suppers. White people in great numbers assemble to witness the gastronomical enjoyments. . . .

When the viands have disappeared, and the hungry maws of the children of toil are satisfied, then, next in the order of amusement, is the Christmas dance. My business on these gala days always was to play on the violin. The African race is a music-loving one, proverbially; and many there were among my fellow-bondsmen whose organs of tune were strikingly developed, and who could thumb the banjo with dexterity. . . .

On that particular Christmas I have now in my mind, Miss Lively and Mr. Sam, the first belonging to Stewart, the latter to Roberts, started the ball. It was well known that Sam cherished an ardent passion for Lively, as also did one of Marshall's and another of Carey's boys; for Lively was lively indeed, and a heart-breaking coquette withal. It was a victory for Sam Roberts, when, rising from the repast, she gave him her hand for the first "figure" in preference to either of his rivals. They were somewhat crest-fallen, and shaking their heads angrily, rather intimated they would like to pitch into Mr. Sam and hurt him badly.

But not an emotion of wrath ruffled the placid bosom of Samuel as his legs flew like drum-sticks down the outside and up the middle, by the side of his bewitching partner. The whole company cheered them vociferously, and, excited with the applause, they continued "tearing down" after all the others had become exhausted and halted a moment to recover breath. But

Sam's superhuman exertions overcame him finally, leaving Lively
alone, yet whirling like a top. Thereupon one of Sam's rivals,
Pete Marshall, dashed in, and, with might and main, leaped
and shuffled and threw himself into every conceivable shape,
as if determined to show Miss Lively and all the world that
Sam Roberts was of no account. . . .

One "set" off, another takes its place, he or she remaining
longest on the floor receiving the most uproarious commen-
dation, and so the dancing continues until broad daylight. It
does not cease with the sound of the fiddle, but in that case
they set up a music peculiar to themselves. This is called "patting," accompanied with one of those unmeaning songs, composed rather for its adaption to a certain tune or measure, than
for the purpose of expressing any distinct idea. The patting is
performed by striking the hands on the knees, then striking
the hands together, then striking the right shoulder with one
hand, the left with the other—all the while keeping time with
the feet, and singing, perhaps this song:

> *Harper's creek and roarin' ribber,*
> *Thar, my dear, we'll live forebber;*
> *Den we'll go to de Ingin nation,*
> *All I want in dis creation,*
> *Is pretty little wife and big plantation.*

Or, if these words are not adapted to the tune called for, it
may be that *Old Hog Eye* is—a rather solemn and startling
specimen of versification, not, however, to be appreciated unless heard at the South. It runneth as follows:

> *Who's been here since I've been gone?*
> *Pretty little girl wid a josey on.*
> > *Hog Eye!*
> > *Old Hog Eye!*
> > *And Hosey too!*

Never see de like since I was born,
Here comes a little gal wid a josey on.
Hog Eye!
Old Hog Eye!
And Hosey too!

During the remaining holidays succeeding Christmas, they are provided with passes, and permitted to go where they please within a limited distance, or they may remain and labor on the plantation, in which case they are paid for it. It is very rarely, however, that the latter alternative is accepted. They may be seen at these times hurrying in all directions, as happy looking mortals as can be found on the face of the earth. They are different beings from what they are in the field; the temporary relaxation, the brief deliverance from fear, and from the lash, producing an entire metamorphosis in their appearance and demeanor. In visiting, riding, renewing old friendships, or, perchance, reviving some old attachment, or pursuing whatever pleasure may suggest itself, the time is occupied.

Such is "southern life as it is," three days in the year, as I found it—the other three hundred and sixty-two being days of weariness, and fear, and suffering, and unremitting labor.

From Twelve Years a Slave, by Solomon Northup, 1853.

On the Underground Railroad

If you have read Uncle Tom's Cabin, *you remember how the fugitive slave Eliza crossed the ice on the Ohio River to freedom on the other side.*

There was a real Eliza who crossed the Ohio early in the 1830's, giving Harriet Beecher Stowe the idea for that incident. Eliza was welcomed at the house of John Rankin, a Tennessee minister who made his home on the riverbank, one of the most important stations on the Underground Railroad.

The "railroad" was a term for the series of stopping points that ran northward along many paths. The slave's friends— Black and white—gave him food and a bed for the night and started him toward the next station. Thousands of brave men and women defied the federal fugitive slave laws to operate the Underground Railroad.

Some of the "conductors" aided great numbers to escape. Levi Coffin and Thomas Garret, white Quakers, each speeded almost three thousand runaways. Robert Purvis and William Still, Philadelphia Blacks, were said to have helped nine thousand fugitives.

There were conductors at the Southern end, too, and most of them were Blacks. Josiah Henson brought out a hundred people, and Harriet Tubman, called "Moses," went down deep into "Egypt-land" nineteen times to rescue over three hundred slaves.

Because of the secrecy required to make the passage north safe, few records were kept of the operation. One such record

*is a letter from the fugitive slave J. H. Hill, telling how he was
helped to escape from Virginia in 1853.*

NINE MONTHS I was trying to get away. I was secreted
for a long time in a kitchen of a merchant near the corner of
Franklyn and 7th streets, at Richmond, where I was well taken
care of, by a lady friend of my mother. When I got tired of
staying in that place, I wrote myself a pass to pass myself to
Petersburg, here I stopped with a very prominent colored person, who was a friend to freedom—stayed here until two white
friends told other friends if I was in the city to tell me to go at
once, and stand not upon the order of going, because they had
heard a plot.

I wrote a pass, started for Richmond, reached Manchester,
got off the cars, walked into Richmond, once more got back
into the same old den, stayed here from the 16th of Aug. to
12th Sept. [1853]. On the 11th of Sept. 8 o'clock P.M. a message
came to me that there had been a state room taken on the
steamer *City of Richmond* for my benefit, and I assured the
party that it would be occupied if God be willing.

Before 10 o'clock the next morning, on the 12th, a beautiful
Sept. day, I arose early, wrote my pass for Norfolk, left my
old den with a many a good bye, turned out the back way to
7th St., thence to Main, down Main behind 4 night watch to
old Rockett's and after about 20 minutes of delay I succeeded
in reaching the state room. My conductor was very much excited, but I felt as composed as I do at this moment, for I had
started from my den that morning for liberty or for death providing myself with a brace of pistols.

From *The Underground Railroad*, by William Still, 1878.

A Refusal to
Pay Taxes

A free Black's chance to get an education improved in the North as time went on. But in many places there still were separate schools for black children. The Massachusetts abolitionists stopped segregated schools in Boston and New Bedford by 1855. Most other Jim Crow—that is, officially segregated—Northern states maintained separate schools much longer. Blacks who migrated to the Midwest generally had to wait until after the Civil War for free public education.

Determined Blacks were not content to wait indefinitely for integration. In Boston, the black lawyer Robert Morris teamed with the white Senator Charles Sumner to fight segregation. In Philadelphia, Robert Purvis decided early to dedicate his life and his inherited wealth to ending slavery and discrimination. The son of a Moorish black woman and a wealthy Englishman, he was born in Charleston, South Carolina, and educated in Edinburgh. He helped to organize the first national convention of Blacks. At twenty-three, he was one of the founders of the American Anti-Slavery Society, and later became its president. As a leader of the Pennsylvania abolitionists, he organized the Philadelphia Vigilance Committee, which guided slave runaways through the city and helped pay their way to Canada. His methods became the pattern for the operation of the Underground Railroad.

Purvis gave unselfishly of his time, energy, and money. He never hesitated at personal danger. On his elegant suburban estate he raised blue-ribbon livestock and poultry and entertained abolitionists seeking a rest or his counsel. It was here that his young niece Charlotte Forten learned her abolitionist principles.

In 1853, refusing to pay the local school tax, Robert Purvis wrote this explanation to the tax collector. It helped end the separation policy of the schools.

YOU CALLED YESTERDAY for the tax upon my property in this Township, which I shall pay, excepting the "School Tax." I object to the payment of this tax, on the ground that my rights as a citizen, and my feelings as a man and a parent, have been grossly outraged in depriving me, in violation of law and justice, of the benefits of the school system which this tax was designed to sustain.

I am perfectly aware that all that makes up the character and worth of the citizens of this township look upon the proscription and exclusion of my children from the Public School as illegal, and an unjustifiable usurpation of my right. I have borne this outrage ever since the innovation upon the usual practice of admitting all the children of the Township into the

Public Schools, and at considerable expense have been obliged to obtain the services of private teachers to instruct my children, while my school tax is greater, with a single exception, than that of any other citizen of the township.

It is true (and the outrage is made but the more glaring and insulting), I was informed by a pious Quaker director, with a sanctifying grace, imparting, doubtless, an unctuous glow to his saintly prejudices, that a school in the village of Mechanicsville was appropriated for "thine." The miserable shanty, with all its appurtenances, on the very line of the township, to which this benighted follower of George Fox alluded, is, as you know, the most flimsy and ridiculous sham which any tool of a skin-hating aristocracy could have resorted to, to cover or protect his servility.

To submit by voluntary payment of the demand is too great an outrage upon nature, and, with a spirit, thank God, unshackled by this, or any other wanton and cowardly act, I shall resist this tax, which, before the unjust exclusion, had always afforded me the highest gratification in paying. With no other than the best feeling towards yourself, I am forced to this unpleasant position, in vindication of my rights and personal dignity against an encroachment upon them as contemptibly mean as it is infamously despotic.

From *The Liberator*, December 16, 1853.

Let Him Come and Take Me

J. W. Loguen was the son of a slave mother and the white man who owned her. His mother had been born free in Ohio, but when she was seven, she was kidnapped and sold to a Tennessean

*who ran a whiskey distillery with slave labor. As soon as he
could, the boy rode off to freedom on his master's mare. Fearless
and intelligent, he earned his way through college and became
a minister in Syracuse, New York. When the Fugitive Slave Law
was adopted in 1850, he announced publicly: "I am a fugitive
slave from Tennessee. My master is Manasseth Loguen. The
letter of the law gives him a title to my person—and let him come
and take it. I'll not run, nor will I give him a penny for my
freedom."*

*At a meeting held in Syracuse in October 1850, the Reverend
Mr. Loguen made a speech that forecast how militant Blacks
would meet the new Fugitive Slave Law. One year later, he
proved dramatically that he meant exactly what he said. He took
part in the rescue of the runaway slave Jerry, when crowbars
and a battering ram were used to break into the Syracuse courthouse and free the fugitive under the guns of the marshals. The
episode was a national sensation. Would force alone end slavery?
More and more began to believe it.*

I WAS A SLAVE; I knew the dangers I was exposed to. I
had made up my mind as to the course I was to take. On that
score I needed no counsel, nor did the colored citizens generally. They had taken their stand—they would not be taken
back to slavery. If to shoot down their assailants should forfeit
their lives, such result was the least of the evil. They will have
their liberties or die in their defence.

What is life to me if I am to be a slave in Tennessee? My
neighbors! I have lived with you many years, and you know
me. My home is here, and my children were born here. I am
bound to Syracuse by pecuniary interests, and social and family
bonds. And do you think I can be taken away from you and
from my wife and children, and be a slave in Tennessee? Has
the President and his Secretary sent this enactment up here,
to you, Mr. Chairman, to enforce on me in Syracuse?—and

will you obey him? Did I think so meanly of you—did I suppose the people of Syracuse, strong as they are in numbers and love of liberty—or did I believe their love of liberty was so selfish, unmanly and unchristian—did I believe them so sunken and servile and degraded as to remain at their homes and labors, or, with none of that spirit which smites a tyrant down, to surround a United States Marshal to see me torn from my home and family, and hurled back to bondage—I say did I think so meanly of you, I could never come to live with you. . . .

I tell you the people of Syracuse and of the whole North must meet this tyranny and crush it by force, or be crushed by it. This hellish enactment has precipitated the conclusion that white men must live in dishonorable submission, and colored men be slaves, or they must give their physical as well as intellectual powers to the defence of human rights. The time has come to change the tones of submission into tones of defiance—and to tell Mr. Fillmore and Mr. Webster, if they propose to execute this measure upon us, to send on their blood-hounds.

Mr. President, long ago I was beset by over prudent and good men and women to purchase my freedom. Nay, I was frequently importuned to consent that they purchase it, and present it as an evidence of their partiality to my person and character. Generous and kind as those friends were, my heart recoiled from the proposal. I owe my freedom to the God who made me, and who stirred me to claim it against all other beings in God's universe. I will not, nor will I consent, that anybody else shall countenance the claims of a vulgar despot to my soul and body. Were I in chains, and did these kind people come to buy me out of prison, I would acknowledge the boon with inexpressible thankfulness. But I feel no chains, and am in no prison. I received my freedom from Heaven, and with it came the command to defend my title to it. I have long since resolved to do nothing and suffer nothing that can in any way imply that I am indebted to any power but the Almighty for my manhood and personality.

Now, you are assembled here, the strength of this city is here to express their sense of this fugitive act, and to proclaim to the despots at Washington whether it shall be enforced here—whether you will permit the government to return me and other fugitives who have sought an asylum among you, to the Hell of slavery. The question is with you. If you will give us up, say so, and we will shake the dust from our feet and leave you. But we believe better things. We know you are taken by surprise. The immensity of this meeting testifies to the general consternation that has brought it together, necessarily, precipitately, to decide the most stirring question that can be presented, to wit, whether, the government having transgressed constitutional and natural limits, you will bravely resist its aggressions, and tell its soulless agents that no slave-holder shall make your city and county a hunting field for slaves.

Whatever may be your decision, my ground is taken. I have declared it everywhere. It is known over the State and out of the State—over the line in the North, and over the line in the South. I don't respect this law—I don't fear it—I won't obey it! It outlaws me, and I outlaw it, and the men who attempt to enforce it on me. I place the governmental officials on the ground that they place me. I will not live a slave, and if force is employed to re-enslave me, I shall make preparations to meet the crisis as becomes a man.

If you will stand by me—and I believe you will do it, for your freedom and honor are involved as well as mine—it requires no microscope to see that—I say if you will stand with us in resistance to this measure, you will be the saviours of your country.

Your decision to-night in favor of resistance will give vent to the spirit of liberty, and it will break the bands of party, and shout for joy all over the North. Your example only is needed to be the type of public action in Auburn, and Rochester, and Utica, and Buffalo, and all the West, and eventually in the Atlantic cities. Heaven knows that this act of noble daring will

break out somewhere—and may God grant that Syracuse be
the honored spot, whence it shall send an earthquake voice
through the land!

From *The Rev. J. W. Loguen, As a Slave and As a Freeman.
A Narrative of Real Life*, 1859.

What Is Your Fourth of July to Me?

NEGROES
FOR SALE.

Will be sold at public
auction, at Spring Hill, in the
County of Hempstead, on a
credit of twelve months, on Fri
day the 28th day of this present month, 15 young and valuable Slaves, consisting of 9
superior Men & Boys, between
12 and 27 years of age, one
woman about 43 years who is
a good washer and cook, one woman about twenty-seven, and one
very likely young woman with three children.
Also at the same time, and on the same terms, three Mules, about
forty head of Cattle, plantation tools, one waggon, and a first rate
Gin stand, manufactured by Pratt &Co.
Bond with two or more approved securities will be required.
Sale to commence at 10 o'clock.
E. E. Hundley,
W. Robinson,
H. M. Robinson.

*Young America began celebrating the birthday of its national
independence almost before the new republic was out of its cradle. Annually the Fourth of July orators thundered tributes to
the Founding Fathers and to the Declaration of Independence.
Prayers were made, hymns sung, and sermons preached in honor
of those who had shed their blood for justice, liberty, and humanity.*

The ex-slave Frederick Douglass was one of the most prominent citizens of Rochester, New York. Here he edited his abolitionist newspaper, The North Star, *and was stationmaster for the Underground Railroad. In 1852 the city honored him with an invitation to deliver the Fourth of July oration. But Douglass was no mouthpiece for dead history. "We have to do with the past," he said, "only as we can make it useful to the present and the future. You have no right to enjoy a child's share in the labor of your fathers, unless your children also are to be blest by your labors." He then went on to fling this challenge from Black Americans.*

FELLOW CITIZENS: Pardon me, and allow me to ask, why am I called upon to speak here today? What have I or those I represent to do with your national independence? Are the great principles of political freedom and of natural justice, embodied in that Declaration of Independence, extended to us? And am I, therefore, called upon to bring our humble offering to the national altar, and to confess the benefits, and express devout gratitude for the blessings resulting from your independence to us? . . .

What to the American slave is your Fourth of July? I answer, a day that reveals to him more than all other days of the year, the gross injustice and cruelty to which he is the constant victim. To him your celebration is a sham; your boasted liberty an unholy license; your national greatness, swelling vanity; your sounds of rejoicing are empty and heartless; your denunciation of tyrants, brass-fronted impudence; your shouts of liberty and equality, hollow mockery; your prayers and hymns, your sermons and thanksgivings, with all your religious parade and solemnity, are to him mere bombast, fraud, deception, impiety, and hypocrisy—a thin veil to cover up crimes which would disgrace a nation of savages. There is not a nation of the earth guilty of practices more shocking and bloody than are the people of these United States at this very hour.

Go where you may, search where you will, roam through all the monarchies and despotisms of the Old World, travel through South America, search out every abuse and when you have found the last, lay your facts by the side of the everyday practices of this nation, and you will say with me that, for revolting barbarity and shameless hypocrisy, America reigns without a rival. . . .

From *The Life and Writings of Frederick Douglass*,
Volume II, edited by Philip S. Foner, 1950.

Is Money the Answer?

Frances Harper

Frances Ellen Watkins Harper spent a lonely childhood in Baltimore. She was born a free Black in that city in 1825. Orphaned early, she was raised by an aunt who sent her to a school for free black children until she was thirteen. Then she was obliged to earn her own way, making dresses, taking care of children, and all the while trying to learn to write. At twenty-five she became a schoolteacher, finding work in Ohio and then Pennsylvania. Newspapers and magazines began publishing her poems. Many were on antislavery themes, for she had helped fugitives on the Underground Railroad wherever she was. In 1854 she became a lecturer for the Maine abolitionists. She traveled widely in the North until the Civil War, and then went south to help the freedmen. She was the most popular black poet of her time. In 1859, in The Anglo-African *magazine, she warned that no virtue lay in making money for its own sake. Gathering riches would not be the Black's salvation.*

WHEN WE HAVE a race of men whom this blood-stained government cannot tempt or flatter, who would sternly refuse every office in the nation's gift, from a president down to a tide-waiter, until she shook her hands from complicity in the guilt of cradle plundering and man stealing, then for us the foundations of an historic character will have been laid.

We need men and women whose hearts are the homes of a high and lofty enthusiasm, and a noble devotion to the cause of emancipation, who are ready and willing to lay time, talent and money on the altar of universal freedom.

We have money among us, but how much of it is spent to bring deliverance to our captive brethren? Are our wealthiest men the most liberal sustainers of the Anti-slavery enterprise? Or does the bare fact of their having money really help mould public opinion and reverse its sentiments?

We need what money cannot buy and what affluence is too beggarly to purchase. Earnest, self sacrificing souls that will stamp themselves not only on the present but the future. Let us not then defer all our noble opportunities till we get rich. And here I am, not aiming to enlist a fanatical crusade against the desire for riches, but I do protest against chaining down the soul, with its Heaven endowed faculties and God given attributes to the one idea of getting money as stepping into power or even gaining our rights in common with others.

The respect that is only bought by gold is not worth much. It is no honor to shake hands politically with men who whip women and steal babies. If this government has no call for our services, no aim for our children, we have the greater need for them to build up a true manhood and womanhood for ourselves.

The important lesson we should learn, and be able to teach, is how to make every gift, whether gold or talent, fortune or genius, subserve the cause of crushed humanity and carry out the greatest idea of the present age, the glorious idea of human brotherhood.

From *The Anglo-African*, May, 1859.

Could I Die in a More Noble Cause?

Copeland's trial

Five Blacks were with John Brown's band on the rainy Sunday night of October 16, 1859, when they attacked the federal arsenal at Harpers Ferry in Virginia. Their plan was to capture the town, give arms to the slaves in that region, and spread the revolt through the South. They took the arsenal, but superior troops overwhelmed them. Most of the twenty-two men were killed, a few escaped, and some were captured.

Two of the Blacks, Dangerfield Newby, forty-four, and Shields Green, twenty-three, had been born slaves. Newby was shot dead

*in the raid; he left a wife and seven children in slavery. Green
was captured. Osborn Perry Anderson, twenty-nine, escaped
and fought later in the Civil War. Lewis Sheridan Leary, twenty-
four, left a wife and a baby at Oberlin to join Brown's men. He
died in the attack.*

*The fifth Black, John A. Copeland, Jr., was born of free
parents in North Carolina. They moved to Oberlin, where he
became a student at the college. When his uncle, Lewis Leary,
joined John Brown, Copeland enlisted too.*

*John Brown was tried, and hanged for treason on December
2, 1859. Two weeks later, after trial, both Shields Green and
John Copeland were hanged on the same gallows, going to their
deaths just as John Brown had, "with the most unflinching firm-
ness," said the reporter for the Associated Press.*

*In prison, awaiting execution, Copeland wrote to his family
these words.*

DEAR PARENTS,—My fate as far as man can seal it is
sealed, but let this not occasion you any misery, for remember
the cause in which I was engaged, remember that it was a "Holy
Cause," one in which men who in every point of view [were]
better than I am have suffered and died. Remember that if I
must die I die in trying to liberate a few of my poor and oppressed people from my condition of servitude which God in
his Holy Writ has hurled his most bitter denunciations against
and in which men who were by the color of their faces removed
from the direct injurious effect, have already lost their lives
and still more remain to meet the same fate which has been
by man decided that I must meet. . . .

I am not terrified by the gallows, which I see staring me in
the face, and upon which I am soon to stand and suffer death
for doing what George Washington was made a hero for
doing. . . . For having lent my aid to a general no less brave,

and engaged in a cause no less honorable and glorious, I am to suffer death. Washington entered the field to fight for the freedom of the American people—not for the white man alone, but for both black and white. Nor were they white men alone who fought for the freedom of this country. The blood of black men flowed as freely as that of white men. . . . And some of the very last blood shed was that of black men. . . .

It was a sense of the wrongs which we have suffered that promoted the noble but unfortunate Captain Brown and his associates to attempt to give freedom to a small number, at least, of those who are now held by cruel and unjust laws and by no less cruel and unjust men. . . .

And now, dear brother, could I die in a more noble cause? Could I die in a manner and for a cause which would induce true and honest men more to honor me, and the angels more ready to receive me to their happy home of everlasting joy above?

I imagine that I hear you, and all of you, mother, father, sisters, and brothers, say—"No, there is not a cause for which we, with less sorrow, could see you die." Believe me when I tell you, that though shut up in prison and under sentence of death, I have spent more happy hours here, and were it not that I know that the hearts of those to whom I am at-tached . . . will be filled with sorrow, I would almost as lief die now as at any time, for I feel that I am prepared to meet my Maker. . . .

From *John Brown and His Men*, by Richard J. Hinton, 1894.

Men of Color, to Arms!

As soon as Fort Sumter was fired upon, the abolitionists tried to make clear to Lincoln and the North that the Union cause would not triumph unless the war was fought to end slavery. It was "freedom for all, or chains for all," they said. From the beginning Frederick Douglass, the powerful spokesman of Black Americans, insisted that both slave and free Blacks should be called into service to fight in an army of liberation.

For almost eighteen months there was grave doubt of the course Lincoln was taking on slavery. He seemed to move so slowly, although he never took a step backward. When the Emancipation Proclamation was announced, the friends of freedom around the world knew that the course the abolitionists had advocated was at last to be followed.

The Union Army ranks were opened to Blacks, and through his newspaper, on March 2, 1863, Douglass issued a flaming call, "Men of Color, To Arms!" His own sons, Lewis and Charles, were among the first to respond. The assurances of equal treatment Douglass had been told he could give were not carried out. Black soldiers suffered unequal pay, allowances, and opportunities throughout the war. They had to fight a double battle, against slavery in the South, and against Jim Crow in the North.

When the Civil War ended, 180,000 black troops had served in Lincoln's Army and 30,000 in the Navy. A quarter of a million had helped the military as laborers. To put an end to slavery, 38,000 Blacks gave their lives in battle.

*

WHEN FIRST THE rebel cannon shattered the walls of Sumter and drove away its starving garrison, I predicted that the war then and there inaugurated would not be fought out entirely by white men. Every month's experience during these weary years has confirmed that opinion. A war undertaken and brazenly carried on for the perpetual enslavement of colored men, calls logically and loudly for colored men to help suppress it. Only a moderate share of sagacity was needed to see that the arm of the slave was the best defense against the arm of the slaveholder. Hence with every reverse to the national arms, with every exulting shout of victory raised by the slaveholding rebels, I have implored the imperiled nation to unchain against her foes her powerful black hand.

Slowly and reluctantly that appeal is beginning to be heeded. Stop not now to complain that it was not heeded sooner. . . .

By every consideration which binds you to your enslaved fellow-countrymen, and the peace and welfare of your country; by every aspiration which you cherish for the freedom and equality of yourselves and your children; by all the ties of blood and identity which make us one with the brave black men now fighting our battles in Louisiana and in South Carolina, I urge you to fly to arms, and smite with death the power that would bury the government and your liberty in the same hopeless grave.

I wish I could tell you that the State of New York calls you to this high honor. For the moment her constituted authorities are silent on the subject. They will speak by and by, and doubtless on the right side; but we are not compelled to wait for her. We can get at the throat of treason and slavery through the State of Massachusetts. She was first in the War of Independence; first to break the chains of her slaves; first to make the black man equal before the law; first to admit colored children to her common schools, and she was first to answer with her blood the alarm cry of the nation, when its capital was menaced by rebels. You know her patriotic governor, and you know Charles Sumner. I need not add more.

Massachusetts now welcomes you to arms as soldiers. She has but a small colored population from which to recruit. She has full leave of the general government to send one regiment to the war, and she has undertaken to do it. Go quickly and help fill up the first colored regiment from the North. I am authorized to assure you that you will receive the same wages, the same rations, the same equipments, the same protection, the same treatment and the same bounty, secured to the white soldiers. You will be led by able and skillful officers, men who will take especial pride in your efficiency and success. They will be quick to accord to you all the honor you shall merit by your valor, and see that your rights and feelings are respected by other soldiers. I have assured myself on these points, and can speak with authority.

More than twenty years of unswerving devotion to our common cause may give me some humble claim to be trusted at this momentous crisis. I will not argue. To do so implies hesitation and doubt, and you do not hesitate. You do not doubt. The day dawns; the morning star is bright upon the horizon! The iron gate of our prison stands half open. One gallant rush from the North will fling it wide open, while four millions of our brothers and sisters shall march out into liberty. The chance is now given you to end in a day the bondage of centuries, and to rise in one bound from social degradation to the plane of common equality with all other varieties of men.

Remember Denmark Vesey of Charleston; remember Nathaniel Turner of Southampton; remember Shields Green and Copeland, who followed noble John Brown, and fell as glorious martyrs for the cause of the slave. Remember that in a contest with oppression, the Almighty has no attribute which can take sides with oppressors.

The case is before you. This is our golden opportunity. Let us accept it, and forever wipe out the dark reproaches unsparingly hurled against us by our enemies. Let us win for ourselves the gratitude of our country, and the best blessings of our posterity through all time.

From *The Life and Writings of Frederick Douglass*,
Volume III, edited by Philip S. Foner, 1950.

It Was a Glorious Day!

In the fall of 1861 the Union fleet captured Port Royal harbor off the South Carolina coast and took control of that district and the Sea Islands. The slave owners had fled inland, leaving about ten thousand slaves who became "contrabands of war" in the

hands of the Northern army. Isolated for generations from the rest of the world, the former slaves had been given few chances for education. Lincoln's government decided to send teachers south to demonstrate that the freedmen could be educated and trained to become useful, independent citizens. It was a chance to refute the old argument that Blacks were fit only for slavery. The next spring fifty-three teachers—all white—arrived from the North and took their posts on plantations. They taught the former slaves to read and write, distributed clothing, helped the sick, and did all they could to prepare them for new responsibilities.

Six months later, twenty-four-year-old Charlotte Forten arrived from Philadelphia as the first black teacher to join in the experiment to prove Blacks were as capable of self-improvement as whites. She came just as the army had begun to raise a "black regiment" from the young freedmen of the islands. General Rufus Saxton had chosen Colonel Thomas Wentworth Higginson, a Massachusetts abolitionist, to command and train the new black troops. Miss Forten was invited to the army camp to watch the ceremony on January 1, 1863, the day the Emancipation Proclamation went into effect.

NEW-YEAR'S DAY, Emancipation Day, was a glorious one to us. General Saxton and Colonel Higginson had invited us to visit the camp of the First Regiment of South Carolina Volunteers on that day, "the greatest day in the nation's history." We enjoyed perfectly the exciting scene on board the steamboat *Flora*. There was an eager, wondering crowd of the freed people, in their holiday attire, with the gayest of headkerchiefs, the whitest of aprons, and the happiest of faces. The band was playing, the flags were streaming, and everybody was talking merrily and feeling happy. The sun shone brightly, and the very waves seemed to partake of the universal gayety, for they danced and sparkled more joyously than ever before. Long before we reached Camp Saxton, we could see the beautiful grove and the ruins of the old fort near it.

Some companies of the First Regiment were drawn up in line under the trees near the landing, ready to receive us. They were a fine, soldierly looking set of men, and their brilliant dress made a splendid appearance among the trees. It was my good fortune to find an old friend among the officers. He took us over the camp and showed us all the arrangements. Everything looked clean and comfortable; much neater, we were told, than in most of the white camps.

An officer told us that he had never seen a regiment in which the men were so honest. "In many other camps," said he, "the Colonel and the rest of us would find it necessary to place a guard before our tents. We never do it here. Our tents are left entirely unguarded, but nothing has ever been touched." We were glad to know that. It is a remarkable fact, when we consider that the men of this regiment have all their lives been slaves; for we all know that Slavery does not tend to make men honest.

The ceremony in honor of Emancipation took place in the beautiful grove of live-oaks adjoining the camp. I wish it were possible to describe fitly the scene which met our eyes, as we sat upon the stand, and looked down on the crowd before us. There were the black soldiers in their blue coats and scarlet pantaloons; the officers of the First Regiment, and of other regiments, in their handsome uniforms; and there were crowds of lookers-on, men, women, and children, of every complexion, grouped in various attitudes, under the moss-hung trees. The faces of all wore a happy, interested look.

The exercises commenced with a prayer by the chaplain of the regiment. An ode, written for the occasion, was then read and sung. President Lincoln's Proclamation of Emancipation was then read, and enthusiastically cheered. The Rev. Mr.

French presented Colonel Higginson with two very elegant flags, a gift to the First Regiment, from the Church of the Puritans, in New York. He accompanied them by an appropriate and enthusiastic speech. As Colonel Higginson took the flags, before he had time to reply to the speech, some of the colored people, of their own accord, began to sing,—

"My country, 'tis of thee,
Sweet land of liberty,
Of thee we sing!"

It was a touching and beautiful incident, and sent a thrill through all our hearts. The Colonel was deeply moved by it. He said that reply was far more effective than any speech he could make. But he did make one of those stirring speeches which are "half battles." All hearts swelled with emotion as we listened to his glorious words, "stirring the soul like the sound of a trumpet." His soldiers are warmly attached to him, and he evidently feels toward them all as if they were his children.

General Saxton spoke also, and was received with great enthusiasm. Throughout the morning, repeated cheers were given for him by the regiment, and joined in heartily by all the people. They know him to be one of the best and noblest men in the world. His unfailing kindness and consideration for them, so different from the treatment they have sometimes received at the hands of United States officers, have caused them to have unbounded confidence in him.

At the close of Colonel Higginson's speech, he presented the flags to the color-bearers, Sergeant Rivers and Sergeant Sutton, with an earnest charge, to which they made appropriate replies.

Mrs. Gage uttered some earnest words, and then the regiment sang John Brown's Hallelujah Song.

After the meeting was over, we saw the dress-parade, which

was a brilliant and beautiful sight. An officer told us that the men went through the drill remarkably well, and learned the movements with wonderful ease and rapidity. To us it seemed strange as a miracle to see this regiment of blacks, the first mustered into the service of the United States, thus doing itself honor in the sight of officers of other regiments, many of whom doubtless came to scoff. The men afterward had a great feast; ten oxen having been roasted whole, for their especial benefit.

In the evening there was the softest, loveliest moonlight. We were very unwilling to go home; for, besides the attractive society, we knew that the soldiers were to have grand shouts and a general jubilee that night. But the steamboat was coming, and we were obliged to bid a reluctant farewell to Camp Saxton and the hospitable dwellers therein. We walked the deck of the steamer singing patriotic songs, and we agreed that moonlight and water had never looked so beautiful as they did that night.

At Beaufort we took the row-boat for St. Helena. The boatmen as they rowed sang some of their sweetest, wildest hymns. It was a fitting close to such a day. Our hearts were filled with an exceeding great gladness; for although the government had left much undone, we knew that Freedom was surely born in our land that day. It seemed too glorious a good to realize, this beginning of the great work we had so longed for and prayed for. It was a sight never to be forgotten, that crowd of happy black faces from which the shadow of Slavery had forever passed.

"Forever free! forever free!"—those magical words in the President's Proclamation were constantly singing themselves in my soul.

From *The Freedmen's Book*, by Lydia Maria Child, 1865.

A Letter from the Front

Black troops met their first major battle test in the storming of Fort Wagner. It was a Confederate stronghold on Morris Island, South Carolina, just six miles away from St. Helena Island, where Charlotte Forten was teaching the former slaves.

Placed at the head of the assault was the Massachusetts Fifty-

fourth. Not a man of this first black regiment to be raised in the free states had held a musket in his hand eighteen weeks before. Without training in storming a fort, they were sent headlong into a badly planned night attack. The Confederate batteries answered with volcanic blasts of shots and shell, but the black soldiers climbed up the parapet to a desperate bayonet struggle at the top. Outnumbered and outgunned, they were ordered back after two assaults.

The Union casualties were great, and the Fifty-fourth bore the heaviest losses in dead and wounded. But the black troops had proved their courage and their soldiership.

Letters from the front gave the folks back home some idea of what the black troops were going through. One from Lewis Douglass (son of Frederick Douglass) told his sweetheart, Amelia Loguen (daughter of J. W. Loguen), of the battle at Fort Wagner.

My Dear Amelia:

I have been in two fights, and am unhurt. I am about to go in another I believe tonight. Our men fought well on both occasions. The last was desperate. We charged that terrible battery on Morris island known as Fort Wagner, and were repulsed. . . . De Forest of your city is wounded, George Washington is missing, Jacob Carter is missing, Charles Reason wounded, Charles Whiting, Charles Creamer all wounded.

I escaped unhurt from amidst that perfect hail of shot and shell. It was terrible. I need not particularize, the papers will give a better [account] than I have time to give. My thoughts are with you often, you are as dear as ever, be good to remember it as I no doubt you will. As I said before we are on the eve of another fight and I am very busy and have just snatched a moment to write you. I must necessarily be brief. Should I fall in the next fight killed or wounded I hope I fall with my face to the foe.

This regiment has established its reputation as a fighting regiment, not a man flinched, though it was a trying time. Men fell all around me. A shell would explode and clear a space of twenty feet. Our men would close up again, but it was no use, we had to retreat, which was a very hazardous undertaking. How I got out of that fight alive I cannot tell, but I am here.

My Dear girl I hope again to see you. I must bid you farewell should I be killed. Remember if I die I die in a good cause. I wish we had a hundred thousand colored troops we would put an end to this war.

Good Bye to all. Your own loving—Write soon—

LEWIS

From *The Mind of the Negro as Reflected in Letters Written During the Crisis, 1800–1860*, edited by Carter G. Woodson, 1926.

To My Old Master

When the war ended in 1865, the South was a wreck. Its cities were shelled and burned, its fields and crops ruined, its men dead or wounded. The freed slaves wandered over the land, desperately trying to survive without the help of masters upon whom they had depended all their lives. Food for the table, a roof overhead, education for the children, care for the old folks, work, jobs—where would it come from, in a desolate and bitter South?

Thousands and thousands of Blacks had left their old places, sometimes because they wanted something different, someplace else, whatever it might be. Sometimes because no one was left to take charge. Sometimes because old masters had returned but had driven them off. One ex-slaveholder, typical of many, tried

to get back a former slave who had slipped away to freedom during the war. Here is the freedman's reply.

> *To my old Master, Colonel P. H. Anderson,*
> *Big Spring, Tennessee.*

Sir. I got your letter, and was glad to find that you had not forgotten Jourdon, and that you wanted me to come back and live with you again, promising to do better for me than anybody else can. I have often felt uneasy about you. I thought the Yankees would have hung you long before this, for harboring Rebs they found at your house. I suppose they never heard about your going to Colonel Martin's to kill the Union soldier that was left by his company in their stable. Although you shot at me twice before I left you, I did not want to hear of your being hurt, and am glad you are still living. It would do me good to go back to the dear old home again, and see Miss Mary and Miss Martha and Allen, Esther, Green, and Lee. Give my love to them all, and tell them I hope we will meet in the better world, if not in this. I would have gone back to see you all when I was working in the Nashville Hospital, but one of the neighbors told me that Henry intended to shoot me if he ever got a chance.

I want to know particularly what the good chance is you propose to give me. I am doing tolerably well here. I get twenty-five dollars a month, with victuals and clothing; have a comfortable home for Mandy,—the folks call her Mrs. Anderson,—and the children—Milly, Jane, and Grundy—go to school and are learning well. The teacher says Grundy has a head for a preacher. They go to Sunday school, and Mandy and me attend church regularly. We are kindly treated. Sometimes we overhear others saying, "Them colored people were slaves" down in Tennessee. The children feel hurt when they hear such remarks; but I tell them it was no disgrace in Tennessee to belong to Colonel Anderson. Many darkeys would have been proud, as I used to be, to call you master. Now if you will write and say what wages you will give me, I will be better able to decide whether it would be to my advantage to move back again.

As to my freedom, which you say I can have, there is nothing to be gained on that score, as I got my free papers in 1864 from the Provost-Marshal-General of the Department of Nashville. Mandy says she would be afraid to go back without some proof that you were disposed to treat us justly and kindly; and we have concluded to test your sincerity by asking you to send us our wages for the time we served you. This will make us forget and forgive old scores, and rely on your justice and friendship in the future. I served you faithfully for thirty-two years, and Mandy twenty years. At twenty-five dollars a month for me, and two dollars a week for Mandy, our earnings would amount to eleven thousand six hundred and eighty dollars. Add to this the interest for the time our wages have been kept back, and deduct what you paid for our clothing, and three doctor's visits to me, and pulling a tooth for Mandy, and the balance will show what we are in justice entitled to. Please send the money by Adam's Express, in care of V. Winters, Esq., Dayton, Ohio. If you fail to pay us for faithful labors in the past, we can have little faith in your promises in the future. We trust the good Maker has opened your eyes to the wrongs which you and your fathers have done to me and my fathers, in making us toil for you for generations without recompense. Here I draw my wages every Saturday night; but in Tennessee there was never any pay-day for the Negroes any more than for the horses and cows. Surely there will be a day of reckoning for those who defraud the laborer of his hire.

In answering this letter, please state if there would be any safety for my Milly and Jane, who are now grown up, and both good-looking girls. You know how it was with poor Matilda and Catherine. I would rather stay here and starve—and die, if it come to that—than have my girls brought to shame by the violence and wickedness of their young masters. You will also please state if there has been any schools opened for the colored children in your neighborhood. The great desire of my life now is to give my children an education, and have them form virtuous habits.

Say howdy to George Carter, and thank him for taking the pistol from you when you were shooting at me.

From your old servant,

Jourdon Anderson

From *The Freedmen's Book*, by Lydia Maria Child, 1865.

When Freedom Come

When Lee's army surrendered, American slavery came to an end. By the close of 1865, the Thirteenth Amendment, abolishing slavery, became part of the Constitution. A war that had begun with the limited aim of preserving the Union had been turned into a revolutionary crusade for freedom. It was a glorious victory for the abolitionists, Black and white. For over a generation they had labored together to rouse the country's conscience to the sin of slavery. They had been shunned and stoned, beaten, jailed, lynched. But they had gone on, talking, writing, organizing to overthrow the "peculiar institution." And now, 246 years after the first Blacks had been landed in Virginia, the dream of universal emancipation had come true.

The freedom of 4,000,000 slaves had been dearly bought. They paid heavily with their own blood, for of the quarter of a million Blacks who served in the Union forces, 38,000 lost their lives, a death rate 40 percent greater than the whites'. If their valor needed more proof, there were twenty black soldiers and sailors who earned the Congressional Medal of Honor.

So they were free at last. But what would freedom be like? How would they live? Where would they work? And what about old master? How would he take the change?

In the recollections of those first freedom days taken down from the lips of ex-slaves many years later, you can see the breaking up of old ways and the forming of new. The first passage is from a woman who had been a slave in Mississippi and Tennessee, the second came from South Carolina, and the third from Georgia.

*

WHEN FREEDOM COME, folks left home, out in the streets, crying, praying, singing, shouting, yelling, and knocking down everything. Some shot off big guns. Then come the calm. It was sad then. So many folks done dead, things tore up, and nowheres to go and nothing to eat, nothing to do. It got squally. Folks got sick, so hungry. Some folks starved nearly to death. Ma was a cripple woman. Pa couldn't find work for so long when he mustered out.

Toby and Govie

I worked for Massa 'bout four years after freedom, 'cause he forced me to, said he couldn't 'ford to let me go. His place was near ruint, the fences burnt, and the house would have been, but it was rock. There was a battle fought near his place, and I taken Missy to a hideout in the mountains to where her father was, 'cause there was bullets flying everywhere. When the war was over, Massa come home and says, "You son of a gun, you's supposed to be free, but you ain't, 'cause I ain't gwine give you freedom." So I goes on working for him till I gits the chance to steal a hoss from him. The woman I wanted to marry, Govie, she 'cides to come to Texas with me. Me and Govie, we rides that hoss 'most a hundred miles, then we turned him a-loose and give him a scare back to his house, and come on foot the rest of the way to Texas.

All we had to eat was what we could beg, and sometimes we went three days without a bite to eat. Sometimes we'd pick a few berries. When we got cold we'd crawl in a brushpile and hug up close together to keep warm. Once in a while we'd come to a farmhouse, and the man let us sleep on cottonseed in his barn, but they was far and few between, 'cause they wasn't many houses in the country them days like now.

When we gits to Texas, we gits married, but all they was to our wedding am we just 'grees to live together as man and wife. I settled on some land, and we cut some trees and split them open and stood them on end with the tops together for our house. Then we deadened some trees, and the land was ready to farm. There was some wild cattle and hogs, and that's the way we got our start, caught some of them and tamed them.

I don't know as I 'spected nothing from freedom, but they turned us out like a bunch of stray dogs, no homes, no clothing, no nothing, not 'nough food to last us one meal. After we settles on that place, I never seed man or woman 'cept Govie, for six years, 'cause it was a long ways to anywhere. All we had to farm with was sharp sticks. We'd stick holes and plant corn, and when it come up we'd punch up the dirt round it. We didn't plant cotton, 'cause we couldn't eat that. I made bows and arrows to kill wild game with, and we never went to a store for nothing. We made our clothes out of animal skins.

I Stayed in Peonage

After Sherman come through Atlanta, he let the slaves go, and when he did, me and some of the other slaves went back to our old masters. Old Man Governor Brown was my boss man. After the war was over, Old Man Gordon took me and some of the others out to Mississippi. I stayed in peonage out there for 'bout forty years. I was located at just 'bout forty miles south of Greenwood, and I worked on the plantations of Old Man Sara Jones and Old Man Gordon.

I couldn't git away 'cause they watched us with guns all the time. When the levee busted, that kinda freed me. Man, they was devils; they wouldn't 'low you to go nowhere—not even to church. You done good to git something to eat. They wouldn't give you no clothes, and if you got wet you just had to lay down in what you got wet in.

And, man, they would whup you in spite of the devil. You had to ask to git water—if you didn't they would stretch you 'cross a barrel and wear you out. If you didn't work in a hurry, they would whup you with a strap that had five–six holes in it. I ain't talking 'bout what I heard—I'm talking 'bout what I done seed.

One time they sent me on Old Man Mack Williams' farm here in Jasper County, Georgia. That man would kill you sure. If that little branch on his plantation could talk it would tell many a tale 'bout folks being knocked in the head. I done seen Mack Williams kill folks, and I done seen him have folks killed. One day he told me that if my wife had been good looking, I never would sleep with her again 'cause he'd kill me and take her and raise childrens offen her. They used to take women away from their husbands, and put with some other man to breed just like they would do cattle. They always kept a man penned up, and they used him like a stud hoss.

When you didn't do right, Old Mack Williams would shoot you or tie a chain round your neck and throw you in the river. He'd git them other niggers to carry them to the river, and if they didn't he'd shoot 'em down. Any time they didn't do what he said, he would shoot 'em down. He'd tell 'em to "Catch that nigger," and they would do it. Then he would tell 'em to put the chain round their neck and throw 'em in the river. I ain't heard this—I done seen it.

From *Lay My Burden Down*, edited by B. A. Botkin,
University of Chicago Press, 1945.

From Memphis to New Orleans

The riot in New Orleans—platform in Mechanics' Institute after
the riot (from a contemporary sketch)

*The Union armies had smashed the old order. The slaveholding
economy of the South lay in ruins. At the war's close, eleven
states were out of the Union. Conquered they were—but not
subdued, as one Southerner warned. Now they faced the task*

of rebuilding their life with the land and without the slave labor they had always relied on.

But in what direction would the South move? Would it adopt the conqueror's ideas and institutions? His politics and principles? Or would it hold fast to its own, and try to nourish old roots back into life?

Much depended upon what the North would do. The soldiers in blue returned home to prospering farms, humming factories, and spreading cities, to an economy that had grown incredibly fast and strong under the pressures and opportunities of war. The manufacturers and merchants, bankers and brokers who held the controls saw limitless horizons for expansion and profits. They wanted to sell their new goods, and sell them anywhere to anybody. As their profits had piled up during the war they had begun putting the surplus into western lands, mines, and railroads. Now they looked south, to see how they could "northernize" the stricken land. From its coal and iron, timber and turpentine, plantations and railroads, money could be made. As Yankee businessmen prepared to send their dollars south, they thought about how to reconstruct the region to attain the calm conditions required for investments to prosper.

That term—"Reconstruction"—came into popular use during the Civil War. Then it meant the restoration in the South of state governments that would be loyal to the Union. Historians today, however, give it a broader meaning, to cover all the major changes of the postwar period. A new United States was being born out of the old, and men and parties tried to mold its shape. There were many plans for how to reconstruct the South. Each President, from Lincoln to Johnson to Grant to Hayes, had his ideas, and so did various factions in Congress. Outside Washington other forces were pressing their own policies, from Northern abolitionists at one end to Confederate officials at the other.

Lincoln believed that the seceded states should be speedily restored to the Union under presidential guidance. His first plan for Reconstruction, developed in the middle of the war, excluded all Blacks from voting or holding office.

Only a few days before his death, however, Lincoln had told a friend that "the restoration of the Rebel states to the Union must rest upon the principle of civil and political equality of both races." He believed that the Blacks had "demonstrated in blood their right to the ballot." But a man who had been a slaveholder succeeded him in the presidency. Andrew Johnson granted pardons swiftly to many leaders of the Confederacy and made it clear he would let their states back into the Union on very lenient terms. Federal troops were rapidly withdrawn from the South, with only a handful left behind.

Encouraged to set up their own governments and apply for readmission to the Union, the Southern states framed new constitutions and elected their officials. But nowhere was the ballot offered to the Black. As in slavery times, Southerners—and many in the North—still believed that Blacks were born inferior, and therefore not only unfit to take part in politics but unable ever to learn how. Only the white race—the superior race—could vote, and in the fall elections of 1865 prominent Confederates were put in office everywhere and the great task of Reconstruction placed in their hands. The sign of how they planned to carry it out was visible at once. "Black codes" were adopted by the state legislatures which in all but name restored the Black to his old position of slave. The codes permitted Blacks to be sold into temporary bondage for "vagrancy." This is a "white man's government," said the new governor of South Carolina, "and intended for white men only." To which all the other new governments said Amen.

If this was what "home rule" meant, the North would not tolerate it. Republican politicians knew that riveting the chains back on the Black would make the Democratic Party dominant again. Businessmen did not care to put money into a slave economy. And abolitionists were enraged by the attempt to make a mockery of an emancipation bought by four terrible years of war.

In one state after another Blacks held rallies and conventions to protest these bitter fruits of Reconstruction Southern style. They demanded that oppressive laws be wiped off the statute books and that all political and legal barriers based upon color be torn down. They wanted the right to vote and federal protection from the bands of white hoodlums trying to terrorize the Black.

Under the Republican leadership of Congressman Thaddeus Stevens and Senator Charles Sumner, Congress refused to seat the new Southern congressmen and rejected the President's Reconstruction program. It set up a Joint Committee of Fifteen to get the facts on what was going on in the South and to work out a better Reconstruction plan. The Committee's proposals included a Freedmen's Bureau and a Civil Rights Bill, both of which Congress passed over President Johnson's veto, and the Fourteenth Amendment to the Constitution. It declared Blacks were citizens of the United States and entitled to equal treatment before the law. If any state denied or abridged the franchise on account of race or color, that state would lose representation in Congress proportionately.

To get back into the Union, Southern states had to ratify the Amendment. Although the Amendment did not make a direct grant of black suffrage, every state but Tennessee at once rejected it.

If further evidence was needed of how the South felt, two spectacular anti-Black riots broke out that year. In May of 1866, after some dispute between black soldiers and the white police force of Memphis, a mob joined the police in a drunken assault upon the city's black population that was put down by federal troops only after three days of burning, raping, and pillaging. The toll showed forty-six Blacks killed and over eighty wounded; one white man was injured.

Violence against the Blacks continued into the summer. On July 30 a riot erupted in New Orleans when a white mob containing many policemen and ex-Confederate soldiers attacked a black-white convention called to consider a black suffrage amendment to Louisiana's constitution. Some thirty-four Blacks and four of their white allies were killed and more than two hundred injured.

This was no riot, said Union General Philip Sheridan, "but an absolute massacre by the police." Congress sent investigators to both Memphis and New Orleans. From the testimony of the ex-slaves Sarah Song and J. B. Jourdain come the following two excerpts:

Sarah Song

Q. Were you in Memphis at the time of the riots?

A. Yes, sir; I was.

Q. What did you see of the rioting?

A. I saw them kill my husband; it was on Tuesday night, between ten and eleven o'clock.

Q. Who shot him?

A. I do not know. There were between twenty and thirty men who came to the house. When they first came, they hallo'd to us to open the doors. My husband was sick in bed and could not get up; he had been sick in bed two weeks—he had the jaundice. I lay there, I was so scared; we have two children who were with us. They broke the outside doors open. I staid in bed till they came in. The inside door was open. They came into the room and asked if we had any pistols or shot guns in the house. My husband said he had one, but it was only a rusty pistol that his little boy had found—it was fit for nothing but the child to play with. Then they told my husband to get up and get it; he got up and gave it to them. I then lighted a lamp after they got the pistol. They told my husband to get up and come out, that they were going to shoot him. They made him get up and go out of doors and told him if he had anything to say to say it quick, for they were going to kill him. If he said anything, I did not hear it.

He stood outside, perhaps a quarter of an hour. They asked him if he had been a soldier; he said he never had been. One of them said, "You are a damned liar; you have been in the government service for the last twelve or fourteen months." "Yes," said he, "I have been in the government service, but not as a soldier." Then another said, "Why did you not tell us that at first?" Then one stepped back and shot him as quick as he said that; he was not a yard from him; he put the pistol to his head and shot him three times. This was between ten and eleven o'clock. When my husband fell he scuffled about a little, and looked as if he tried to get back into the house. Then they told him if he did not make haste and die, they would shoot him again. Then one of them kicked him, and another shot him again when he was down; they shot him through the head every time, as far as I could see. He never spoke after he fell. They then went running right off and did not come back again. . . .

From "Memphis Riots and Massacres,"
Report No. 101, House of Representatives,
39th Congress, 1st Session (Serial No. 1274).

J. B. Jourdain

Q. What is your age?

A. I am thirty-four.

Q. How long have you lived in New Orleans?

A. I was born here.

Q. Were you in this city on the thirtieth of July last?

A. Yes, sir; I was here the whole month of July.

Q. Were you in the Mechanics' Institute on that day?

A. Yes, sir; I was there about 12 o'clock. My attention was called to something going on outside; I heard a drum beating as if the military were coming, and I was much satisfied that it was so. As I looked up the street to where I heard the drum, I saw the United States flag flying, and I recognized a procession of colored persons with the flag. Then I went towards them, and as I got to the corner of Canal and Dryades the procession was coming up Dryades Street from below.

When the tail part of the procession, which consisted of boys, came up, there was a pistol fired from a man who was standing on the corner of the banquette [sidewalk]; it was fired by an officer with whom I am well acquainted . . . he was detailed by the police. He fired at the procession—at those colored boys; when he shot, the boys wheeled around. There were two or three shots fired by the same person; I believe it was by the same person. Then the police from the other side rushed and arrested one of these boys, and jerked him and took him to the calaboose. The drum had kept on with the flag, and the boys all ran.

I stood at the corner and did not go any further; I thought I would not go back to the Mechanics' Institute, and I remained there for perhaps ten minutes. On the corner where I was standing I saw the police from Dauphin Street turning up Canal Street, and running with pistols in their hands. I got on the side of the banquette and let them go by. As they passed Dryades Street they were firing in the street there, and the loafers that were there were throwing bricks at the Negroes, and the Negroes, too, were throwing bricks, and as the people came up they commenced firing. They fired to scare the people, but they fired with bullets. After firing some time the street got a little clear, so that they could go in. I followed them. When they got to the Mechanics' Institute they found the door fastened and they could not get in; then they backed out and fired several times through the windows.

Q. Were the windows up or down?

A. They were shut—some of them might have been open—

and as they fired they broke the glass. Then the fire bells began to ring and the firemen began to come. The policemen then succeeded in bursting open the doors and went inside. What they did inside I do not know, but in about a quarter of an hour after there were a good many came out wounded, cut up, shot in the face and head, and there were police taking them to the calaboose. As they passed with them the crowd would knock them down and kill them, and some of the police were helping them kill them on the street.

I spoke to the lieutenant of police, with whom I am acquainted—I am acquainted with them all somewhat—and I begged him "For God's sake, stop your men from killing these men so." He gave me no answer, but walked away to the Mechanics' Institute. After a while I spoke to him again; said I, "For God's sake, stop these men from this; I could arrest them all myself." His reply was, "Yes, God damn them; I'll set fire to the building and burn them all." I said no more, but went away. Afterwards I saw a man come out. He was led by a man at each arm; he had no hat on, and his face was all covered with blood. I was looking straight at him, and I said, "That's somebody I know"—I was speaking to myself. When he appeared the crowd cried out, "Kill him." "Kill the damned son of a bitch." I saw it was Dr. Dostie. The officers had him, and were taking him towards Canal Street. The shots were fired while the police had hold of him, and some of the police were wounded by their own men. It was a volley of shots; I saw he dropped, he must have been more than half dead. I remarked, "There is one more." They then rushed back to the Mechanics' Institute, and every man that came out of the Institute was shot or knocked down with a loaded pistol, and when he was down they would shoot him.

From "New Orleans Riots," Report No. 16, House of Representatives, 39th Congress, 2nd Session (Serial No. 1304).

I Shall Not Beg for My Rights

Henry MacNeal Turner

Angered by the violence in the South, Northerners voted more Stevens-Sumner Republicans into Congress in the fall elections of 1866. As soon as Congress met, it gave the right to vote to Blacks in the District of Columbia. In March 1867, again over President Johnson's veto, it launched its own program (called Radical Reconstruction) by dividing the South into five districts under military command, ordering elections for conventions that would rewrite state constitutions, and giving Blacks the right to vote.

Beginning that fall the Southern states, under the eye of the military, held the constitutional conventions the Reconstruction

*Acts called for. About a million Blacks were now enfranchised,
and nearly the same number of whites. Most of the Blacks, long
forbidden education whether slave or free, were illiterate, as were
about a third of the whites. When registration was ended, 660,000
whites had qualifed to vote, and 700,000 Blacks.*

*Illiterate though most of the Blacks were, they were no less
qualified to vote than the immigrants now being herded to the
polls in the thousands by the political bosses of Northern cities.
Given time, they would learn to read and write. Only two years
out of bondage, they had the courage to risk the vengeance of
former masters and to stand up for their rights as free citizens.
Frederick Douglass, granting all that was being said of the freedman's ignorance, pointed out that "if the Negro knows enough
to fight for his country, he knows enough to vote; if he knows
enough to pay taxes for the support of the government, he knows
enough to vote."*

*Even after centuries of oppression, leaders could and did arise.
They came from the plantations and the towns to take their seats
in constitutional conventions and in state legislatures, seats that
had always been reserved for white planters. A few had the
benefit of formal training; others were almost wholly self-
educated. Many were preachers, some teachers, a few lawyers,
the others farmers or artisans. Fears of the white South that
Blacks, once in office, would seek bloody revenge proved
groundless. Over the South Carolina convention, the first assembly with a majority of black delegates, rippled a banner with
the slogan "United we stand, divided we fall."*

*Among the new leaders of the black people was Henry MacNeal
Turner. Born free in South Carolina, on his father's death he
had been bound out to a planter and had lived his young years
in conditions little different from slavery. By the age of twelve
he had shown his fearlessness in refusing to permit overseers to
beat him. At fifteen he ran away. He learned his ABC's from
friendly whites, but when others interfered, he taught himself to*

read and write out of Bible and hymnbook. As messenger in a
lawyer's office and then handyman in a Baltimore medical school,
he devoured every book and magazine at hand to learn all he
could of law, medicine, and theology. When the Civil War came
he was the first Black to be commissioned an army chaplain,
serving with a black regiment. Turner was elected to the first
Reconstruction legislature of Georgia. While he tried to secure
better wages for black workers, he also moved to assist the whites'
economic recovery. But the legislature was dominated by a white
majority, and in September 1868 it expelled all its members who
were blacks. Here is Representative Turner's defense of the Black's
right to hold office, made on September 3.

BEFORE PROCEEDING TO argue this question upon its in-
trinsic merits, I wish the members of this House to understand
the position that I take. I hold that I am a member of this
body. Therefore, sir, I shall neither fawn or cringe before any
party, nor stoop to beg them for my rights. Some of my colored
fellow members, in the course of their remarks, took occasion
to appeal to the sympathies of members on the opposite side,
and to eulogize their character for magnanimity. It reminds me
very much, sir, of slaves begging under the lash. I am here to
demand my rights. . . .

The scene presented in this House, to-day, is one unparalleled in the history of the world. . . . Never has a man been
arraigned before a body clothed with legislative, judicial or
executive functions, charged with the offense of being of a
darker hue than his fellowmen . . . charged with an offense
committed by the God of Heaven Himself. Cases may be found
where men have been deprived of their rights for crimes and
misdemeanors; but it has remained for the State of Georgia,
in the very heart of the nineteenth century, to call a man before
the bar, and there charge him with an act for which he is no

more responsible than for the head which he carries upon his shoulders. . . .

Whose Legislature is this? Is it a white man's Legislature, or is it a black man's Legislature? Who voted for a Constitutional Convention, in obedience to the mandate of the Congress of the United States? Who first rallied around the standard of Reconstruction? Who set the ball of loyalty rolling in the State of Georgia? And whose voice was heard on the hills and in the valleys of his State? It was the voice of the brawny-armed Negro, with the few humanitarian-hearted white men who came to our assistance. I claim the honor, sir, of having been the instrument of convincing hundreds—yea, thousands—of white men, that to reconstruct under the measures of the United States Congress was the safest and the best course for the interest of the State.

Let us look at some facts in connection with this matter. Did half the white men of Georgia vote for this Legislature? Did not the great bulk of them fight, with all their strength, the Constitution under which we are acting? And did they not fight against the organization of this Legislature? And further, sir, did they not vote against it? Yes, sir! And there are persons in this Legislature today, who are ready to spit their poison in my face, while they themselves opposed, with all their power, the ratification of this Constitution. They question my right to a seat in this body, to represent the people whose legal votes elected me. . . . We are told that if black men want to speak, they must speak through white trumpets; if black men want their sentiments expressed, they must be adulterated and sent through white messengers, who will quibble, and equivocate, and evade, as rapidly as the pendulum of a clock. If this be not done, then the black men have committed an outrage, and their Representatives must be denied the right to represent their constituents.

The great question, sir, is this: Am I a man? If I am such,

I claim the rights of a man. Am I not a man because I happen to be of a darker hue than honorable gentlemen around me?

We have pioneered civilization here; we have built up your country; we have worked in your fields, and garnered your harvests, for two hundred and fifty years! And what do we ask of you in return? Do we ask you for compensation for the sweat our fathers bore for you—for the tears you have caused, and the hearts you have broken, and the lives you have curtailed, and the blood you have spilled? Do we ask retaliation? We ask it not. We are willing to let the dead past bury its dead; but we ask you now for our rights.

You have all the elements of superiority upon your side; you have our money and your own; you have our education and your own; and you have your land and our own, too. We, who number hundreds of thousands in Georgia, including our wives and families, with not a foot of land to call our own—strangers in the land of our birth; without money, without education, without aid, without a roof to cover us while we live, nor sufficient clay to cover us when we die! . . .

You may expel us, gentlemen, but I firmly believe that you will someday repent it. The black man cannot protect a country, if the country doesn't protect him; and if, tomorrow, a war should arise, I would not raise a musket to defend a country where my manhood is denied. The fashionable way in Georgia when hard work is to be done, is, for the white man to sit at his ease, while the black man does the work; but, sir, I will say this much to the colored men of Georgia, as if I should be killed in this campaign, I may have no opportunity of telling them at any other time: Never lift a finger nor raise a hand in defense of Georgia, unless Georgia acknowledges that you are men, and invests you with the rights pertaining to man-hood. . . .

From "Participation of Negroes in the Government 1867–1870," by Ethel M. Christler, unpublished master's thesis, Atlanta University, 1932.

His Crime Was
His Color

Printing shop at Tuskegee Institute, where
young Blacks learned the craft

*It was a great thing to be free, but it was terribly hard to make
your own way in the world, without money, without land, without friends. It was "root, hog, or die" in the beginning. Now
the four million Blacks released from slavery were thrown on
the job market to compete with white labor. It was a situation
made for trouble. Some white planters, embittered by the loss
of their human chattels, drove the ex-slaves off the plantations.
Others, eager to get labor at the lowest possible cost, were en-*

*raged by freedmen who asserted their right to refuse work if they
didn't like the pay.*

*Many Blacks had had enough of plantation life under any
terms. To them it would always be tainted with memories of
slavery. They moved into the cities, going north as well as south.
Others, skilled as blacksmiths, cabinetmakers, bricklayers, tried
to find work in their craft or trade but met iron resistance from
white artisans who feared their competition. Some employers
did not draw the color line, however, especially if it helped them
to undermine the new white unions. Northerners looked south
for cheap labor and imported Blacks to beat down a higher
standard of living or to break unions. The exploitation of the
Black for such purposes only sharpened the cleavage between
black and white workers. Very few unions welcomed Blacks into
their ranks.*

*In Rochester, New York, Frederick Douglass, the foremost
leader of his people for a generation, saw his own son discrim-
inated against by a union. In 1869 he made these remarks about
it in a speech.*

DOUGLASS [his son Lewis] is made a transgressor for
working at a low rate of wages by the very men who prevented
his getting a high rate. He is denounced for not being a member
of a Printers' Union by the very men who would not permit
him to join such Union. He is not condemned because he is
not a good printer, but because he did not become such in a
regular way, that regular way being closed against him by the
men now opposing him.

Suppose it were true that this young man had worked for
lower wages than white printers receive, can any printer be
fool enough to believe that he did so from choice? What me-
chanic will ever work for low wages when he can possibly obtain
higher? Had he been a white young man, with his education

and ability, he could easily have obtained employment, and could have found it on the terms demanded by the Printers' Union.

There is no disguising the fact—his crime was his color. It was his color in Denver, it was his color in Rochester, and it is his color in Washington to-day. In connection with this subject I have now a word to say of the goodly city in which I have lived for the last twenty years, and where I still reside, a city than which not one in the country is more civilized, refined and cultivated. It abounds in both educational and religious institutions, and its people are generally as liberal and friendly to the colored race as any other in this State, and far more so than most cities outside of the State. Here the common schools have been open to all classes alike for a dozen years, and colored and white children have sat on the same benches, and played in the same school-yards, and at the same sports and games, and they have done so in peace. I can say many good things of Rochester. The Fugitive-Slave bill never took a slave out of its limits, though several attempts were made to do so. When colored people were mobbed and hunted like wild beasts in other cities, and public fury was fanned against them by a malignant pro-slavery press, the colored man was always safe and well protected in Rochester.

And yet I have something against it. One of the saddest spectacles that ever assailed my eyes or pained my heart was presented in that city, and you will pardon me for making mention of it, though it is clearly personal. The same young man who is now at work at the Government printing office in Washington and against whose employment so much feeling has been shown, was the subject. He had just returned from the war; had stood on the walls of Fort Wagner with Colonel Shaw; had borne himself like a man on the perilous edge of battle, and now that the war was nearly over, he had returned to Rochester, somewhat broken in health, but still able and willing to work at his trade. But alas! he begged in vain of his fellow-worms to give him leave to toil. Day after day, week after week, and month after month he sought work, found none, and came home sad and dejected.

I had felt the iron of Negro hate before, but the case of this young man gave it a deeper entrance into my soul than ever before. For sixteen years I had printed a public journal in Rochester; I had employed white men and white apprentices during all this time; had paid out, in various ways, to white men in that city little less than $100,000, and yet here was my son, who had learned his trade in my office, a young man of good character, and yet unable to find work at his trade because of his color and race. Walking among my fellow-citizens in the street, I have never failed to receive due courtesy and kindness. Some men have even shown an interest in saving my soul; but of what avail are such manifestations where one sees himself ostracized, degraded and denied the means of obtaining his daily bread?

From *The New York Times*, August 8, 1869.

KKK

The legal power to punish had been the slaveholder's primary method of control. The flogging, branding, mutilation, and mob violence commonly reported in slavery days did not end with Emancipation. Violence had been deeply embedded in Southern life and now it was used to put down all those whom the former Confederates saw as enemies. Anyone who tried to educate the Blacks on their political rights and to help them vote, or who preached black-white equality, was a fit target. By 1867 the Ku

Klux Klan and several other secret organizations had combined their terror in an attempt to destroy Radical Reconstruction throughout the South. They rode under the banner of white supremacy. Business pressure, vote buying, the lash, the hangman's noose, the torch, and the gun were their weapons. They meant to crush the Black and his white allies.

The first selection to follow comes from a transcription, taken many years later, of an ex-slave's reminiscences of the Klan in North Carolina.

If the struggling new governments were to make any headway, they had to fight back. They passed laws against the night riders and with their state militias tried to stop the outrages. But the violence did not let up, and their very survival as governments was threatened. Appeals to President Grant for federal intervention brought little relief. When cases were pressed, witnesses were usually too scared to testify, and even if they did, juries refused to convict.

Finally, in April 1871, Congress passed a law known as the Ku Klux Act that empowered the President to declare martial law where the secret organizations were deemed "in rebellion against the government of the United States." A joint committee

of Congress went south to hold hearings on the counterrecon-
struction. Black witnesses by the score told what was happening
to their people.

  The second selection is part of the testimony on South Carolina
that Willis Johnson gave the committee on July 3, 1871.

North Carolina

AFTER US COLORED FOLKS was 'sidered free and turned
loose, the Ku Klux broke out. Some colored people started to
farming, like I told you, and gathered the old stock. If they
got so they made good money and had a good farm, the Ku
Klux would come and murder 'em. The government builded
schoolhouses, and the Ku Klux went to work and burned 'em
down. They'd go to the jails and take the colored men out and
knock their brains out and break their necks and throw 'em in
the river.

  There was a colored man they taken, his name was Jim
Freeman. They taken him and destroyed his stuff and him
'cause he was making some money. Hung him on a tree in his
front yard, right in front of his cabin.

  There was some colored young men went to the schools
they'd opened by the government. Some white woman said
someone had stole something of hers, so they put them young
men in jail. The Ku Klux went to the jail and took 'em out
and killed 'em. That happened the second year after the war.

  After the Ku Kluxes got so strong, the colored men got
together and made the complaint before the law. The governor
told the law to give 'em the old guns in the commissary, what
the Southern soldiers had used, so they issued the colored men
old muskets and said protect themselves. They got together
and organized the militia and had leaders like regular soldiers.
They didn't meet 'cept when they heared the Ku Kluxes were
coming to get some colored folks. Then they was ready for

'em. They'd hide in the cabins, and then's when they found out who a lot of them Ku Kluxes was, 'cause a lot of 'em was kilt. They wore long sheets and covered the hosses with sheets so you couldn't recognize 'em. Men you thought was your friend was Ku Kluxes, and you'd deal with 'em in stores in the daytime, and at night they'd come out to your house and kill you. I never took part in none of the fights, but I heared the others talk 'bout them, but not where them Ku Kluxes could hear 'em.

From *Lay My Burden Down*, edited by B. A. Botkin,
University of Chicago Press, 1945.

South Carolina

When I awoke, as near as I can tell, it was between 12 and 1 o'clock. I heard some one call "Sims." I held still and listened, and heard them walk from his door to my door. I was upstairs, and I got up and came downstairs. They walked back to his house again and asked him to put his head out. He did not answer, but his wife asked them who they were. They said they were friends. They walked back to my door again, and just as they got to the door they blew a whistle. Another whistle off a piece answered, and then men seemed to surround the house and all parts of the yard. Then they hallooed, "Open the door."

I said nothing. I went to the head of the bed and got my pistol, and leaned forward on the table with the pistol just at the door. They tried with several surges to get the door open, but it did not come open. They went to the wood-pile and got the axe, and struck the front-door some licks, bursted it open, and then went to the back door and burst it open. Nobody had yet come into the house. They said, "Strike a light." Then I dropped down on my knees back of the table, and they struck some matches and threw them in the house, and two of them stepped in the front door, and that brought them within arm's length of me as they stood there. As soon as they did that, I raised my pistol quickly, right up one's back, and shot, and he fell and hallooed, and the other tried to pull him out. As he pulled him I shot again. As they were pulling, others ran up and pulled him out in the yard, and when the whole party was out in the yard I stepped to the door and shot again, and then jumped to the back door and ran.

I got off. I stayed away until the next morning; then I came back and tracked them half a mile where they had toted this man and laid him down. I was afraid to go further. Mr. Sims and I were together, and I would not go any further, and he told me to go away, that I ought not to stay there, that he saw the men and saw the wounded man, and was satisfied that he was dead or mortally wounded, and I must leave.

Mr. John Calmes, the candidate of the Democrats for the legislature, advised me to take a paper and go around the settlement to the white people, stating that I would never vote the radical ticket, and he said he did not think they would interfere with me then. He said that all they had against me was that on election day I took the tickets around among the black people; and he said: "You knocked me out of a good many votes, but you are a good fellow and a good laborer, and we want labor in this country." I told him I would not do that. . . .

From "Testimony Taken by the Joint Select Committee to Inquire Into the Condition of Affairs in the Late Insurrectionary States."

We Did Not Discriminate

*Reconstruction has often been called the era of "black rule."
How mistaken this is can be seen from a quick look at a few
facts. Most black officeholders of the Reconstruction served in
local and state governments. Only twenty-two sat in Congress
between 1869 and 1901. Two of these represented Mississippi in
the Senate; the rest were in the lower house. Most served only
one or two terms. Only two, Joseph Rainey and Robert Smalls,
served five. All had not only the powerful opposition of the white
Democrats to contend with, but found many whites in their own
Republican Party just as determined to keep political power for
themselves. With important committee posts closed to them, the
twenty-two black members of Congress could have little influence
on lawmaking.*

*In the state governments, too, Blacks never held control. They
won high office and made large contributions to public life, but
they never dominated or ruled any state in the South. Their
greatest numerical strength was in South Carolina. In the lower
house of the first Reconstruction legislature the Blacks held eighty-
seven seats and the whites forty. But whites always controlled
the state senate and the governorship.*

*Among these whites were two groups, called "carpetbaggers"
and "scalawags." The first term was used against the Northerners
who were in the South during Reconstruction. It was a label that
implied empty-handed, greedy men had come down to grab the
belongings of Southerners and stuff them into their carpetbags.*

Certainly there were such dishonest Northerners bent on ex-
ploiting the South. But thousands of others settled in the South
after the war to help the freedmen and to build democracy. Often
theirs was a strong influence on politics because they had both
the education and experience that the freedmen and the loyal
Southern whites lacked, and they had, too, the support of the
party in power in Washington.

Alongside these "carpetbaggers" stood the "scalawags"—
Southern whites who had opposed secession and hated the rich
planters who had led the Confederate cause. Because they took
part in the new Reconstruction program, they were reviled by
the former Confederates. It was these three groups—the Blacks,
the Northern whites, and the loyal Southern whites—who figured
in the Reconstruction governments. Blacks were never domi-
nant.

The largest number of Blacks to be sent to Congress from any
one state came from South Carolina. One of them, Joseph Rai-
ney, was the first Black to be elected to Congress. Born in slav-
ery, his freedom—and his whole family's—had been purchased
by the earnings of his father, a barber. Joseph too became a
barber in Charleston and had his private schooling there. Forced
to work on Confederate fortifications when the war began, he
fled to the West Indies. He returned when the war was over, and
was elected to the state constitutional convention and then the
state senate before going to Congress. On March 5, 1872, he
rose in Congress to make this answer to attacks on "black rule"
in his state.

Now, SIR, I have not time to vindicate fully the course
of action of the colored people of South Carolina. We are
certainly in the majority there; I admit that we are as two to
one. Sir, I ask this House, I ask the country, I ask white men,
I ask Democrats, I ask Republicans whether the Negroes have

presumed to take improper advantage of the majority they hold in that State by disregarding the interest of the minority? They have not. Our convention which met in 1868, and in which the Negroes were in a large majority, did not pass any proscriptive or disfranchising acts, but adopted a liberal constitution, securing alike equal rights to all citizens, white and black, male and female, as far as possible. Mark you, we did not discriminate, although we had a majority.

Our constitution towers up in its majesty with provisions for the equal protection of all classes of citizens. Notwithstanding our majority there, we have never attempted to deprive any man in that State of the rights and immunities to which he is entitled under the Constitution of this Government. You cannot point to me a single act passed by our Legislature, at any time, which had a tendency to reflect upon or oppress any white citizen of South Carolina. You cannot show me one enactment by which the majority in our State have undertaken to crush the white men because the latter are in a minority.

From *Congressional Globe*, 1872.

I Had Reached the Promised Land

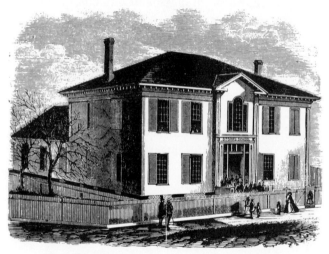

Freedmen's school at Atlanta, Georgia

One goal of the Freedmen's Bureau was to establish schools in the South. In its five short years of life, with the help of religious and philanthropic groups, it founded 4,300 schools, from the elementary grades through college. With tuition free, and often schoolbooks too, over a quarter of a million Blacks were able to start their education. Early in the Civil War, when the Sea Islands off south Carolina had been captured by the Union forces, Yankee schoolmarms had headed south to teach black children and adults to read and write. The institution of slavery had kept back the development of the black people, and the abolitionist and missionary teachers hoped to demonstrate that the widely held notions—in the North as well as in the South— of the inherent superiority and inferiority of races were wrong. Slave codes had forbidden the Blacks education, and the vast majority were therefore still illiterate. The teachers were joyously welcomed by them everywhere. Within a few years some schools had progressed so rapidly that they were training Blacks to go out and teach.

Probably a majority of the teachers who came south were abolitionists. These veterans of the antislavery crusade were also the backbone of the freedmen's aid societies that helped raise funds, recruit teachers, write textbooks, and open the schools in the South. Their zeal was notable, and necessary, for they had to overcome many obstacles in the first years of freedom. One was the fact that the children knew little or nothing of the world beyond the plantation or the village boundaries. Many had never seen a book or newspaper; some did not know right from left, or had no concept of time. Yet they learned to read, well and swiftly, under the guidance of teachers who cared.

But it was outside the school walls that the greatest barrier to education stood. It was the grim resolve of many Southern whites that these "aliens," these Yankee schoolteachers, should not meddle with "their" Blacks. The "nigger teachers," as they were called, were suspected of spreading notions of political and social equality. They were often ostracized, insulted, and whipped, and their schoolhouses were burned.

Perhaps one of the best-known instances of the Blacks' powerful desire for education is the story of Booker T. Washington. Born a slave in Virginia, freed at the age of nine, he never slept in a bed or ate at a table until after Emancipation. In his au-tobiography, Up from Slavery, *he tells how he used Webster's* Speller *to teach himself to read, and attended the first colored school opened in the neighborhood by a Northern Black. For*

five years, from the age of nine, he worked from 4:00 A.M. to
9:00 A.M. in a coal mine, went to school, and returned to the
mine for another two hours. In the passage that follows, he
describes how he got to Hampton Institute in 1872.

ONE DAY, while at work in the coal-mine, I happened
to overhear two miners talking about a great school for coloured people somewhere in Virginia. This was the first time
that I had ever heard anything about any kind of school or
college that was more pretentious than the little coloured school
in our town.

In the darkness of the mine I noiselessly crept as close as I
could to the two men who were talking. I heard one tell the
other that not only was the school established for the members
of my race, but that opportunities were provided by which poor
but worthy students could work out all or a part of the cost of
board, and at the same time be taught some trade or industry.

As they went on describing the school, it seemed to me that
it must be the greatest place on earth, and not even Heaven
presented more attractions for me at that time than did the
Hampton Normal and Agricultural Institute in Virginia about
which these men were talking. I resolved at once to go to that
school, although I had no idea where it was, or how many miles
away, or how I was going to reach it; I remembered only that
I was on fire constantly with one ambition, and that was to go
to Hampton. This thought was with me day and night. . . .

Finally the great day came, and I started for Hampton. . . . I
reached Hampton, with a surplus of exactly fifty cents with
which to begin my education. To me it had been a long, eventful
journey; but the first sight of the large, three-story, brick school
building seemed to have rewarded me for all that I had under-
gone in order to reach the place. . . . It seemed to me to be
the largest and most beautiful building I had ever seen. The

sight of it seemed to give me new life. I felt that a new kind of existence had now begun—that life would now have a new meaning. I felt that I had reached the promised land, and I resolved to let no obstacle prevent me from putting forth the highest effort to fit myself to accomplish the most good in the world. . . .

Life at Hampton was a constant revelation to me; was constantly taking me into a new world. The matter of having meals at regular hours, of eating on a tablecloth, using a napkin, the use of the bath-tub and of the tooth-brush, as well as the use of sheets upon the bed, were all new to me. . . .

The charge for my board at Hampton was ten dollars per month. I was expected to pay a part of this in cash and to work out the remainder. To meet this cash payment, as I have stated, I had just fifty cents when I reached the institution. Aside from a very few dollars that my brother John was able to send me once in a while, I had no money with which to pay my board. I was determined from the first to make my work as janitor so valuable that my services would be indispensable. This I succeeded in doing to such an extent that I was soon informed that I would be allowed the full cost of my board in return for my work. The cost of tuition was seventy dollars a year. This, of course, was wholly beyond my ability to provide. If I had been compelled to pay the seventy dollars for tuition, in addition to providing for my board, I would have been compelled to leave the Hampton school. General Armstrong, however, very kindly got Mr. S. Griffitts Morgan, of New Bedford, Mass., to defray the cost of my tuition during the whole time that I was at Hampton. . . .

After having been for a while at Hampton, I found myself in difficulty because I did not have books and clothing. Usually, however, I got around the trouble about books by borrowing from those who were more fortunate than myself. As to clothes, when I reached Hampton I had practically nothing. Everything that I possessed was in a small hand satchel. . . .

In some way I managed to get on till the teachers learned that I was in earnest and meant to succeed, and then some of them were kind enough to see that I was partly supplied with second-hand clothing that had been sent in barrels from the North. These barrels proved a blessing to hundreds of poor but deserving students. Without them I question whether I should ever have gotten through Hampton. . . .

I was among the youngest of the students who were in Hampton at that time. Most of the students were men and women—some as old as forty years of age. As I now recall the scene of my first year, I do not believe that one often has the opportunity of coming into contact with three or four hundred men and women who were so tremendously in earnest as these men and women were. Every hour was occupied in study or work. Nearly all had had enough actual contact with the world to teach them the need of education. Many of the older ones were, of course, too old to master the text-books very thoroughly, and it was often sad to watch their struggles; but they made up in earnestness much of what they lacked in books. Many of them were as poor as I was, and, besides having to wrestle with their books, they had to struggle with a poverty which prevented their having the necessities of life. Many of them had aged parents who were dependent upon them, and some of them were men who had wives whose support in some way they had to provide for.

The great and prevailing idea that seemed to take possession of every one was to prepare himself to lift up the people at his home. No one seemed to think of himself. And the officers and teachers, what a rare set of human beings they were! They worked for the students night and day, in season and out of season. They seemed happy only when they were helping students in some manner. Whenever it is written—and I hope it will be— the part that the Yankee teachers played in the ed-

ucation of the Negroes immediately after the war will make
one of the most thrilling parts of the history of this country.

From *Up from Slavery*, by Booker T. Washington, 1900.

Justice Demands it

Robert B. Elliott delivering his speech on civil rights

*Blacks were citizens entitled to equal treatment before the law.
So the new Fourteenth Amendment to the Constitution, finally
passed in 1868, said. But it was all too plain that few people*

*were paying any attention to it. In 1872–1873 Congress tried
again, this time spelling it out and confining the application to
the District of Columbia. It passed laws providing that a "respectable well-behaved" person had to be served without regard
to race, color, or previous condition of servitude by proprietors
of hotels and other public places in the nation's capital.*

*Still, racial segregation persisted. Whites were resolved to keep
the Black in an inferior position. Racial separation was a means
to that end. Senator Charles Sumner of Massachusetts, one of
the few Radical Republicans remaining in Congress who were
still militantly outspoken, worked hard for adoption of a federal
civil rights law, but met defeat again and again. In March of
1875 enough strength was finally mustered to pass the bill.*

*The new Civil Rights Act gave citizens of every race and color
the right to equal treatment in inns, public conveyances, theaters,
and other places of public amusement. But in the trading that
took place to get the needed votes, some of the bill's key provisions, including desegregation of the schools, were knocked
out.*

*Several black congressmen took part in the debate on the
measure. One was Robert Brown Elliott of South Carolina.
Born in Boston and educated in England at Eton, Elliott had
studied law in London and come to South Carolina to practice.
He had mastered several languages and collected one of the finest
private libraries in the state. He helped write the state constitution
and was elected to the legislative assembly at twenty-six. By
twenty-eight, he was serving in the United States House of Representatives.*

*When the handsome, dark-skinned congressman rose to speak
on January, 6, 1874, the floor of the House and the galleries
were packed. Senators too were there to watch the dramatic
confrontation between "Anglo-Saxon and the undoubted African," as one observer put it. When the eloquent speech was
ended, great applause rolled over the chamber. Even his political
enemies were impressed.*

Before his term was up, Elliott resigned and returned home, believing state politics were a better arena. He became speaker of South Carolina's assembly. Two Blacks had risen to the lieutenant-governorship of the state, and it was said Elliott meant to become the country's first black governor. But his hopes ended when Reconstruction was overthrown in South Carolina by 1876.

IT IS A MATTER of regret to me that it is necessary at this day that I should rise in the presence of an American Congress to advocate a bill which simply asserts equal rights and equal public privileges for all classes of American citizens. I regret, sir, that the dark hue of my skin may lend a color to the imputation that I am controlled by motives personal to myself in my advocacy of this great measure of a national justice. Sir, the motive that impels me is restricted by no such narrow boundary, but is as broad as your Constitution. I advocate it, sir, because it is right. . . .

In the events that led to the achievement of American independence the Negro was not an inactive or unconcerned spectator. He bore his part bravely upon many battle-fields, although uncheered by that certain hope of political elevation which victory would secure to the white man. The tall granite shaft, which a grateful State has reared above its sons who fell in defending Fort Griswold against the attack of Benedict Arnold, bears the name of Jordan, Freeman, and other brave men of the African race who there cemented with their blood the corner-stone of the Republic. In the State which I have the honor in part to represent the rifle of the black man rang out against the troops of the British crown in the darkest days of the American Revolution. . . .

At the battle of New Orleans, under the immortal Jackson, a colored regiment held the extreme right of the American line unflinchingly, and drove back the British column that pressed upon them, at the point of the bayonet. So marked was their valor on that occasion that it evoked from their great commander the warmest encomiums, as will be seen from his dispatch announcing the brilliant victory. . . .

But, sir, we are told by the distinguished gentleman from Georgia [Mr. Alexander Stephens] that Congress has no power under the Constitution to pass such a law, and that the passage of such an act is in direct contravention of the rights of the States. I cannot assent to any such proposition. The constitution of a free government ought always to be construed in favor of human rights. Indeed, the thirteenth, fourteenth, and fifteenth amendments, in positive words, invest Congress with the power to protect the citizen in his civil and political rights. . . .

Are we then, sir, with the amendments to our Constitution staring us in the face, with these grand truths of history before our eyes, with innumerable wrongs daily inflicted upon five million citizens demanding redress, to commit this question to the diversity of State legislation? . . .

These amendments, one and all . . . have as their all-pervading design and end the security to the recently enslaved race, not only their nominal freedom, but their complete protection from those who had formerly exercised unlimited dominion over them. It is in this broad light that all these amendments must be read, the purpose to secure the perfect equality before the law of all citizens of the United States. What you give to one class you must give to all; what you deny to one class you shall deny to all, unless in the exercise of the common and universal police power of the State you find it needful to confer exclusive privileges on certain citizens, to be held and exercised still for the common good of all. . . .

There are privileges and immunities which belong to me as a citizen of the United States, and there are other privileges and immunities which belong to me as a citizen of my State. The former are under the protection of the Constitution and laws of the United States, and the latter are under the protection of the constitution and laws of my State. But what of that? Are the rights which I now claim—the right to enjoy the common public conveniences of travel on public highways, of rest and refreshment at public inns, of education in public schools, of burial in public cemeteries—rights which I hold as a citizen of the United States or of my State? Or, to state the question more exactly, is not the denial of such privileges to me a denial to me of the equal protection of the laws? For it is under this clause of the fourteenth amendment that we place the present bill, no State shall "deny to any person within its jurisdiction the equal protection of the laws." No matter, therefore, whether his rights are held under the United States or under his particular State, he is equally protected by this amendment. He is always and everywhere entitled to the equal protection of the laws. All discrimination is forbidden; and while the rights of citizens of a State as such are not defined or conferred by the Constitution of the United States, yet all discrimination, all denials of equality before the law, all denial of the equal protection of the laws, whether State or national laws, is forbidden.

The distinction between the two kinds of citizenship is clear, and the Supreme Court have clearly pointed out this distinction, but they have nowhere written a word or line which denies to Congress the power to prevent a denial of equality of rights, whether those rights exist by virtue of citizenship of the United States or of a State. Let honorable members mark well this distinction. There are rights which are conferred on us by the United States. There are other rights conferred on us by the States of which we are individually the citizens. The fourteenth amendment does not forbid a State to deny to all its citizens any of those rights which the State itself has conferred, with certain exceptions, which are pointed out in the decision which we are examining. What it does forbid is inequality, is discrimination, or, to use the words of the amendment itself, is the denial "to any person within its jurisdiction the equal protection of the laws."

If a State denies to me rights which are common to all her other citizens, she violates this amendment, unless she can show . . . that she does it in the legitimate exercise of her police power. If she abridges the rights of all her citizens equally, unless those rights are specially guarded by the Constitution of the United States, she does not violate this amendment. This is not to put the rights which I hold by virtue of my citizenship of South Carolina under the protection of the national Government; it is not to blot out or overlook in the slightest particular the distinction between rights held under the United States and the rights held under the States; but it seeks to secure equality, to prevent discrimination, to confer as complete and ample protection on the humblest as on the highest. . . .

If the States . . . continue to deny to any person within their jurisdiction the equal protection of the laws, or as the Supreme Court has said, "deny equal justice in its courts," then Congress is here said to have power to enforce the constitutional guarantee by appropriate legislation. That is the power which this bill now seeks to put in exercise. It proposes to enforce the constitutional guarantee against inequality and discrimination by appropriate legislation. It does not seek to confer new rights, nor to place rights conferred by State citizenship under the protection of the United States, but simply to prevent and forbid inequality and discrimination on account of race, color, or previous condition of servitude. Never was there a bill more completely within the constitutional power of congress. Never was there a bill which appealed for support more strongly to that sense of justice and fairplay which has been said, and in the main with justice, to be a characteristic of the Anglo-Saxon race. The Constitution warrants it; the Supreme Court sanctions it; justice demands it.

From *Congressional Record*, 1874.

You All Must Live Agreeable

The Blacks who came out of slavery knew well that the source of their old masters' power had been their ownership of the land. Very soon after Emancipation, the freedmen voiced the hope that their new liberty would be rooted deep in a plot of ground they could call their own. They had tilled their native soil for generations, putting their sweat and blood into other men's profit and ease. Now that slavery was dead, they believed they had a right to a piece of land on which they could support their families.

During the war, Congress passed confiscation laws providing that property could be seized for treason, but only during the lifetime of the owner. Some of these lands were sold in lots, but often open competition put the moneyless freedmen out of the bidding.

The federal government stumbled toward the future with no clear solutions for the enormous problems of the freedmen. It made vague and often contradictory promises and reneged on many of them. In the end, Reconstruction brought no real change in the economic relations of the South. The Congress and the state legislatures did not face up to redistribution of the land. And when Reconstruction faltered to its end, the small class of planters who had owned most of the land before the war still sat atop their rich acres.

If the black farmer was to live, he had to work for others. So he went back into cotton and tobacco and rice and sugar, living under the rule of the planter, still lord of the manor. There was no breakup of the plantation system, either during Reconstruction or after. Instead of slave labor, there was now day labor, or tenant farming and sharecropping. These were changes, to be sure, but to the freedmen life did not feel much different from slavery. The law was made by the planter and for the planter— especially as the Reconstruction governments were forced out— and when the law did not suffice, he used force to gain his ends.

What sharecropping meant to the freedman is told by three Blacks who gave their affidavit on August 3, 1875, to a congressional committee investigating conditions in Caddo Parish, Louisiana.

WE WORKED, or made a contract to work, and make a crop on shares on Mr. McMoring's place, and worked for one-third of the crop, and he was to find us all of our provisions; and in July, 1875, we was working alone in the field, and Mr.

McMoring and McBounton came to us and says, "Well, boys, you all got to get away from here"; and that they had gone as far as they could go, and "you all must live agreeable, or you shall take what follows"; and the two white men went and got sticks and guns, and told us that we must leave the place; and we told them that we would not leave it, because we don't want to give up our crop for nothing; and they told us that we had better leave, or we would not get anything; and we wanted justice, but he would not let us have justice; and we told them that we would get judges to judge the crop, to say what it is worth; and the white men told us that no judge should come on his place; and we did not want to leave the place, but they beat Isaiah Fuller, and whipped him, and then we got afraid, and we left the place; and we got about thirty acres in cotton, and the best cotton crop in that part of the parish; and we have about twenty-nine acres of corn, and about the best corn in the parish, and it is ripe, and the fodder ready to pull, and our cotton laid by; and runned us off from the place, and told us not to come back any more; and we were due McMoring the sum of one hundred and eighty dollars and they told us that if they ever heard of it any more that they would fix us; and all the time that we were living and working on the place they would not half feed us; and we had to pay for all, or half of our rashings, or what we had to eat, and that is all that we due them for; and we worked for them as though we were slaves, and then treated like dogs all the time.

From Executive Document No. 30,
44th Congress, 2nd Session (Serial No. 1755).

Exodus

All Colored People

THAT WANT TO

GO TO KANSAS,

On September 5th, 1877,

Can do so for $5.00

"You must make peace at any price." That was the message
Black Americans got from the election of 1876. Its outcome
marked the end of Reconstruction. In the early returns, the Democratic candidate backed by the South, Samuel J. Tilden, seemed
to have defeated the Republican, Rutherford B. Hayes. But
although Tilden had won the popular vote, a complicated dispute
rose over the last crucial electoral votes, and was settled in Hayes'
favor by a bipartisan electoral commission. Behind the dubious
victory of the Republicans and its acceptance by the Democrats
was an elaborate and secret maneuver between spokesmen for
the two candidates. The Republicans got the Presidency and the
Democrats got a pledge to let the South have "home rule" and
the economic aid it badly needed.

Hayes took office in March 1877 and promptly withdrew the
last federal troops from the South. The white Democrats were
now in complete control of everything, including the constitu-

tional rights Blacks might exercise. Hayes went south in September on a "goodwill" tour. He would follow a hands-off policy, he said, having faith in "the great mass of intelligent white men" to protect the Blacks' rights.

How little that faith was worth! The whole South, said one black leader, had got into the hands of the very men who had held them slaves. If they stayed where they were, under these men, they might as well be slaves. And so alone, in families, by hundreds and then by thousands, they began to go north. It was an exodus like the Hebrew flight from slavery on the Nile.

Black conventions in New Orleans and Nashville urged systematic and organized emigration of Blacks to parts of the country where they could enjoy all the rights granted by the Constitution and the laws. Southerners, alarmed by the loss of both plantation hands and skilled artisans, tried persuasion and then force to keep Blacks at home. Among black leaders a debate developed over the exodus. Frederick Douglass hoped the Blacks would give democracy a bit more time to take hold in the South, while Richard T. Greener, dean of Howard University's law school, said only the North and the West would give Blacks a chance to show what they could do under freedom.

The "exodusters," as they were called, swarmed from even the deepest reaches of the South up into Kansas. Many met disaster there, for they came without money and shivered and starved on the bleak plains.

Some Kansans welcomed the immigrants, but others tore down or burned their rude barracks. Their plight reached the outside world, and relief societies formed to send assistance. Many of the exodusters stopped in states along the way or settled in Chicago. But few, whether they prospered or not, ever thought of going back south.

When the wave of migration rose higher and higher, the United States Senate decided to investigate it. The Democrats said the movement was only a Republican plot to swell the party rolls in

the Midwest, and that greedy rail and shipping companies were
encouraging it to get the business.

The true story came in 1880 from the lips of Henry Adams,
a witness before the committee. He was an illiterate Black, a
veteran of the U.S. Army, and he had taken a leading part in
the great migration.

Q. Now TELL US, Mr. Adams, what, if anything, you
know about the exodus of the colored people from the Southern
to the Northern and Western States; and be good enough to
tell us in the first place what you know about the organization
of any committee or society among the colored people themselves for the purpose of bettering their condition, and why it
was organized. Just give us a history of that as you understand
it.

A. I went into the Army in 1866 and came out the last of
1869—and went right back home again where I went from,
Shreveport. . . . After we have come out a parcel of we men
that was in the Army and other men thought that the way our
people had been treated during the time we was in service—
we heard so much talk of how they had been treated and
opposed so much and there was no help for it. That caused me
to go into the Army at first, the way our people was opposed.
There was so much going on that I went off and left it; when
I came back it was still going on, part of it, not quite so bad
as at first. So a parcel of us got together and said that we would
organize ourselves into a committee and look into affairs and
see the true condition of our race, to see whether it was possible
we could stay under a people who had held us under bondage. . . . We organized a committee.

Q. What did you call your committee?

A. We just called it a committee. . . . Some of the members
of the committee was ordered by the committee to go into

every State in the South where we had been slaves there, and post one another from time to time about the true condition of our race, and nothing but the truth.

Q. I want to know how many traveled in that way to get at the condition of your people in the Southern States?

A. I think about one hundred or one hundred and fifty went from one place or another.

Q. And they went from one place to another, working their way and paying their expenses and reporting to the common center at Shreveport, do you mean?

A. Yes, sir.

Q. What was the character of the information that they gave you?

A. . . . . They said in several parts where they was that the land rent was still higher there in that part of the country than it was where we first organized it, and the people was still being whipped, some of them, by the old owners, the men that had owned them as slaves, and some of them was being cheated out of their crops just the same as they was there.

Q. Was anything said about their personal and political rights in these reports, as to how they were treated about these?

A. Yes, some of them stated that in some parts of the country where they voted they would be shot. Some of them stated that if they voted the Democratic ticket they would not be injured.

Q. But that they would be shot, or might be shot, if they voted the Republican ticket?

A. Yes, sir.

Q. I am speaking now of the period from 1870 to 1874, and you have given us the general character of the reports that you got from the South; what did you do in 1874?

A. Well, along in August sometime in 1874, after the white league sprung up, they organized and said this is a white man's government, and the colored men should not hold any offices; they were no good but to work in the fields and take what they would give them and vote the Democratic ticket. That's what they would make public speeches and say to us, and we would hear them. We then organized an organization called the colonization council.

Q. What was the difference between that organization and your committee, as to its objects?

A. Well, the committee was to investigate the condition of our race.

Q. And this organization was then to better your condition after you had found out what that condition was?

A. Yes, sir.

Q. In what way did you propose to do it?

A. We first organized and adopted a plan to appeal to the President of the United States and to Congress to help us out of our distress, or protect us in our rights and privileges.

Q. Well, what other plan had you?

A. And if that plan failed our idea was then to ask them to set apart a territory in the United States for us, somewhere where we could go and live with our families.

Q. You preferred to go off somewhere by yourselves?

A. Yes.

Q. Well, what then?

A. If that failed, our other object was to ask for an appropriation of money to ship us all to Liberia, in Africa; somewhere where we could live in peace and quiet.

Q. Yes, and what after that?

A. When that failed then our idea was to appeal to other governments outside of the United States to help us get away from the United States and go there and live under their flag.

Q. Now when you organized the council what kind of people were taken into it?

A. Nobody but laboring men. . . . When we met in committee there was not any of us allowed to tell our name. . . . We first appealed to President Grant. . . . That was in September, 1874 . . . at other times we sent to Congress. . . . We told them our condition, and asked Congress to help us out of our distress and protect us in our lives and property, and pass some law or provide some way that we might get our rights in the South, and so forth. . . . After the appeal in 1874, we appealed when the time got so hot down there they stopped our churches from having meetings after nine o'clock at night. They stopped them from sitting up and singing over the dead, and so forth, right in the little town where we lived, in Shreveport. I know that to be a fact; and after they did all this, and we saw it was getting so warm—killing our people all over the whole country—there was several of them killed right down in our parish—we appealed. . . .

We had much rather stayed there [in the South] if we could have had our rights. . . . In 1877 we lost all hopes . . . we found ourselves in such condition that we looked around and we seed that there was no way on earth, it seemed, that we could better our condition there, and we discussed that thoroughly in our organization along in May. We said that the whole South—every State in the South—had got into the hands of the very men that held us slaves—from one thing to another and we thought that the men that held us slaves was holding the reins of government over our heads in every respect almost, even the constable up to the governor. We felt we had almost as well be slaves under these men. . . .

We said there was no hope for us and we had better go. . . . Then, in 1877 we appealed to President Hayes and to Congress, to both Houses. I am certain we sent papers there; if they didn't get them that is not our fault; we sent them. . . .

Mighty few ministers would allow us to have their churches [for meetings]; some few would in some of the parishes. . . . When we held our meetings we would not allow the politicians to speak. . . .

It is not exactly five hundred men belonging to the coun-

cil . . . they have now got at this time 98,000 names en-
rolled . . . men and women, and none under twelve years
old . . . some in Louisiana—the majority of them in Louisiana,
and some in Texas, and some in Arkansas . . . a few in Mississippi . . . a few in Alabama [and] in a great many of the
others. . . .

Q. Now, Mr. Adams, you know, probably, more about the
causes of the exodus from that country than any other man,
from your connection with it; tell us in a few words what you
believe to be the causes of these people going away?

A. Well, the cause is, in my judgment, and from what information I have received, and what I have seen with my own
eyes—it is because the largest majority of the people, of the
white people, that held us as slaves treats our people so bad
in many respects that it is impossible for them to stand it. Now,
in a great many parts of that country there our people most as
well be slaves as to be free; because, in the first place, I will
state this: that in some times, in times of politics, if they have
any idea that the Republicans will carry a parish or ward, or
something of that kind, why, they would do anything on God's
earth. There ain't nothing too mean for them to do to prevent
it; nothing I can make mention of is too mean for them to
do. . . .

From Senate Report No. 693, 46th Congress, 2nd Session, part 2.

Cast Down Your Bucket Where You Are

Students of Forestry at Booker T. Washington's
Tuskegee Institute

*The abilities Booker T. Washington had shown at Hampton
Institute, the first successful agricultural and industrial school
for Blacks, won for him the post of principal of the new black
school founded at Tuskegee in 1881. The Institute started with
almost nothing, and was built into a large and flourishing school
by the leadership of Washington and the labors of the students.
With their own bricks they built the workshops where they were*

trained to be carpenters, blacksmiths, printers, shoemakers. Work was no disgrace, but an honor, Washington preached. Blacks must start where slavery left them, at the bottom, and work their way up to equality with the whites. Tuskegee taught black farmers how to get the most out of their land and black businessmen how to organize for their mutual benefit.

This emphasis on industrial and agricultural education for Blacks was not new, of course. Schools for manual labor and the domestic sciences had been advocated for the past sixty years. To overcome barriers raised against black progress by white employers and workers, Frederick Douglass and the black conventions had argued that a policy of self-help and trade schools would make Blacks valuable to society and win its respect. Most of the early black schools fostered programs of industrial education whose theme was help yourself—with white guidance—and you will acquire property and high moral standards. Along the road, somewhere in the dim future, the blessings of full citizenship will be bestowed upon you.

The "uplift" program had a natural appeal for whites both North and South. It expressed the Yankee virtues of hard work and individual initiative and promised to provide a trained and docile labor supply. And since it accepted an inferior position for Blacks in the long period while they would be straining to lift themselves up by their bootstraps, it pleased the Southern whites, too.

At Tuskegee, Washington assured white neighbors that the school was there to serve the community. Gradually he overcame their suspicions by providing the services and the produce that they needed. He won the support of white leaders by counseling the Blacks to obey the laws and keep the peace. Northern philanthropists gave large sums to Tuskegee, and Southern politicians, who had feared education would "ruin our Negroes," relaxed when they heard no demands for equality.

At the Cotton States Exposition in Atlanta in 1895, Washing-

ton was invited to make a speech. It was an unusual honor to
be tendered by whites. Still, there was only polite handclapping
when he was introduced. But when Washington finished, the
ovation signaled the fact that the policy he voiced would over-
night make him the most famous Black in the country and the
most influential among powerful whites.

A SHIP LOST AT SEA for many days suddenly sighted a
friendly vessel. From the mast of the unfortunate vessel was
seen the signal: "Water, water, we die of thirst." The answer
from the friendly vessel at once came back, "Cast down your
bucket where you are." A second time the signal, "Water,
water, send us water," ran up from the distressed vessel and
was answered, "Cast down your bucket where you are," and
a third and fourth signal for water was answered "Cast down
your bucket where you are." The captain of the distressed
vessel, at last heeding the injunction, cast down his bucket and
it came up full of fresh, sparkling water from the mouth of the
Amazon River. To those of my race who depend on bettering
their condition in a foreign land, or who underestimate the
importance of cultivating friendly relations with the Southern
white man who is their next door neighbor, I would say, cast
down your bucket where you are, cast it down in making friends,
in every manly way, of the people of all races by whom you
are surrounded. Cast it down in agriculture, in mechanics, in
commerce, in domestic service, and in the professions. And in
this connection it is well to bear in mind that, whatever other
sins the South may be called upon to bear, when it comes to
business pure and simple it is in the South that the Negro is
given a man's chance in the commercial world; and in nothing
is this Exposition more eloquent than in emphasizing this chance.
Our greatest danger is, that, in the great leap from slavery to
freedom, we may overlook the fact that the masses of us are

to live by the productions of our hands, and fail to keep in mind that we shall prosper in the proportion as we learn to dignify and glorify common labor and put brains and skill into the common occupations of life; shall prosper in proportion as we learn to draw the line between the superficial and the substantial, the ornamental gewgaws of life and the useful. No race can prosper till it learns that there is as much dignity in tilling a field as in writing a poem. It is at the bottom of life we must begin and not the top. Nor should we permit our grievances to overshadow our opportunities.

To those of the white race who look to the incoming of those of foreign birth and strange tongue and habits for the prosperity of the South, were I permitted, I would repeat what I say to my own race, "Cast down your bucket where you are." Cast it down among the 8,000,000 Negroes whose habits you know, whose loyalty and love you have tested in days when to have proved treacherous meant the ruin of your firesides. Cast it down among those people who have, without strikes and labor wars, tilled your fields, cleared your forests, builded your railroads and cities, and brought forth treasures from the bowels of the earth and helped make possible this magnificent representation of the progress of the South. Casting down your bucket among my people, helping and encouraging as you are doing on these grounds, and with education of head, hand and heart, you will find that they will buy your surplus land, make blossom the waste places in your fields, and run your factories. While doing this you can be sure in the future, as you have been in the past, that you and your families will be surrounded by the most patient, faithful, law-abiding, and unresentful people that the world has seen. As we have proved our loyalty to you in the past, in nursing your children, watching by the sick beds of your mothers and fathers, and often following them with tear-dimmed eyes to their graves, so in the future, in our humble way, we shall stand by you with a devotion that no foreigner can approach, ready to lay down our lives, if need be, in defense of yours; interlacing our industrial, commercial, civil, and religious life with yours in a way that shall make the interests of both races one. In all things that are purely social we can be as separate as the fingers, yet one as the hand in all things essential to mutual progress.

There is no defense or security for any of us except in the highest intelligence and development of all. If anywhere there are efforts tending to curtail the fullest growth of the Negro, let these efforts be turned into stimulating, encouraging and making him the most useful and intelligent citizen. Effort or means so invested will pay a thousand per cent interest. These efforts will be twice blessed—"blessing him that gives and him that takes."

There is no escape, through law of man or God, from the inevitable:

> *"The laws of changeless justice bind*
> *Oppressor with oppressed,*
> *And close as sin and suffering joined*
> *We march to fate abreast."*

Nearly sixteen millions of hands will aid you pulling the load upwards, or they will pull against you the load downwards. We shall constitute one-third and much more of the ignorance and crime of the South, or one-third its intelligence and progress; we shall contribute one-third to the business and industrial prosperity of the South, or we shall prove a veritable body of death, stagnating, depressing, retarding every effort to advance the body politic.

The wisest among my race understand that the agitation of questions of social equality is the extremest folly, and the progress in the enjoyment of all the privileges that will come to us must be the result of severe and constant struggle, rather than of artificial forcing. No race that has anything to contribute to the markets of the world is long in any degree ostracized. It is important that we be prepared for the exercise of these privileges. The opportunity to earn a dollar in a factory just now is worth infinitely more than the opportunity to spend a dollar in an opera house.

In conclusion, may I repeat, that nothing in thirty years has given us more hope and encouragement and drawn us so near to you of the white race as the opportunity offered by this Exposition; here bending, as it were, over the altar that represents the results of the struggles of your race and mine, both starting practically empty-handed three decades ago, I pledge that, in your effort to work out the great and intricate problem which God has laid at the doors of the South, you shall have at all times the patient, sympathetic help of my race. Only let this be constantly in mind, that while, from representations in these buildings of the products of field, of forest, of mine, of factory, letters and art, much good will come—yet, far above and beyond material benefit, will be that higher good, that let us pray God will come, in a blotting out of sectional differences and racial animosities and suspicions, and in a determination, even in the remotest corner, to administer absolute justice in a willing obedience among all classes to the mandates of law, and a spirit that will tolerate nothing but the highest equity in the enforcement of law. This, this, coupled with material prosperity, will bring into our beloved South new heaven and new earth.

From Alice M. Bacon, *The Negro and the Atlanta Exposition*, 1896.

I Want Equality–
Nothing Less!

John Hope

Booker T. Washington's "Atlanta Compromise" speech, as it came to be called, was hailed nationally as the formula for peace between the races. For many whites it put the Black Americans nicely in their "place." They took Washington's program of expediency as the final solution to the black problem and treated him as the spokesman for the millions of his people.

But there were other black leaders who differed with Washington. The foremost spokesman of the previous generation, the militant Frederick Douglass, had died a few months before the Atlanta speech. Now others were coming up. Among them was

John Hope. Born in Georgia in 1868, he worked his way through Worcester Academy and Brown University. Washington then invited him to teach at Tuskegee, but young as Hope was, he knew he was on a different path. Instead, he took a post in Nashville at Roger Williams University, a liberal arts college for Blacks. When he heard that Washington was to speak at Atlanta, he made it a point to go down and hear him. He thought deeply about the implications of Washington's speech, and on February 22 of the next year, 1896, speaking to the black debating society of Nashville, he challenged Washington's "compromise."

Only twenty-eight then, Hope was making a brilliant record as a teacher, and within a few years was asked to come to Atlanta Baptist College to teach the classics. "Going back to Georgia, when for your race Georgia is hell?" his friends asked. And he replied, "It may be hell, but my people are there, and I'm going home." Later Hope was to become the first black president of the college. Because he was a leader of the anti-Bookerite movement, the philanthropists who followed Washingon's advice shut off all funds to Hope's school in retaliation for his independence.

IF WE ARE NOT striving for equality, in heaven's name for what are we living? I regard it as cowardly and dishonest for any of our colored men to tell white people or colored people that we are not struggling for equality. If money, education, and honesty will not bring to me as much privilege, as much equality as they bring to any American citizen, then they are to me a curse, and not a blessing. God forbid that we should get the implements with which to fashion our freedom, and then be too lazy or pusillanimous to fashion it. Let us not fool ourselves nor be fooled by others. If we cannot do what other freemen do, then we are not free. Yes, my friends, I want equality. Nothing less. I want all that my God-given powers will enable me to get, then why not equality? Now, catch your breath, for I am going to use an adjective: I am going to say we demand social equality. In this Republic we shall be less than freemen, if we have a whit less than that which thrift, education, and honor afford other freemen. If equality, political, economic, and social, is the boon of other men in this great country of ours, then equality, political, economic, and social, is what we demand. Why build a wall to keep me out? I am no wild beast, nor am I an unclean thing.

Rise, Brothers! Come let us possess this land. Never say: "Let well enough alone." Cease to console yourselves with adages that numb the moral sense. Be discontented. Be dissatisfied. "Sweat and grunt" under present conditions. Be as restless as the tempestuous billows on the boundless sea. Let your discontent break mountain-high against the wall of prejudice, and swamp it to the very foundation. Then we shall not have to plead for justice nor on bended knee crave mercy; for we shall be men. Then and not until then will liberty in its highest sense be the boast of our Republic.

From *The Story of John Hope,* by Ridgely Torrence, Macmillan, 1948.

A Happy Set of People

By 1900 the myth of white supremacy had gripped the national mind. The belief that the darker races were naturally inferior was spread everywhere by the press. Even the most respected newspapers and literary magazines—from The New York Times *to* Harper's—*were guilty of the crudest racism. The press played up crimes in which Blacks were involved, creating the stereotype*

of the criminal Black. Poems, stories, articles, novels, editorials, cartoons, jokes by the thousand sketched the Black as dull, stupid, ignorant, vicious, lazy; he was the clown, the thief, the liar. There was no attempt to be consistent, for in one "romance" the Black was the faithful plantation hand ready to die for ol' Massa and in the next he was the degraded brute bent on ravishing ol' Missy behind the magnolias.

The superiority of the Anglo-Saxon was universally declaimed. Darwin's theories were twisted to prove that the white, and especially the Anglo-Saxon, was the fittest, destined to rule the colored. It was white America's task to spread its superiority over the earth. It became very easy for white Americans, who were used to imposing their will on Blacks, to take over Cuba and the Philippines and look farther abroad to see what other

darker-skinned people were waiting to be "civilized." America,
by the end of the century, had convinced itself that it was un-
selfishly ready to shoulder the "White Man's Burden."

In a letter to a national magazine in 1902, one black mother
tried to show how little whites knew of black life, and what the
effect was.

I AM A COLORED WOMAN, wife and mother. I have lived
all my life in the South, and have often thought what a peculiar
fact it is that the more ignorant the Southern whites are of us
the more vehement they are in their denunciation of us. They
boast that they have little intercourse with us, never see us in
our homes, churches or places of amusement, but still they
know us thoroughly.

They also admit that they know us in no capacity except as
servants yet they say we are at our best in that single capacity.
What philosophers they are! The Southerners say we Negroes
are a happy, laughing set of people, with no thought of tomorrow. How mistaken they are! The educated, thinking Negro
is just the opposite. There is a feeling of unrest, insecurity,
almost panic among the best class of Negroes in the South. In
our homes, in our churches, wherever two or three are gathered
together, there is a discussion of what is best to do. Must we
remain in the South or go elsewhere? Where can we go to feel
that security which other people feel? Is it best to go in great
numbers or only several families? These and many other things
are discussed over and over. . . .

I know of houses occupied by poor Negroes in which a respectable farmer would not keep his cattle. It is impossible for
them to rent elsewhere. All Southern real estate agents have
"white property" and "colored property." In one of the largest
Southern cities there is a colored minister, a graduate of Harvard, whose wife is an educated, Christian woman, who lived

for weeks in a tumble-down rookery because he could neither
rent nor buy in a respectable locality.

Many colored women, who wash, iron, scrub, cook or sew
all the week to help pay the rent for these miserable hovels
and help fill the many small mouths, would deny themselves
some of the necessaries of life if they could take their little
children and teething babies on the cars to the parks of a Sunday
afternoon and sit under the trees, enjoy the cool breezes and
breathe God's pure air for only two or three hours; but this is
denied them. Some of the parks have signs, "No Negroes allowed on these grounds except as servants." Pitiful, pitiful
customs and laws that make war on women and babes! There
is no wonder that we die; the wonder is that we persist in living.

Fourteen years ago I had just married. My husband had saved
sufficient money to buy a small home. On account of our limited
means we went to the suburbs, on unpaved streets, to look for
a home, only asking for a high, healthy locality. Some real
estate agents were "sorry, but had nothing to suit," some had
"just the thing," but we discovered on investigation that they
had "just the thing" for an unhealthy pigsty. Others had no
"colored property." One agent said that he had what we wanted,
but we should have to go to see the lot after dark, or walk by
and give the place a casual look; for, he said, "all the white
people in the neighborhood would be down on me." Finally
we bought this lot. When the house was being built we went
to see it. Consternation reigned. We had ruined this neighborhood of poor people; poor as we, poorer in manners at
least. The people who lived next door received the sympathy
of their friends. When we walked on the street (there were no
sidewalks) we were embarrassed by the stare of many un-
friendly eyes.

Two years passed before a single woman spoke to me, and
only then because I helped one of them when a little sudden
trouble came to her. Such was the reception I, a happy young

woman, just married, received from people among whom I wanted to make a home. Fourteen years have now passed, four children have been born to us, and one has died in this same home, among these same neighbors. Although the neighbors speak to us, and occasionally one will send a child to borrow the morning's paper or ask the loan of a pattern, not one woman has ever been inside of my house, not even at the times when a woman would doubly appreciate the slightest attention of a neighbor.

The Southerner boasts that he is our friend; he educates our children, he pays us for work and is most noble and generous to us. Did not the Negro by his labor for over three hundred years help to educate the white man's children? Is thirty equal to three hundred? Does a white man deserve praise for paying a black man for his work?

The Southerner also claims that the Negro gets justice. Not long ago a Negro man was cursed and struck in the face by an electric car conductor. The Negro knocked the conductor down and although it was clearly proven in a court of "justice" that the conductor was in the wrong the Negro had to pay a fine of $10. The judge told him "I fine you that much to teach you that you must respect white folks." The conductor was acquitted. "Most noble judge! A second Daniel!" This is the South's idea of justice. . . .

Whenever a crime is committed, in the South the policemen look for the Negro in the case. A white man with face and hands blackened can commit any crime in the calendar. The first friendly stream soon washes away his guilt and he is ready to join in the hunt to lynch the "big, black burly brute." When a white man in the South does commit a crime, that is simply one white man gone wrong. If his crime is especially brutal he is a freak or temporarily insane. If one low, ignorant black wretch commits a crime, that is different. All of us must bear his guilt. A young white boy's badness is simply the overflowing of young animal spirits; the black boy's badness is badness, pure and simple. . . .

Someone will at last arise who will champion our cause and compel the world to see that we deserve justice; as other heroes compelled it to see that we deserved freedom.

From *The Independent*, September 18, 1902.

No Cowards or Trucklers

Born in 1868, five years after Emancipation, W. E. B. DuBois was the great-great-grandson of an African slave who won his freedom as a Revolutionary soldier against the British. DuBois was schooled in his home state of Massachusetts and took his degrees at Fisk, Harvard—where he was the first Black to receive the Doctorate of Philosophy—and the University of Berlin.

He launched Harvard's Historical Series in 1896 with a study of the African slave trade, and three years later published The Philadelphia Negro, *one of the earliest scientific studies of an urban minority. Teaching and writing at Atlanta University, he soon demonstrated a quality of mind that placed him in the front ranks of America's intellectuals.*

In 1903 DuBois published a book that had an enormous influence on American thinking about Blacks. Called The Souls of Black Folk, *it criticized Booker T. Washington's policy of relying on the goodwill of Southern whites and attacked the disfranchisement and segregation that it had failed to stop. Young as the century was, DuBois foresaw that its problem was the problem of the color line. He urged black leaders to demand*

Founders of the Niagara Movement, photographed at the first meeting in June 1905. W. E. B. DuBois is in the second row, second from the right.

every right pledged in the Declaration of Independence and the Constitution.

Two years later, in June 1905, DuBois and about thirty other Blacks—most of them college educated—met at Niagara Falls to announce a program based upon the principles of human brotherhood, freedom of speech and criticism, and exercise of all rights without regard to race. They would never stop protesting, they said, until America redressed its shameful treatment of Black Americans.

In August 1906 the Niagara Movement, as it was called, met again, this time at Harpers Ferry, where John Brown and his black and white men had laid down their lives to liberate the slaves. From this meeting came a burning manifesto to the country, written by DuBois.

*

THE MEN OF the Niagara Movement coming from the toil of the year's hard work and pausing a moment from the earning of their daily bread turn toward the nation and again ask in the name of ten million the privilege of a hearing. In the past year the work of the Negro hater has flourished in the land. Step by step the defenders of the rights of American citizens have retreated. The work of stealing the black man's ballot has progressed and the fifty and more representatives of stolen votes still sit in the nation's capital. Discrimination in travel and public accommodation has so spread that some of our weaker brethren are actually afraid to thunder against color discrimination as such and are simply whispering for ordinary decencies.

Against this the Niagara Movement eternally protests. We will not be satisfied to take one jot or tittle less than our full manhood rights. We claim for ourselves every single right that belongs to a freeborn American, political, civil and social; and until we get these rights we will never cease to protest and assail the ears of America. The battle we wage is not for ourselves alone but for all true Americans. It is a fight for ideals, lest this, our common fatherland, false to its founding, become in truth the land of the thief and the home of the Slave—a by-word and a hissing among the nations for its sounding pretentions and pitiful accomplishment.

Never before in the modern age has a great and civilized folk threatened to adopt so cowardly a creed in the treatment of its fellow-citizens born and bred on its soil. Stripped of verbiage and subterfuge and in its naked nastiness the new American creed says: Fear to let black men even try to rise lest they become the equals of the white. And this is the land that professes to follow Jesus Christ. The blasphemy of such a course is only matched by its cowardice.

In detail our demands are clear and unequivocal.

First, we would vote; with the right to vote goes everything: Freedom, manhood, the honor of your wives, the chastity of your daughters, the right to work, and the chance to rise, and let no man listen to those who deny this.

We want full manhood suffrage, and we want it now, henceforth and forever.

Second. We want discrimination in public accommodation to cease. Separation in railway and street cars, based simply on race and color, is un-American, undemocratic, and silly. We protest against all such discrimination.

Third. We claim the right of freemen to walk, talk, and be with them that wish to be with us. No man has a right to choose another's man's friends, and to attempt to do so is an impudent interference with the most fundamental human privilege.

Fourth. We want the laws enforced against rich as well as poor; against Capitalist as well as Laborer; against white as well as black. We are not more lawless than the white race, we are more often arrested, convicted and mobbed. We want justice even for criminals and outlaws. We want the Constitution of the country enforced. We want Congress to take charge of Congressional elections. We want the Fourteenth Amendment carried out to the letter and every State disfranchised in Congress which attempts to disfranchise its rightful voters. We want the Fifteenth Amendment enforced and no State allowed to base its franchise simply on color.

The failure of the Republican Party in Congress at the session just closed to redeem its pledge of 1904 with reference to suffrage conditions at the South seems a plain, deliberate, and premeditated breach of promise, and stamps that party as guilty of obtaining votes under false pretense.

Fifth. We want our children educated. The school system in the country districts of the South is a disgrace and in few towns and cities are the Negro schools what they ought to be. We want the national government to step in and wipe out illiteracy in the South. Either the United States will destroy ignorance or ignorance will destroy the United States.

And when we call for education we mean real education. We believe in work. We ourselves are workers, but work is not necessarily education. Education is the development of power and ideal. We want our children trained as intelligent human beings should be, and we will fight for all time against any proposal to educate black boys and girls simply as servants and underlings, or simply for the use of other people. They have a right to know, to think, to aspire.

These are some of the chief things which we want. How shall we get them? By voting where we may vote, by persistent, unceasing agitation, by hammering at the truth, by sacrifice and work.

We do not believe in violence, neither in the despised violence of the raid nor the lauded violence of the soldier, nor the barbarous violence of the mob, but we do believe in John Brown, in that incarnate spirit of justice, that hatred of a lie, that willingness to sacrifice money, reputation, and life itself on the altar of right. And here on the scene of John Brown's martyrdom we reconsecrate ourselves, our honor, our property to the final emancipation of the race which John Brown died to make free.

Our enemies, triumphant for the present, are fighting the stars in their courses. Justice and humanity must prevail. We live to tell these dark brothers of ours—scattered in counsel, wavering and weak—that no bribe of money or notoriety, no promise of wealth or fame, is worth the surrender of a peoples' manhood or the loss of a man's self-respect. We refuse to surrender the leadership of this race to cowards and trucklers. We are men; we will be treated as men. On this rock we have planted our banners. We will never give up, though the trump of doom find us still fighting.

And we shall win. The past promised it, the present foretells it. Thank God for John Brown; Thank God for Garrison and Douglass! Sumner and Phillips, Nat Turner and Robert Gould Shaw, and all the hallowed dead who died for freedom! Thank God for all those today, few though their voices be, who have not forgotten the divine brotherhood of all men, white and black, rich and poor, fortunate and unfortunate.

We appeal to the young men and women of this nation, to those whose nostrils are not yet befouled by greed and snobbery and racial narrowness: Stand up for the right; prove yourselves worthy of your heritage and whether born north or south dare to treat men as men. Cannot the nation that has absorbed ten million foreigners into its political life without catastrophe absorb ten million Negro Americans into that same political life at less cost than their unjust and illegal exclusion will involve?

Courage, brothers! The battle for humanity is not lost or losing. All across the skies sit signs of promise. The Slav is rising in his might, the yellow millions are tasting liberty, the black Africans are writhing toward the lights, and everywhere the laborer, with ballot in his hand, is voting open the gates of Opportunity and Peace. The morning breaks over blood-stained hills. We must not falter, we may not shrink. Above are the everlasting stars.

Reprinted in *An ABC of Color*, by W. E. B. DuBois, 1963.

Mob Law in Lincoln's State

Ida B. Wells

In the young twentieth century Blacks did not walk in green pastures. Many people might be living better on the strength of America's industrial machine, but not the millions born with the stigma of color.

Theodore Roosevelt's reform program was an empty promise for Blacks. As they moved from farm to city seeking jobs and decent housing, they were packed into ghettoes that intensified all the ills of slum life. And almost everywhere they went, Jim Crow and the lyncher followed. In the first decade of the new century violence lurked at every corner, exploding in individual assaults or mass race riots that crazed whole cities throughout the North as well as the South.

One of the most passionate voices of protest in this period was Ida B. Wells. She was born in Mississippi four years after the end of the Civil War. At fourteen, while a student in a Freedmen's Aid Society school, she lost both parents and took over the support of four younger children. Somehow she managed to get more schooling while carrying this burden. Later she went as a teacher to Memphis and began to write for a local black paper, the Living War. *Finally she quit the classroom to edit her own paper,* Free Speech. *Her courageous fight against racial injustice brought her many readers in the Mississippi Delta until 1892, when she exposed white businessmen who had instigated the lynching of three young black competitors. A mob wrecked her press during the night and she was forced to flee the city.*

She carried her antilynch crusade to New York, writing for the Age *and publishing her* Red Book, *the first definitive study of lynching in the United States. In 1892 she went to England to raise international support for the campaign, and the next year to Chicago, where she began organizing black youth and women's clubs. She married the lawyer Ferdinand Barnett, founder of the city's first black newspaper. At twenty-five she said, "Our work has only begun; our race—hereditary bondsmen—must strike the blow if they would be free." With her husband she worked unceasingly against the mob mania, running great risks to report social injustice on the scene and to defend its victims.*

The result of one of her investigations of a double lynching is contained in this article she wrote in 1910.

*

THE RECORD OF the past ten years shows a surprising increase in lynchings and riot even in the North. No Northern state has more frequently offended in this crime than Illinois, the State of Lincoln. . . . Since 1893 there have been sixteen lynchings within the State, including the Springfield riot. With each repetition there has been increased violence, rioting and barbarism. . . .

On the morning of November 11th last year, a double lynching was reported from Cairo, Ill.—a white man and a Negro. A white girl had been found murdered two days before. The bloodhounds which were brought led to a Negro's house three blocks away. A Negro who had stayed in that house the night before was arrested and sweated for twenty-four hours. Although the only clew found was that the gag in the girl's mouth was of the same kind of cloth as the handkerchief of the prisoner, threats of lynching him became so frequent that the Sheriff took him away from the city, back in the woods twenty-five miles away.

When the mob had increased its numbers, they chartered a train, went after the Sheriff, brought him and his prisoner back to Cairo. A rope was thrown over Will James' neck, he was dragged off the train to the main business corner of the town. The rope was thrown over a steel arch, which had a double row of electric lights. The lights were turned on and the body hauled up in view of the assembled thousands of men, women and children. The rope broke before James was strangled to death and before hundreds of waiting bullets could be fired into his body. However, as many as could crowd around emptied their revolvers into the quivering mass of flesh as it lay on the ground. Then seizing the rope the mob dragged the corpse a mile up Washington Street, the principal thoroughfare, to where the girl's body had been found. They were followed by a jeering, hooting, laughing throng of all ages and of both sexes of white people. There they built a fire and placed this body on the flames. It was then dragged out of the fire, the head cut off and stuck on a nearby fence post. The trunk was cut open, the heart and other organs were cut out, sliced up and passed around as souvenirs of the ghastly orgy and our American civilization.

Having tasted blood, a voice in the crowd said, "Let's get Salzner." Away went the mob to the county jail. Salzner, a white man, had been indicted for wife murder and was in jail awaiting trial. The suggestion is said to have come from the brother of Salzner's murdered wife. The mob demanded that the Sheriff, who had repaired to his office in the jail when Will James had been taken from him an hour before, get Salzner for them. He begged them to go away, but when they began battering in the doors he telephoned the Governor for troops. The lynchers got Salzner, hanged him in the court yard in front of the jail, emptied their remaining bullets in his body and went away. When troops reached the scene six hours later, they found, as the leading morning paper said next day, that "the fireworks were all over."

In mass meeting assembled the Negro citizens of Chicago called on Governor Deneen to do his duty and suspend the Sheriff. Two days later the Sheriff's office was vacated. Ten days more and Sheriff Davis had filed his petition for reinstatement, and on December 1st, argument was had before Governor Deneen both for and against the Sheriff.

The Sheriff's counsel, an ex-state Senator, and one of the leading lawyers of Southern Illinois, presented the Sheriff's petition for reinstatement, which declared he had done all in his power to protect the prisoners in his charge. . . . As representing the people who had sent me to Cairo to get the facts, I told of the lynching, of visiting the scenes thereof, of the three days' interview with the colored people of Cairo, and of reading the files of every newspaper in the city published during the lynching to find some account of the steps that had been taken to protect the prisoner. I told of the mass meeting of the Negroes of Cairo in which a resolution was passed declaring that from Tuesday morning when Will James was arrested, until Thursday night when he was lynched—the Sheriff had neither sworn in deputies to aid him in defending the prisoners, nor called on the Governor for troops. We said that a reinstatement of the Sheriff would be an encouragement to mobs to hang, shoot, burn and pillage whenever they felt inclined in the future, as they had done in the past.

Governor Deneen rendered his decision a week later, removing the Sheriff. After reviewing the case he said:

> The sole question presented is, does the evidence show that the said Frank E. Davis, as Sheriff of Alexander County, did all in his power to protect the life of the prisoners and perform the duties required of him by existing laws for the protection of prisoners? . . .
>
> Only one conclusion can be reached, and that is that the Sheriff failed to take the necessary precaution for the protection of his prisoners. Mob violence has no place in Illinois. It is denounced in every line of the Constitution and in every Statute. Instead of breeding respect for the law it breeds contempt. For the suppression of mob violence our Legislature has spoken in no uncertain terms. When such mob violence threatens the life of a prisoner in the custody of the Sheriff, the law charged the Sheriff, at the penalty of the forfeiture of his office, to use the utmost human endeavor to protect the life of his prisoner. The law may be severe. Whether severe or not it must be enforced.
>
> Believing as I do that Frank E. Davis, as Sheriff of Alexander County, did not do all within his

power to protect the lives of William James and Henry Salzner, I must deny the petition of said Frank E. Davis, for reinstatement as Sheriff of Alexander County, and the same is done accordingly.

. . . It is believed that this decision with its slogan "Mob law can have no place in Illinois" has given lynching its death blow in this State.

From "How Enfranchisement Stops Lynching,"
by Ida B. Wells-Barnett, *Original
Rights Magazine*, June, 1910.

My Soul Is Full of Color

Langston Hughes was born in 1902, in Joplin, Missouri. It was just at the time the Niagara Movement was crystallizing out of the opposition to Booker T. Washington's policies. He grew up in Lawrence, Kansas, the town that had been a battlefield in John Brown's struggle to make Kansas a free state. His grandmother, who raised him till he was twelve, was the widow of Sheridan Leary, one of John Brown's men killed in the raid on Harpers Ferry. The boy's first job was to clean the lobby and toilets of an old hotel near his school, for which he got fifty cents a week. Then his grandmother died, and his mother took care of him, moving the family to Illinois and then to Ohio.

When he graduated from elementary school, his classmates elected him Class Poet—although he had never written a poem—

Langston Hughes, aged seventeen, in the uniform
of his high school ROTC

because there was no one else around to fill the post and Blacks
were all supposed to have rhythm. He had to produce something
for the occasion, and that was how he started to write poetry.
A little later, in the twenties, a new black movement developed
in which dozens of young writers flowered. Most of them wrote
on black themes, and used every literary form. The young Lang-
ston Hughes, who had moved to Harlem, became the unofficial
laureate of his people and one of America's leading writers. He
wrote poems, plays, short stories, novels, essays, history, bi-

ography, lyrics for opera composers, newspaper columns.

In his autobiography, Hughes tells what it was like in 1916 to be a high school boy, and a Black American, in Cleveland as the First World War was going on in Europe.

WE MOVED FROM Illinois to Cleveland. My step-father sent for us. He was working in a steel mill during the war, and making lots of money. But it was hard work, and he never looked the same afterwards. Every day he worked several hours overtime, because they paid well for overtime. But after a while, he couldn't stand the heat of the furnaces, so he got a job as caretaker of a theater building, and after that as janitor of an apartment house.

Rents were very high for colored people in Cleveland, and the Negro district was extremely crowded, because of the great migration. It was difficult to find a place to live. We always lived, during my high school years, either in an attic or a basement, and paid quite a lot for such inconvenient quarters. White people on the east side of the city were moving out of their frame houses and renting them to Negroes at double and triple the rents they could receive from others. . . .

But Negroes were coming in in a great dark tide from the South, and they had to have some place to live. Sheds and garages and store fronts were turned into living quarters. As always, the white neighborhoods resented Negroes moving closer and closer—but when the whites did give way, they gave way at very profitable rentals. The landlords and the banks made it difficult for them to buy houses, so they had to pay the exorbitant rents required. When my step-father quit the steel mill job, my mother went out to work in service to help him meet expenses. She paid a woman to take care of my little brother while she worked as a maid.

I went to Central High School in Cleveland. We had a mag-

azine called the *Belfry Owl*. I wrote poems for the *Belfry Owl*.
We had some wise and very good teachers, Miss Roberts and
Miss Weimer in English, Miss Chesnutt, who was the daughter
of the famous colored writer, Charles W. Chesnutt, and Mr.
Hitchcock, who taught geometry with humor, and Mr. Ozanne,
who spread the whole world before us in his history classes.
Also Clara Dieke, who painted beautiful pictures and who
taught us a great deal about many things that are useful to
know—about law and order in art and life, and about sticking
to a thing until it is done.

Ethel Weimer discovered Carl Sandburg for me. Although
I had read of Carl Sandburg before—in an article, I think, in
the Kansas City *Star* about how bad free verse was—I didn't
really know him until Miss Weimer in second-year English
brought him, as well as Amy Lowell, Vachel Lindsay, and
Edgar Lee Masters, to us. Then I began to try to write like
Carl Sandburg.

Little Negro dialect poems like Paul Lawrence Dunbar's and
poems without rhyme like Sandburg's were the first real poems
I tried to write. I wrote about love, about the steel mills where
my step-father worked, the slums where we lived, and the
brown girls from the South, prancing up and down Central
Avenue on a spring day.

> *Just because I loves you—*
> *That's de reason why*
> *My soul is full of color*
> *Like de wings of a butterfly.*

> *Just because I loves you*
> *That's de reason why*
> *My heart's a fluttering aspen leaf*
> *When you pass by.*

I was fourteen then. And another of the poems was this
about the mills:

The mills
That grind and grind,
That grind out steel
And grind away the lives
Of men—
In the sunset their stacks
Are great black silhouettes
Against the sky.
In the dawn
They belch red fire.
The mills—
Grinding new steel,
Old men.

And about Carl Sandburg, my guiding star, I wrote:

Carl Sandburg's poems
Fall on the white pages of his books
Like blood-clots of song
From the wounds of humanity.
I know a lover of life sings
When Carl Sandburg sings.
I know a lover of all the living
Sings then.

Central was the high school of students of foreign-born parents—until the Negroes came. It is an old high school with many famous graduates. It used to be long ago the high school of the aristocrats, until the aristocrats moved farther out. Then poor whites and foreign-born took over the district. Then during the war, the Negroes came. Now Central is almost entirely a Negro school in the heart of Cleveland's vast Negro quarter.

When I was there, it was very nearly entirely a foreign-born school, with a few native white and colored American students mixed in. By foreign, I mean children of foreign-born parents.

Although some of the students themselves had been born in Poland or Russia, Hungary or Italy. And most were Catholic or Jewish.

Although we got on very well, whenever class elections would come up, there was a distinct Jewish-Gentile division among my classmates. That was perhaps why I held many class and club offices in high school, because often when there was a religious deadlock, a Negro student would win the election. They would compromise on a Negro, feeling, I suppose, that a Negro was neither Jew nor Gentile!

I wore a sweater covered with club pins most of the time. I was on the track team, and for two seasons, my relay team won the city-wide championships. I was a lieutenant in the military training corps. Once or twice I was on the monthly honor roll for scholarship. And when we were graduated, Class of '20, I edited the Year Book.

My best pal in high school was a Polish boy named Sartur Andrzejewski. His parents lived in the steel mill district. His mother cooked wonderful cabbage in sweetened vinegar. His rosy-cheeked sisters were named Regina and Sabina. And the whole family had about them a quaint and kindly foreign air, bubbling with hospitality. They were devout Catholics, who lived well and were very jolly.

I had lots of Jewish friends, too, boys named Nathan and Sidney and Herman, and girls named Sonya and Bess and Leah. I went to my first symphony concert with a Jewish girl—for these children of foreign-born parents were more democratic than native white Americans, and less anti-Negro. They lent me *The Gadfly* and *Jean-Christophe* to read, and copies of the *Liberator* and the *Socialist Call*. The were almost all interested in more than basketball and the glee club. They took me to hear Eugene Debs. And when the Russian Revolution broke out, our school almost held a celebration.

Since it was during the war, and Americanism was being

stressed, many of our students, including myself, were then called down to the principal's office and questioned about our belief in 'Americanism. Police went to some of the parents' homes and took all their books away. After that, the principal organized an Americanism Club in our school, and, I reckon, because of the customary split between Jews and Gentiles, I was elected president. But the club didn't last long, because we were never quite clear about what we were supposed to do. Or why. Except that none of us wanted Eugene Debs locked up. But the principal didn't seem to feel that Debs fell within the scope of our club. So the faculty let the club die.

Four years at Central High School taught me many invaluable things. From Miss Dieke, I learnt that the only way to get a thing done is to start to do it, then keep on doing it, and finally you'll finish it, even if in the beginning you think you can't do it at all. From Miss Weimer I learnt that there are ways of saying or doing things, which may not be the currently approved ways, yet that can be very true and beautiful ways, that people will come to recognize as such in due time. In 1916, the critics said Carl Sandburg was no good as a poet, and free verse was no good. Nobody says that today—yet 1916 is not a lifetime ago.

From the students I learnt that Europe was not so far away, and that when Lenin took power in Russia, something happened in the slums of Woodlawn Avenue that the teachers couldn't tell us about, and that our principal didn't want us to know. From the students I learnt, too, that lots of painful words can be flung at people that aren't nigger. Kike was one; spick, and hunky, others.

But I soon realized that the kikes and the spicks and the hunkies—scorned though they might be by the pure Americans—all had it on the niggers in one thing. Summer time came and they could get jobs quickly. For even during the war, when help was badly needed, lots of employers would not hire Negroes. A colored boy had to search and search for a job.

My first summer vacation from high school, I ran a dumb-waiter at Halle's, a big department store. The dumb-waiter carried stock from the stock room to the various departments of the store. I was continually amazed at trays of perfume that cost fifty dollars a bottle, ladies' lace collars at twenty-five, and useless little gadgets like gold cigarette lighters that were worth more than six months' rent on the house where we lived. Yet some people could afford to buy such things without a thought. And did buy them.

The second summer vacation I went to join my mother in Chicago. Dad and my mother were separated again, and she was working as cook for a lady who owned a millinery shop in the Loop, a very fashionable shop where society leaders came by appointment and hats were designed to order. I became a delivery boy for that shop. It was a terrifically hot summer, and we lived on the crowded Chicago South Side in a house next to the elevated. The thunder of the trains kept us awake at night. We could afford only one small room for my mother, my little brother, and me.

South State Street was in its glory then, a teeming Negro street with crowded theaters, restaurants, and cabarets. And excitement from noon to noon. Midnight was like day. The street was full of workers and gamblers, prostitutes and pimps, church folks and sinners. The tenements on either side were very congested. For neither love nor money could you find a decent place to live. Profiteers, thugs, and gangsters were coming into their own. The first Sunday I was in town, I went out walking alone to see what the city looked like. I wandered too far outside the Negro district, over beyond Wentworth, and was set upon and beaten by a group of white boys, who said they didn't allow niggers in that neighborhood. I came home with both eyes blacked and a swollen jaw. That was the summer before the Chicago riots.

I managed to save a little money, so I went back to high school in Cleveland, leaving my mother in Chicago. I couldn't afford to eat in a restaurant, and the only thing I knew how to cook myself in the kitchen of the house where I roomed was rice, which I boiled to a paste. Rice and hot dogs, rice and hot dogs, every night for dinner. Then I read myself to sleep.

I was reading Schopenhauer and Nietzsche, and Edna Ferber and Dreiser, and de Maupassant in French. I never will forget the thrill of first understanding the French of de Maupassant. The soft snow was falling through one of his stories in the little book we used in school, and that I had worked over so long, before I really felt the snow falling there. Then all of a sudden one night the beauty and the meaning of the words in which he made the snow fall, came to me. I think it was de Maupassant who made me really want to be a writer and write stories about Negroes, so true that people in far-away lands would read them—even after I was dead.

From *The Big Sea*, by Langston Hughes, Hill and Wang, 1940.

I Want to Get Out

It began with the boll weevil. That hungry pest crossed over from Mexico into Texas, "jes' a-lookin' for a home," and he found it in the cotton fields of the South. By 1916 the invader, aided by storms and floods, had ruined vast stretches of Southern land. Sharecroppers hungered and shivered in their rickety cabins as landlords, too broke to extend credit, cut off supplies. Families wondered what to do, where to go, how to live.

One way out pointed north. There were jobs up there, people said. And they let you live a little. The war that had exploded

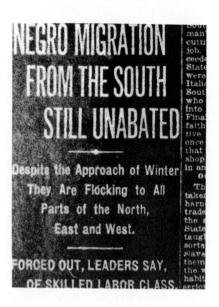

in Europe in 1914 had cut off the flow of immigrants from the old countries. Northern factories, booming on war orders, were short of labor. Manufacturers sent agents south to recruit black workers. They came with free railroad passes in hand or offered cheap tickets to groups of migrants. A "Northern fever" seized the Blacks of the South. The dream of decent jobs, of a house with a floor and windows, of schools and escape from insult and humiliation, led half a million to move north in 1916–1918 Chicago was the mecca for many. The rail lines of the deep-South states led straight there. And out of the big city came a powerful voice, arguing, pleading, challenging, insisting that Blacks join "The Great Northern Drive." It was Robert S. Abbott, using his Chicago Defender to penetrate every cabin and slum with a message of hope. From black hand to black hand went the tattered pages reporting in grisly detail the rising tide of Dixieland lynchings while they pictured the prosperity of Southern Blacks who had made good in the North.

Letters from Blacks—many of them illiterate scrawls from men and women desperate to learn and be free—flooded into *the* Defender's *office, checking on rumors of the exodus, begging to know how to come. From them you can understand why so many were looking for a promised land.*

TROY, ALA., OCT. 17, 1916.
Dear Sirs: I am enclosing a clipping of a lynching again which speaks for itself. I do wish there could be sufficient pressure brought about to have federal investigation of such work. I wrote you a few days ago if you could furnish me with the addresses of some firms or co-opporations that needed common labor. So many of our people here are almost starving . . . quite a number here would go any where to better their conditions. If you can do any thing for us write me as early as possible.

ANNISTON, ALA., APRIL 23, 1917.
Dear Sir: Please gave me some infamation about coming north i can do any kind of work from a truck gardin to farming i would like to leave here and i cant make no money to leave i ust make enough to live one please let me here from you at once i want to get where i can put my children in schol.

Dear Sir: I saw your add in the Chicago *Defender* for laborers. I am a young man and want to finish school. I want you to look out for me a job on the place working morning and evening. I would like to get a job in some private family so I could continue taking my piano lesson I can do anything around the house but drive and can even learn that. Send me the name of the best High School in Chicago. How is the Wendell Phillips College. I have finish the grammar school.

MOBILE, ALA., APRIL 25, 1917.
Sir: I am a poor woman and have a husband and five children living and three dead one single and two twin girls six months

old today and my husband can hardly make bread for them in Mobile. This is my native home but it is not fit to live in just as the Chicago *Defender* say it says the truth and my husband only get $1.50 a day and pays $7.50 a month for house rent and can hardly feed me and his self and children. . . . I want to get out of this dog hold because I don't know what I am raising them up for in this place and I want to get to Chicago where I know they will be raised and my husband crazy to get there because he know he can get more to raise his children and will you please let me know where the cars is going to stop so that he can come where he can take care of me and my children. He get there a while and then he can send for me. I heard they wasn't coming here so I sent to find out and he can go and meet them at the place they are going and go from there to Chicago. No more at present. hoping to hear from you soon from your needed and worried friend.

NEW ORLEANS, LA., MAY 2, 1917.
Dear Sir: Please Sir will you kindly tell me what is meant by the great Northern Drive to take place May the 15th on Tuesday. It is a rumor all over town to be ready for the 15th of May to go in the drive. the *Defender* first spoke of the drive the 10th of February. My husband is in the north already preparing for our family but hearing that the excursion will be $6.00 from here north on the 15th and having a large family, I could profit by it if it is really true. Do please write me at once and say is there an excursion to leave the south. Nearly the whole of the south is getting ready for the drive or excursion as it is termed. Please write at once. We are sick to get out of the solid south.

BHAM, ALA., MAY 1917.
Sir: i am in the darkness of the south and i am trying my best to get out do you no where about i can get a job in new york.

i wood be so glad if cood get a good job . . . o please help me
to get out of this low down county i am counted no more thin
a dog help me please help me o how glad i wood be if some
company wood send me a ticket to come and work for them
no joking i mean business i work if i can get a good job.

BRYAN, TEX., SEPT. 13, 1917.
Dear Sir: I am writing you as I would like to no if you no of
any R. R. Co and Mfg. that are in need for colored labors. I
want to bring a bunch of race men out of the south we want
work some whear north will come if we can git passe any whear
across the Mason & Dickson. please let me hear from you at
once if you can git passes for 10 or 12 men. send at once.

From *Journal of Negro History*, July and October, 1919.

My First Lesson

*To the letters of Southern Blacks yearning to come north can
be added the testimony of Richard Wright. His father, a laborer,
had left his mother when Richard was very young, and at fifteen
the boy decided to run away from home. His schooling had
stopped in the eighth grade. From Natchez he wandered up to
Memphis, where he worked as errand boy and as porter. "But
all I really wanted to do in those days," he said, "was to read."
Up along the Mississippi he moved, finding jobs here and there
until finally he reached Chicago. "There I worked first at sweeping streets and then at digging ditches." After a while he started
to write, seeing a few of his articles and stories appearing in the
little literary magazines. Now it was the years of the Great
Depression, and the federal government's job relief program—*

Richard Wright

the Works Progress Administration—opened projects for writ-
ers, actors, artists, musicians. Richard Wright went to work on
the Federal Writers Project in Chicago. In 1937 his Uncle Tom's
Children *won a contest among WPA writers. In it he transformed*
his young years into powerful short stories. One of his early
pieces was "The Ethics of Living Jim Crow," a moving memory
of his youth. From it comes this section telling how a boy of
those days (around 1917) learned to live as a Black American.

MY FIRST LESSON in how to live as a Negro came when
I was quite small. We were living in Arkansas. Our house stood
behind the railroad tracks. Its skimpy yard was paved with black
cinders. Nothing green ever grew in that yard. The only touch
of green we could see was far away, beyond the tracks, over
where the white folks lived. But cinders were good enough for
me, and I never missed the green growing things. And, anyhow,

cinders were fine weapons. You could always have a nice hot war with huge black cinders. All you had to do was crouch behind the brick pillars of a house with your hands full of gritty ammunition. And the first woolly black head you saw pop out from behind another row of pillars was your target. You tried your very best to knock it off. It was great fun.

I never fully realized the appalling disadvantages of a cinder environment till one day the gang to which I belonged found itself engaged in a war with the white boys who lived beyond the tracks. As usual, we laid down our cinder barrage, thinking that this would wipe the white boys out. But they replied with a steady bombardment of broken bottles. We doubled our cinder barrage, but they hid behind trees, hedges, and the sloping embankments of their lawns. Having no such fortifications, we retreated to the brick pillars of our homes. During the retreat a broken milk bottle caught me behind the ear, opening a deep gash which bled profusely. The sight of blood pouring over my face completely demoralized our ranks. My fellow combatants left me standing paralyzed in the center of the yard and scurried for their homes. A kind neighbor saw me and rushed me to a doctor, who took three stitches in my neck.

I sat brooding on my front steps, nursing my wound and waiting for my mother to come from work. I felt that a grave injustice had been done me. It was all right to throw cinders. The greatest harm a cinder could do was leave a bruise. But broken bottles were dangerous; they left you cut, bleeding, and helpless.

When night fell my mother came from the white folks' kitchen. I raced down the street to meet her. I could just feel in my bones that she would understand. I knew she would tell me exactly what to do next time. I grabbed her hand and babbled out the whole story. She examined my wound, then slapped me.

"How come yoh didn't hide?" she asked me. "How come yoh always fightin'?"

I was outraged, and bawled. Between sobs I told her that I didn't have any trees or hedges to hide behind. There wasn't a thing I could have used as a trench. And you couldn't throw very far when you were hiding behind the brick pillars of a house. She grabbed a barrel stave, dragged me home, stripped me naked, and beat me till I had a fever of one hundred and two. She would smack my rump with the stave and, while the skin was still smarting, impart to me gems of Jim Crow wisdom. I was never to throw cinders any more. I was never to fight any more wars. I was never, never, under any conditions, to fight white folks again. And they were absolutely right in clouting me with the broken milk bottle. Didn't I know she was working hard every day in the hot kitchens of the white folks to make money to take care of me? When was I ever going to learn to be a good boy? She couldn't be bothered with my fights. She finished by telling me that I ought to be thankful to God as long as I lived that they didn't kill me.

All that night I was delirious and could not sleep. Each time I closed my eyes I saw monstrous white faces suspended from the ceiling, leering at me.

From that time on the charm of my cinder yard was gone. The green trees, the trimmed hedges, the cropped lawns grew very meaningful, became a symbol. Even today, when I think of white folks, the hard, sharp outlines of white houses surrounded by trees, lawns, and hedges are present somewhere in the background of my mind. Through the years they grew into an overreaching symbol of fear.

It was a long time before I came in close contact with white folks again. We moved from Arkansas to Mississippi. Here we had the good fortune not to live behind the railroad tracks or close to white neighborhoods. We lived in the very heart of the local Black Belt. There were black churches and black preachers; there were black schools and black teachers, black groceries and black clerks. In fact, everything was so solidly black that for a long time I did not even think of white folks, save in remote and vague terms. But this could not last forever. As one grows older one eats more. One's clothing costs more. When I finished grammar school I had to go to work. My mother could no longer feed and clothe me on her cooking job.

There is but one place where a black boy who knows no trade can get a job. And that's where the houses and faces are white, where the trees, lawns, and hedges are green. My first job was with an optical company in Jackson, Mississippi. The morning I applied I stood straight and neat before the boss, answering all his questions with sharp yessirs and nosirs. I was very careful to pronounce my sirs distinctly, in order that he might know that I was polite, that I knew where I was, and that I knew he was a white man. I wanted that job badly.

He looked me over as though he were examining a prize poodle. He questioned me closely about my schooling, being particularly insistent about how much mathematics I had had. He seemed very pleased when I told him I had had two years of algebra.

"Boy, how would you like to try to learn something around here?" he asked me.

"I'd like it fine, sir," I said, happy. I had visions of "working my way up." Even Negroes have those visions.

"All right," he said. "Come on."

I followed him to the small factory.

"Pease," he said to a white man of about thirty-five, "this is Richard. He's going to work for us."

Pease looked at me and nodded.

I was then taken to a white boy of about seventeen.

"Morrie, this is Richard, who's going to work for us."

"Whut yuh sayin' there, boy!" Morrie boomed at me.

"Fine!" I answered.

The boss instructed these two to help me, teach me, give me jobs to do, and let me learn what I could in my spare time.

My wages were five dollars a week.

I worked hard, trying to please. For the first month I got along O.K. Both Pease and Morrie seemed to like me. But one thing was missing. And I kept thinking about it. I was not learning anything, and nobody was volunteering to help me. Thinking they had forgotten that I was to learn something about the mechanics of grinding lenses, I asked Morrie one day to tell me about the work. He grew red.

"Whut yuh tryin' t' do, nigger, get smart?" he asked.

"Naw, I ain't tryin' t' git smart," I said.

"Well, don't, if yuh know whut's good for yuh!"

I was puzzled. Maybe he just doesn't want to help me, I thought. I went to Pease.

"Say, are you crazy, you black bastard?" Pease asked me, his gray eyes growing hard.

I spoke out, reminding him that the boss had said I was to be given a chance to learn something.

"Nigger, you think you're white, don't you?"

"Naw sir!"

"Well, you're acting mighty like it!"

"But, Mr. Pease, the boss said——"

Pease shook his fist in my face.

"This is a white man's work around here, and you better watch yourself!"

From then on they changed toward me. They said good morning no more. When I was just a bit slow in performing some duty, I was called a lazy black son-of-a-bitch.

Once I thought of reporting all this to the boss. But the mere idea of what would happen to me if Pease and Morrie should learn that I had "snitched" stopped me. And after all, the boss was a white man too. What was the use?

The climax came at noon one summer day. Pease called me to his workbench. To get to him I had to go between two narrow benches and stand with my back against a wall.

"Yes sir," I said.

"Richard, I want to ask you something," Pease began pleasantly, not looking up from his work.

"Yes sir," I said again.

Morrie came over, blocking the narrow passage between the benches. He folded his arms, staring at me solemnly.

I looked from one to the other, sensing that something was coming.

"Yes sir," I said for the third time.

Pease looked up and spoke very slowly.

"Richard, Mr. Morrie, here, tells me you called me Pease."

I stiffened. A void seemed to open up in me. I knew this was the showdown.

He meant that I had failed to call him Mr. Pease. I looked at Morrie. He was gripping a steel bar in his hands. I opened my mouth to speak, to protest, to assure Pease that I had never called him simply Pease and that I had never had any intentions of doing so, when Morrie grabbed me by the collar, ramming my head against the wall.

"Now, be careful, nigger!" snarled Morrie, baring his teeth. "I heard yuh call 'im Pease. 'N' if yuh say yuh didn't, you're callin' me a liar, see?" He waved the steel bar threateningly.

If I had said, "No sir, Mr. Pease, I never called you Pease," I would have been automatically calling Morrie a liar. And if I had said, "Yes sir, Mr. Pease, I called you Pease," I would have been pleading guilty to having uttered the worst insult that a Negro can utter to a Southern white man. I stood hesitating, trying to frame a neutral reply.

"Richard, I asked you a question!" said Pease. Anger was creeping into his voice.

"I don't remember calling you Pease, Mr. Pease," I said

cautiously. "And if I did, I sure didn't mean——"

"You black son-of-a-bitch! You called me Pease, then!" he spat, slapping me till I bent sideways over a bench. Morrie was on top of me, demanding:

"Didn't yuh call 'im Pease? If yuh say yuh didn't I'll rip yo' gut string loose with this bar, yuh black granny dodger! Yuh can't tell a white man a lie 'n' git erway with it, you black son-of-a-bitch!"

I wilted. I begged them not to bother me. I knew what they wanted. They wanted me to leave.

"I'll leave," I promised. "I'll leave right now."

They gave me a minute to get out of the factory. I was warned not to show up again or tell the boss.

I went.

When I told the folks at home what had happened, they called me a fool. They told me that I must never again attempt to exceed my boundaries. When you are working for white folks, they said, you got to "stay in your place" if you want to keep working. . . .

From *Uncle Tom's Children*, by Richard Wright, Harper, 1938

The One-Room Kitchenette

By 1928 almost a million and a quarter migrants had come up from the South to find a new life in the Northern cities. Young Richard Wright was one of them. In Chicago he learned to be a writer and became one of the most eloquent spokesmen for his generation. In 1938 he published his first novel, Native Son,

describing the life of a young Black in a Chicago slum. It was
a great success critically and financially. The book was soon
converted into both play and movie. The next year he published
12 *Million Black Voices, a "folk history." From it comes this*
passage in which Wright tells what the great exodus from the
South during World War I was like and what the migrants found
when they arrived on the pavements of the city.

LORD IN HEAVEN! Good God Almighty! Great Day in
the Morning! It's here! Our time has come! We are leaving!
We are angry no more; we are leaving! We are bitter no more;
we are leaving! We are leaving our homes, pulling up stakes
to move on. We look up at the high southern sky and remember
all the sunshine and the rain and we feel a sense of loss, but

we are leaving. We look out at the wide green fields which our eyes saw when we first came into the world and we feel full of regret, but we are leaving. We scan the kind black faces we have looked upon since we first saw the light of day, and, though pain is in our hearts, we are leaving. We take one last furtive look over our shoulders to the Big House—high upon a hill beyond the railroad tracks—where the Lord of the Land lives, and we feel glad, for we are leaving. . . .

Night and day, in rain and in sun, in winter and in summer, we leave the land. Already, as we sit and look broodingly out over the turning fields, we notice with attention and hope that the dense southern swamps give way to broad, cultivated wheat farms. The spick-and-span farmhouses done in red and green and white crowd out the casual, unpainted gingerbread shacks. Silos take the place of straggling piles of hay. Macadam highways now wind over the horizon instead of dirt roads. The cheeks of the farm people are full and ruddy, not sunken and withered like soda crackers. . . .

We see white men and women get on the train, dressed in expensive new clothes. We look at them guardedly and wonder will they bother us. Will they ask us to stand up while they sit down? Will they tell us to go to the back of the coach? Even though we have been told that we need not be afraid, we have lived so long in fear of all white faces that we cannot help but sit and wait. We look around the train and we do not see the old familiar signs: For Colored and For White. The train speeds north and we cannot sleep. Our heads sink in a doze, and then we sit bolt-upright, prodded by the thought that we must watch these strange surroundings. But nothing happens; these white men seem impersonal and their very neutrality reassures us—for a while. Almost against our deeper judgment, we try to force ourselves to relax, for these brisk men give no sign of what they feel. They are indifferent. O sweet and welcome *indifference*!

The miles click behind us. Into Chicago, Indianapolis, New York, Cleveland, Buffalo, Detroit, Toledo, Philadelphia, Pittsburgh, and Milwaukee we go, looking for work. We feel freer than we have ever felt before, but we are still a little scared. It is like a dream. Will we wake up suddenly and find that none of this is really true, that we are merely daydreaming behind the barn, snoozing in the sun, waiting to hear the hoarse voice of the riding boss saying: "Nigger, where do you think you are? Get the hell up from there and move on!"

Timidly, we get off the train. We hug our suitcases, fearful of pickpockets, looking with unrestrained curiosity at the great big brick buildings. We are very reserved, for we have been warned not to act "green," that the city people can spot a "sucker" a mile away. Then we board our first Yankee street car to go to a cousin's home, a brother's home, a sister's home, a friend's home, an uncle's home, or an aunt's home. We pay the conductor our fare and look about apprehensively for a seat. We have been told that we can sit where we please, but we are still scared. We cannot shake off three hundred years of fear in three hours. We ease into a seat and look out of the window at the crowded streets. A white man or a white woman comes and sits beside us, not even looking at us, as though this were a normal thing to do. The muscles of our bodies tighten. Indefinable sensations crawl over our skins and our blood tingles. Out of the corners of our eyes we try to get a glimpse of the strange white face that floats but a few inches from ours. The impulses to laugh and to cry clash in us; we bite our lips and stare out of the window.

There are so many people. For the first time in our lives we feel human bodies, strangers whose lives and thoughts are unknown to us, pressing always close about us. We cannot see or know a *man* because of the thousands upon thousands of *men*. The apartments in which we sleep are crowded and noisy, and soon enough we learn that the brisk, clipped men of the

North, the Bosses of the Buildings, are not at all *indifferent*. They are deeply concerned about us, but in a new way. It seems as though we are now living inside of a machine; days and events move with a hard reasoning of their own. We live amid swarms of people, yet there is a vast distance between people, a distance that words cannot bridge. No longer do our lives depend upon the soil, the sun, the rain, or the wind; we live by the grace of jobs and the brutal logic of jobs. We do not know this world, or what makes it move. In the South life was different; men spoke to you, cursed you, yelled at you, or killed you. The world moved by signs we knew. But here in the North cold forces hit you and push you. It is a world of *things*.

Our defenseless eyes cloud with bewilderment when we learn that there are not enough houses for us to live in. And competing with us for shelter are thousands of poor migrant whites who have come up from the South, just as we have come. The cost of building a house is high, and building activities are on the downgrade. It is wartime; no new labor is coming in from the old countries across the seas. The only district we can live in is the area just beyond the business belt, a transition area where a sooty conglomeration of factories and mills belches smoke that stains our clothes and lungs. . . .

Having been warned against us by the Bosses of the Buildings, having heard tall tales about us, about how "bad" we are, they [the whites] react emotionally as though we had the plague when we move into their neighborhoods. Is it any wonder, then, that their homes are suddenly and drastically reduced in value? They hastily abandon them, sacrificing them to the Bosses of the Buildings, the men who instigate all this for whatever profit they can get in real-estate sales. And in the end we are all the "fall guys." When the white folks move, the Bosses of the Buildings let the property to us at rentals higher than those the whites paid.

And the Bosses of the Buildings take these old houses and

convert them into "kitchenettes," and then rent them to us at rates so high that they make fabulous fortunes before the houses are too old for habitation. What they do is this: they take, say, a seven-room apartment, which rents for $50 a month to whites, and cut it up into seven small apartments, of one room each; they install one small gas stove and one small sink in each room. The Bosses of the Buildings rent these kitchenettes to us at the rate of, say, $6 a week. Hence, the same apartment for which white people—who can get jobs anywhere and who receive higher wages than we—pay $50 a month is rented to us for $42 a week! And because there are not enough houses for us to live in, because we have been used to sleeping several in a room on the plantations in the South, we rent these kitchenettes and are glad to get them. These kitchenettes are our havens from the plantations in the South. We have fled the wrath of Queen Cotton and we are tired.

Sometimes five or six of us live in a one-room kitchenette, a place where simple folk such as we should never be held captive. A war sets up in our emotions: one part of our feelings tells us that it is good to be in the city, that we have a chance at life here, that we need but turn a corner to become a stranger, that we no longer need bow and dodge at the sight of the Lords of the Land. Another part of our feelings tells us that, in terms of worry and strain, the cost of living in the kitchenettes is too high, that the city heaps too much responsibility upon us and gives too little security in return.

The kitchenette is the author of the glad tidings that new suckers are in town, ready to be cheated, plundered, and put in their places.

The kitchenette is our prison, our death sentence without a trial, the new form of mob violence that assaults not only the lone individual, but all of us, in its ceaseless attacks.

The kitchenette, with its filth and foul air, with its one toilet for thirty or more tenants, kills our black babies so fast that in many cities twice as many of them die as white babies.

The kitchenette is the seed bed for scarlet fever, dysentery, typhoid, tuberculosis, gonorrhea, syphilis, pneumonia, and malnutrition.

The kitchenette scatters death so widely among us that our death rate exceeds our birth rate, and if it were not for the trains and autos bringing us daily into the city from the plantations, we black folks who dwell in the northern cities would die out entirely over the course of a few years.

The kitchenette, with its crowded rooms and incessant bedlam, provides an enticing place for crimes of all sort—crimes against women and children or any stranger who happens to stray into its dark hallways. The noise of our living, boxed in stone and steel, is so loud that even a pistol shot is smothered.

The kitchenette throws desperate and unhappy people into an unbearable closeness of association, thereby increasing latent friction, giving birth to never-ending quarrels of recrimination, accusation, and vindictiveness, producing warped personalities.

The kitchenette injects pressure and tension into our individual personalities, making many of us give up the struggle, walk off and leave wives, husbands, and even children behind to shift as best they can.

The kitchenette creates thousands of one-room homes where our black mothers sit deserted, with their children about their knees.

The kitchenette blights the personalities of our growing children, disorganizes them, blinds them to hope, creates problems whose effects can be traced in the characters of its child victims for years afterward.

The kitchenette jams our farm girls, while still in their teens, into rooms with men who are restless and stimulated by the noise and lights of the city; and more of our girls have bastard babies than the girls in any other sections of the city.

The kitchenette fills our black boys with longing and restlessness, urging them to run off from home, to join together with other restless black boys in gangs, that brutal form of city courage.

The kitchenette piles up mountains of profits for the Bosses of the Buildings and makes them ever more determined to keep things as they are.

The kitchenette reaches out with fingers full of golden bribes to the officials of the city, persuading them to allow old firetraps to remain standing and occupied long after they should have been torn down.

The kitchenette is the funnel through which our pulverized lives flow to ruin and death on the city pavements, at a profit. . . .

From *12 Million Black Voices,* by Richard Wright
and Edwin Rosskam, Viking Press, 1941.

We Return-Fighting!

As the wartime industries grew, more and more Blacks rushed north in the hope of finding work. Many got jobs better than anything they had known before. They found places in iron and steel mills, in meatpacking and auto plants; they helped build ships and mine coal and run railroads. But their problems in the crowded black ghettoes multiplied with their numbers. White workers feared their competition on the job and tried to keep them out of their neighborhoods. The government offered no protection against discrimination and segregation. For a while Blacks had put their faith in Woodrow Wilson's 1912 campaign promise to see "justice done to the colored people in every matter." But once in office, the Virginia-born President strung Jim Crow fences throughout the federal government.

In 1917 the United States entered World War I—"to make the world safe for democracy," President Wilson said. The world did not seem to include Black Americans. The same Jim Crow fence cut across the armed forces in which 367,000 Blacks served during the war. The new Air Corps slammed the door tight against Blacks; the Navy rated them fit for menial duty only; and the other armed services segregated them. There were clashes between black and white soldiers in the training camps and between black soldiers and white civilians in the communities surrounding them. When the colored troops reached France, believed to be a prejudice-free haven, they found the Army had warned the French not to treat black soldiers as equals. Nevertheless, Blacks made a great record in combat, winning many citations for bravery. Perhaps some felt that with all the wartime talk of democracy surely things would be different when they got home.

As the packed troopships crossed Atlantic homeward bound, Dr. W. E. B. DuBois put into words the feeling in the hearts of the black soldiers. He published those words in 1919 in The Crisis, *the journal he edited for the National Association for the Advancement of Colored People (NAACP).*

Born in 1868, DuBois was now 51. He was one of America's foremost scholars, but never content to float quietly in an academic backwater. He was fearless in his leadership of the black protest movement, and through his writings had an enormous influence on his own generation and on all those who have followed.

WE ARE RETURNING from war! *The Crisis* and tens of thousands of black men were drafted into a great struggle. For bleeding France and what she means and has meant and will mean to us and humanity and against the threat of German race arrogance, we fought gladly and to the last drop of blood; for America and her highest ideals, we fought in far-off hope; for the dominant southern oligarchy entrenched in Washington, we fought in bitter resignation. For the America that represents and gloats in lynching, disfranchisement, caste, brutality and devilish insult—for this, in the hateful upturning and mixing of things, we were forced by vindictive fate to fight, also.

But today we return! We return from the slavery of uniform which the world's madness demanded us to don to the freedom of civil garb. We stand again to look America squarely in the face and call a spade a spade. We sing: This country of ours, despite all its better souls have done and dreamed, is yet a shameful land.

It lynches.

And lynching is barbarism of a degree of contemptible nastiness unparalleled in human history. Yet for fifty years we have lynched two Negroes a week, and we have kept this up right through the war.

It disfranchises its own citizens.

Disfranchisement is the deliberate theft and robbery of the only protection of poor against rich and black against white. The land that disfranchises its citizens and calls itself a democracy lies and knows it lies.

It encourages ignorance.

It has never really tried to educate the Negro. A dominant minority does not want Negroes educated. It wants servants, dogs, whores and monkeys. And when this land allows a reactionary group by its stolen political power to force as many black folk into these categories as it possibly can, it cries in contemptible hypocrisy: "They threaten us with degeneracy; they cannot be educated."

It steals from us.

It organizes industry to cheat us. It cheats us out of our land; it cheats us out of our labor. It confiscates our savings. It reduces our wages. It raises our rent. It steals our profit. It taxes us without representation. It keeps us consistently and universally poor, and then feeds us on charity and derides our poverty.

It insults us.

It has organized a nation-wide and latterly a worldwide propaganda of deliberate and continuous insult and defamation of
black blood wherever found. It decrees that it shall not be
possible in travel nor residence, work nor play, education nor
instruction for a black man to exist without tacit or open acknowledgment of his inferiority to the dirtiest white dog. And
it looks upon any attempt to question or even discuss this dogma
as arrogance, unwarranted assumption and treason.

This is the country to which we Soldiers of Democracy return.
This is the fatherland for which we fought! But it is our fatherland. It was right for us to fight. The faults of our country
are our faults. Under similar circumstances, we would fight
again. But by the God of Heaven, we are cowards and jackasses
if now that that war is over, we do not marshal every ounce
of our brain and brawn to fight a sterner, longer, more un-
bending battle against the forces of hell in our own land.

We return.

We return from fighting.

We return fighting.

Make way for Democracy! We saved it in France, and by
the Great Jehovah, we will save it in the United States of
America, or know the reason why.

From *The Crisis*, 1919.

Black Men, You Shall Be Great Again

Marcus Garvey

New York City W.P.A. Art Project

Thousands of Blacks were immigrating to Harlem from the West Indies at the same time as Blacks from the South. Among them was a chunky black Jamaican named Marcus Garvey. Two years earlier, in his native island, he had started the Universal Negro Improvement Association (UNIA). On the sidewalks of New

York his talk about redeeming the race made little impression at first. Garvey wandered west from Harlem, touring 38 states to see how Blacks lived in America. Everywhere he found tens of thousands of migrants from the South jammed into rickety tenements, Jim Crowed on their jobs and in their neighborhoods, living in the shadow of the big white world and living on its castoffs.

For a few years he made little progress in winning the black masses with his message—pride in race. But neither had any other organization made headway with the black people. The National Urban League and the NAACP had paid more attention to middle-class than working-class Blacks, and depended upon better-off whites and Blacks for support. But by 1919, the year in which race riots erupted in a deadly rash over the face of America, Blacks were ready for a program that pointed a way out of the prison of the ghetto. Marcus Garvey had the gifts to dramatize his dream of a black world ruled by black men. The Blacks should be proud of their past, he said, proud of the great empires built by black people in Africa's glorious age, proud of their very blackness. Garvey praised everything black. The color was a sign of strength and beauty, he said, not a badge of inferiority.

In his speeches and his newspaper, The Negro World, *he declared the white man's prejudice against Blacks was so strong, it was foolish to believe his sermons on justice and democracy would ever mean anything in practice. This America was a white man's country, he said, and no place for Blacks. The only hope for Blacks was to build an independent nation in Africa, their ancestral homeland.*

Garvey's black nationalist appeal showed amazing success by 1919. The UNIA grew swiftly, its branches spreading to most of the large centers of black population. Garvey gave his followers parades and pageants, uniforms and titles, conventions and conferences. By the mid twenties, he had about a million followers. He organized stores, factories, cooperatives, and a Black Star Steamship Line. It was this last venture that ended his sensational rise. It showed a heavy financial loss and Garvey was tried for fraud. Found guilty, he was sent to prison in 1925. Two years later he was pardoned, but deported as an alien. He lived the rest of his life in obscurity.

Garvey never reached Africa, nor did he ever land any of his followers on that shore. But that was no measure of Garveyism's meaning. It was the first real mass movement among Black Americans in the country's history. Blacks showed they did not want to leave the United States any more than had earlier generations, no matter how angry and bitter they were. What Garvey did was to strengthen their self-respect and pride, to open out the world to them, to show the promise of liberation which the African nations would achieve a generation or two later.

From Garvey's writings of the early 1920's comes this statement of his ideas and beliefs.

IT COMES TO the individual, the race, the nation, once in a lifetime to decide upon the course to be pursued as a career. The hour has now struck for the individual Negro as well as the entire race to decide the course that will be pursued in the interest of our own liberty.

We who make up the Universal Negro Improvement Association have decided that we shall go forward, upward and onward toward the great goal of human liberty. We have determined among ourselves that all barriers placed in the way of our progress must be removed, must be cleared away for we desire to see the light of a brighter day.

The Universal Negro Improvement Association for five years has been proclaiming to the world the readiness of the Negro to carve out a pathway for himself in the course of life. . . . We are organized for the absolute purpose of bettering our con-

dition, industrially, commercially, socially, religiously and politically. We are organized not to hate other men, but to lift
ourselves, and to demand respect of all humanity. We have a
program that we believe to be righteous; we believe it to be
just, and we have made up our minds to lay down ourselves
on the altar of sacrifice for the realization of this great hope
of ours, based upon the foundation of righteousness. We declare to the world that Africa must be free, that the entire
Negro race must be emancipated from industrial bondage,
peonage and serfdom; we make no compromise, we make no
apology in this our declaration. We do not desire to create
offense on the part of the other races, but we are determined
that we shall be heard, that we shall be given the rights to which
we are entitled. . . .

Men of the Negro race, let me say to you that a greater
future is in store for us; we have no cause to lose hope, to
become faint-hearted. We must realize that upon ourselves
depend our destiny, our future; we must carve out that future,
that destiny, and we who make up the Universal Negro Improvement Association have pledged ourselves that nothing in
the world shall stand in our way, nothing in the world shall
discourage us, but opposition shall make us work harder, shall
bring us closer together so that as one man the millions of us
will march on toward the goal that we have set for ourselves.

The new Negro shall not be deceived. The new Negro refuses
to take advice from anyone who has not felt with him, and
suffered with him. We have suffered for three hundred years,
therefore we feel that the time has come when only those who
have suffered with us can interpret our feelings and our spirit.
It takes the slave to interpret the feelings of the slave; it takes
the unfortunate man to interpret the spirit of his unfortunate
brother; and so it takes the suffering Negro to interpret the
spirit of his comrade. . . .

There is many a leader of our race who tells us that everything is well, and that all things will work out themselves and that a better day is coming. Yes, all of us know that a better day is coming; we all know that one day we will go home to Paradise, but whilst we are hoping by our Christian virtues to have an entry into Paradise we also realize that we are living on earth, and that the things that are practiced in Paradise are not practiced here. You have to treat this world as the world treats you; we are living in a temporal, material age, an age of activity, an age of racial, national selfishness. What else can you expect but to give back to the world what the world gives to you, and we are calling upon the four hundred million Negroes of the world to take a decided stand, a determined stand, that we shall occupy a firm position; that position shall be an emancipated race and a free nation of our own. We are determined that we shall have a free country; we are determined that we shall have a flag; we are determined that we shall have a government second to none in the world. . . .

When we come to consider the history of man, was not the Negro a power, was he not great once? Yes, honest students of history can recall the day when Egypt, Ethiopia and Timbuctoo towered in their civilizations, towered above Europe, towered above Asia. When Europe was inhabited by a race of cannibals, a race of savages, naked men, heathens and pagans, Africa was peopled with a race of cultured black men, who were masters in art, science and literature; men who were cultured and refined; men who, it was said, were like the gods. Even the great poets of old sang in beautiful sonnets of the delight it afforded the gods to be in companionship with the Ethiopians. Why, then, should we lose hope? Black men, you were once great; you shall be great again. Lose not courage, lose not faith, go forward. The thing to do is to get organized; keep separated and you will be exploited, you will be robbed, you will be killed. Get organized, and you will compel the world to respect you. If the world fails to give you consideration, because you are black men, because you are Negroes, four hundred millions of you shall, through organization, shake the pillars of the universe and bring down creation, even as Samson brought down the temple upon his head and upon the heads of the Philistines.

So Negroes, I say, through the Universal Negro Improvement Association, that there is much to live for. I have a vision of the future, and I see before me a picture of a redeemed Africa, with her dotted cities, with her beautiful civilization, with her millions of happy children, going to and fro. Why should I lose hope, why should I give up and take a back place in this age of progress? Remember that you are men, that God created you Lords of this creation. Lift up yourselves, men, take yourselves out of the mire and hitch your hopes to the stars; yes, rise as high as the very stars themselves. Let no man pull you down, let no man destroy your ambition, because man is but your companion, your equal; man is your brother; he is not your lord; he is not your sovereign master. . . .

From *Philosophy and Opinions of Marcus Garvey*,
Universal Publishing House, 1923.

The Right to a Home

"I am huntin' for a city, to stay awhile," ran one of the old songs Blacks sang before the Civil War. They might have been dreaming of free Canaan's shore. In the twenties Blacks arriving in Chicago or Cleveland from the country had great trouble finding room to sit down in the new Canaan. All but a few corners of the cities were closed to them. The only housing they could find was in run-down and packed black ghettoes. By 1912 Louisville had put the first housing segregation law on the books. If a block had a majority of whites it was labeled for whites

only, and vice versa. One after another cities followed the pat-
tern, and soon ghettoes were legally sanctioned in many parts
of the country.

Even when Blacks of the professional or business class had
the income to support homes in attractive and quiet neighbor-
hoods, it was very hard for them to find sellers. Such neigh-
borhoods were almost always all white and did not welcome
Blacks. If sales did occur (at prices that went through the ceiling),
disaster often followed for the Black family.

Take the case of Dr. Ossian Sweet. The black physician bought
a home in a white neighborhood of Detroit in 1925. Not peace
and quiet came, but hatred and headlines. Dr. Sweet's family
was besieged by a mob; in self-defense his younger brother Henry
fired back, and one of the attackers fell dead. The Sweet family
and their friends in the house at the time were all arrested and
charged with willful murder. The NAACP took up the cause,
securing the great lawyer Clarence Darrow to defend them.

In The Crisis, *Dr. DuBois discussed the issue of Black Amer-*
icans' right to their home and their right to defend it. The press
gave the case great publicity. In his closing speech to the jury,
Darrow exposed the racial prejudice behind the trial by pointing
out that if white men had killed a Black while protecting their
family and home from a mob of Blacks, "no one would have
dreamed of having them indicted. . . . They would have been
given medals instead."

The jury of twelve white men brought in a verdict of "Not
guilty." A precedent had been set in the law: A man's home was
his castle, even if he was a Black.

IN DETROIT, MICHIGAN, a black man has shot into a mob
which was threatening him, his family, his friends, and his home
in order to make him move out of the neighborhood. He killed
one man and wounded another.

Immediately a red and awful challenge confronts the nation.

Must black folk shoot and shoot to kill in order to maintain their rights or is this unnecessary and wanton bloodshed for fancied ill? The answer depends on the facts. The Mayor of Detroit has publicly warned both mob and Negroes. He has repudiated mob law but he adds, turning to his darker audience, that they ought not to invite aggression by going where they are not wanted. There are thus two interpretations:

1. A prosperous Negro physician of Detroit, seeking to get a way from his people, moves into a white residential section where his presence for social reasons is distasteful to his neighbors.

2. A prosperous Negro physician of Detroit, seeking a better home with more light, air, space and quiet, finds it naturally in the parts of the city where white folk with similar wants have gone rather than in the slums where most of the colored are crowded.

Which version is true? See the figures:

NEGRO POPULATION OF DETROIT

1900 . .   4,111
1910 . .   5,741
1920 . . 40,838
1925 . . 60,000 (estimated)

Two thirds of this population in 1920 were crowded into three wards—the Third, Fifth and Seventh. Meantime the total population of Detroit has more than doubled in ten years and the people have reached out on all sides to new dwelling places. Have the Negroes no right to reach too? Is it not their duty to seek better homes and, if they do, are they not bound to "move into white neighborhoods" which is simply another way of saying "move out of congested slums"?

Why do they not make their own new settlements then? Because no individual can make a modern real estate development; no group of ordinary individuals can compete with organized real estate interests and get a decent deal. When Negroes have tried it they have usually had miserable results. . . . In Macon, Savannah, New Orleans and Atlanta crime and prostitution have been kept and protected in Negro residence districts. In New York City, for years, no Negro could rent or buy a home in Manhattan outside the "Tenderloin"; and white Religion and Respectability, far from stretching a helping hand, turned and cursed the blacks when by bribery, politics and brute force they broke into the light and air of Harlem. . . .

Dear God! Must we not live? And if we live may we not live somewhere? And when a whole city full of white folk led and helped by banks, Chambers of Commerce, mortgage companies and "realtors" are combing the earth for every decent bit of residential property for whites, where in the name of God can we live and live decently if not by these same whites? If some of the horror-struck and law-worshipping white leaders of Detroit instead of winking at the Ku Klux Klan and admonishing the Negroes to allow themselves to be kicked and killed with impunity—if these would finance and administer a decent scheme of housing relief for Negroes it would not be necessary for us to kill white mob leaders in order to live in peace and decency. These whited sepulchres pulled that trigger and not the man that held the gun.

But, wail the idiots, Negroes depress real estate values! This is a lie—an ancient and bearded lie. Race prejudice decreases values both real estate and human; crime, ignorance and filth decrease values. But a decent, quiet, educated family buying property in a decent neighborhood will not affect values a bit unless the people in that neighborhood hate a colored skin more than they regard the value of their own property. This has been proven in a thousand instances. Sudden fall in values comes through propaganda and hysteria manipulated by real estate agents, or by Southern slave drivers who want their labor

to return South, or by ignorant gossip mongers. Usually Negroes do not move into new developments but into districts
which well-to-do whites are deserting. The fall in values is not
due to race but to a series of economic readjustments and often,
as in Baltimore, real estate values were actually saved and
raised, not lowered when black folk bought Druid Hill Avenue
and adjacent streets. Certainly a flood of noisy dirty black folk
will ruin any neighborhood but they ruin black property as well
as white, and the reason is not their color but their condition.
And whom, High Heaven, shall we blame for that?

From *The Crisis*, November, 1925.

Free Within Ourselves

*There was a direct connection between the militancy of Blacks
like Dr. Ossian Sweet—who took up arms to defend his home
from a mob—and the new movement in the arts. The younger
writers published in Alain Locke's anthology* The New Negro
*had turned their backs on Booker T. Washington. They did not
want to "accommodate" or "adjust." With W. E. B. DuBois
they stood for full equality. Many of these younger writers were
the sons of the rising middle class. But they were not dedicated
to making money or to imitating the white folks. Nor did they
want to separate themselves from the black masses. They looked
for and found enduring values in their own people, in their
folkways, in their work and play, in their heart and spirit.*

*In 1926 one of the leading young writers, Langston Hughes
(then 24), published an article calling on black artists to look
closely at the life around them and write it and paint it as it was.
Don't be like the black society woman who pays for a front-row*

Langston Hughes

seat at a concert of European folk songs, he said, but who
wouldn't think of going to hear a black blues singer. His state-
ment was a historic declaration of independence for the black
artist.

. . . THE ROAD FOR the serious black artist who would
produce a racial art is most certainly rocky and the mountain
is high. Until recently he received almost no encouragement
for his work from either white or colored people. The fine
novels of Chesnutt go out of print with neither race noticing
their passing. The quaint charm and humor of Dunbar's dialect
verse brought to him, in his day, largely the same kind of

encouragement one would give a sideshow freak (A colored man writing poetry! How odd!), a clown (How amusing!).

The present vogue in things Negro, although it may do as much harm as good for the budding colored artist, has at least done this: it has brought him forcibly to the attention of his own people among whom for so long, unless the other race had noticed him beforehand, he was a prophet with little honor. . . .

The Negro artist works against an undertow of sharp criticism and misunderstanding from his own group and unintentional bribes from the whites. "O, be respectable, write about nice people, show how good we are," say the Negroes. "Be stereotyped, don't go too far, don't shatter our illusions about you, don't amuse us too seriously. We will pay you," say the whites. . . .

But in spite of the Nordicized Negro intelligentsia and the desires of some white editors we have an honest American Negro literature already with us. Now I await the rise of the Negro theater. Our folk music, having achieved world-wide fame, offers itself to the genius of the great individual American Negro composer who is to come. And within the next decade I expect to see the work of a growing school of colored artists who paint and model the beauty of dark faces and create with new technique the expressions of their own soul-world. And the Negro dancers who will dance like flame and the singers who will continue to carry our songs to all who listen—they will be with us in even greater numbers tomorrow.

Most of my own poems are racial in theme and treatment, derived from the life I know. In many of them I try to grasp and hold some of the meanings and rhythms of jazz. I am sincere as I know how to be in these poems and yet after every reading I answer questions like these from my own people: Do you think Negroes should always write about Negroes? I wish you wouldn't read some of your poems to white folks. How do you find anything interesting in a place like a cabaret? Why do you write about black people? You aren't black. What makes you do so many jazz poems?

But jazz to me is one of the inherent expressions of Negro life in America: the eternal tom-tom beating in the Negro soul— the tom-tom of revolt against weariness in a white world, a world of subway trains, and work, work, work; the tom-tom of joy and laughter, and pain swallowed in a smile. Yet the Philadelphia clubwoman is ashamed to say that her race created it and she does not like me to write about it. The old subconscious "white is best" runs through her mind. Years of study under white teachers, a lifetime of white books, pictures, and papers, and white manners, morals, and Puritan standards made her dislike the spirituals. And now she turns up her nose at jazz and all its manifestations—likewise almost everything else distinctly racial. . . . She does not want a true picture of herself from anybody. She wants the artist to flatter her, to make the white world believe that all Negroes are as smug and as near white in soul as she wants to be. But, to my mind, it is the duty of the younger Negro artist, if he accepts any duties at all from outsiders, to change through the force of his art that old whispering "I want to be white," hidden in the aspirations of his people, to "Why should I want to be white? I am a Negro— and beautiful!"

So I am ashamed for the black poet who says, "I want to be a poet, not a Negro poet," as though his own racial world were not as interesting as any other world. I am ashamed, too, for the colored artist who runs from the painting of Negro faces to the painting of sunsets after the manner of the academicians because he fears the strange un-whiteness of his own features. An artist must be free to choose what he does, certainly, but he must also never be afraid to do what he might choose.

Let the blare of Negro jazz bands and the bellowing voice of Bessie Smith singing blues penetrate the closed ears of the colored near-intellectuals until they listen and perhaps understand. Let Paul Robeson singing *Water Boy*, and Rudolph Fisher writing about the streets of Harlem, and Jean Toomer holding the heart of Georgia in his hands, and Aaron Douglas drawing strange black fantasies cause the smug Negro middle class to turn from their white, respectable, ordinary books and papers to catch a glimmer of their own beauty. We younger Negro artists who create now intend to express our individual dark-skinned selves without fear or shame. If white people are pleased we are glad. If they are not, it doesn't matter. We know we are beautiful. And ugly too. The tom-tom cries and the tom-tom laughs. If colored people are pleased we are glad. If they are not, their displeasure doesn't matter either. We build our temples for tomorrow, strong as we know how, and we stand on top of the mountain, free within ourselves.

From *The Nation*, June 23, 1926.

This Is Me!
I'm Somebody!

Harlem's Blacks numbered 50,000 on the eve of World War I. By 1920 black Harlem stretched from 130th Street to 145th and from Madison to Eighth Avenues and included 80,000 people. Ten years later the southern border had moved down to 110th Street and the black population had swelled to 200,000. (Indeed, by 1940 there were eleven cities with as many as 100,000 Blacks.) Loften Mitchell, author of many plays and essays, provides this personal memoir of what it was like to grow up in Harlem in the thirties.

*

THE SMALL TOWN of black Harlem, though surrounded by hostility, was crowded with togetherness, love, human warmth, and neighborliness. Southern Negroes fled from physical lynchings and West Indians from economic lynchings. They met in the land north of 110th Street and they brought with them their speech patterns, folkways, mores, and their dogged determination. They brought, too, their religiosity and their gregariousness and they created here a distinct nation that was much like a small town. Readily welcomed were newly arrived relatives and strangers, and these were maintained until they found jobs and homes. In this climate everyone knew everyone else. A youngster's misbehavior in any house earned him a beating there plus one when he got home. In this climate the cooking of chitterlings brought a curious neighbor to the door: "Mrs. Mitchell, you cooking chitterlings? I thought you might need a little cornbread to go with 'em." A moment later a West

Indian neighbor appeared with rice and beans. Another neighbor followed with some beer to wash down the meal. What started as a family supper developed into a building party.

This climate created in Harlem a human being with distinct characteristics. The child of Harlem had the will to survive, to "make it." He was taught, "If you're going to be a bum, be the best bum." He was taught, too, a burning distrust for whites, to strike them before they struck, that to "turn the other cheek" was theologically correct, but physically incorrect in dealing with white folks. He learned to hold out his right hand, but to clench his left hand if the "flesh wasn't pinched in a decent handshake." This Harlem child learned to laugh in the face of adversity, to cry in the midst of plentifulness, to fight quickly and reconcile easily. He became a "backcapping" signifying slicker and a suave, sentimental gentleman. From his African, Southern Negro and West Indian heritage, he knew the value of gregariousness and he held group consultations on the street corners to review problems of race, economics, or politics.

He was poor, but proud. He hid his impoverishment with clothes, pseudo-good living, or sheer laughter. Though he complained of being broke, he never admitted his family was poor. "My old man puts all his dough in the bank," was the common complaint. "That's why I'm out here, stashed like a tramp." When the Harlemite stood on breadlines, he had a glib statement: "I'm here, picking up some food for some poor old lady next door to me." If he were seen in the relief office, he let you know he was there trying to get a poor neighbor on relief. This Harlem child had to have something—a car, a sharp wit, sharp clothing, a ready laugh, a loud voice, a beautiful woman. He had the burning need to belong to something, own something, and let the world know: "This is me! I'm somebody!"

I know. I felt it. We had to have that will to survive, for bloody street fighting bruised our bodies and a sadistic school system attempted to destroy our hearts and minds. Sadism was—in the 1920's and 1930's—a pre-requisite for teaching in the public schools. Incompetent, inept teachers sought "butts" for bad jokes. Knowledge-hungry black children were excellent targets. These teachers knew nothing and cared little about Negroes and wondered why they had to put up with them. Since neither teacher nor pupil had been exposed to Negro history, the black child sat in class, unwanted, barely tolerated. . . .

Harlem life was difficult, but it was fun. In the nineteen-thirties we had our own language, sung openly, defiantly. We resorted to it like other groups when we wanted to exclude people. We loved to see the puzzled white faces when one Negro asked: "What you putting down?" The answer was: "I'm putting down all skunks, punks, and a hard hustle!" If someone "backcapped" you, you might tell him: "We ain't cousins, so we can sure play dozens! And you know we ain't brothers, so we can sure talk about mothers!" An inquiry regarding one's welfare brought this response: "I'm like the bear, I ain't no-where. I'm like the bear's brother, I ain't gon' get no further." If someone expressed disbelief, he was told: "If I'm lying, I'm flying. In fact, Jack, if I'm lying, God's gone to Jackson, Mississippi, and you know He wouldn't be hanging out down there!" There were other expressions, too: To be "beat to your sox" was to be penniless. To be "sent" was to be in a heavenly state and if something "sent your brown body," you were in orbit! If you were "taking charge," you were in command of a situation and "coming on like Gang Busters." But, if you were a "lane from Spain," you were "dead out of the country—from Blip, which is down south where if you ain't white, it's a Blip—or from South America, that foreign country known as Alabama, Georgia, or Mississippi." You had to be "hip as a whip, have your boots laced, or else you were a crumb, subject to be swept out of a place!" If your "boots were laced," you

made it to the Apollo Theatre each and every Friday. The new
show started then. Every Harlemite and his brother showed,
defying all truant officers. You had to "fall" into the second
balcony, see someone you knew on the other side of the place,
then yell: "Hey, there, Daddy-O!" The fellow on the other
side—who had been sitting there, praying he would see an
acquaintance—returned your greeting in loud, friendly tones:
"Man! I ain't seen you in a month of Sundays! How's every
little thing?" "Jumping!" you answered. "Pick you up on the
rebound!"

Fortified and recognized, you sat down. Luis Russell, Jimmy
Lunceford, Teddy Hill, Lucky Millinder—or whatever band
played that week—started swinging the Apollo theme song.
You had to show the chick next to you that you knew the
words: "I think you're wonderful. I may be wrong. I think
you're wonderful. I think you're swell!" And, of course, if you
could get the next line, you really rated: "Your smiling face
and shining eyes—"

By the end of the first number you were either "spieling" to
the chick next to you, or you had struck up an acquaintance
with someone close to you. As the music played, you stomped
your feet and the whole balcony rocked.

Pigmeat Markham, George Wiltshire, Johnny Lee Long,
Johnny Hudgins, Eddie Green, Eddie Hunter, Ralph Cooper,
Jimmy Baskette and Dusty Fletcher fed us a thousand laughs.
We roared at our economic plight, our race problem, and at
life itself. One skit during the height of the depression indicated
our willingness to laugh at our economic plight: The lights came
up on Pigmeat and Ralph Cooper, strolling on stage, counting
rolls of bills they held: "Twenty. Forty. Sixty," they counted
in unison. Suddenly Pigmeat froze, then exploded, angrily:
"What the hell is this one dollar bill doing here?" He ripped
the bill into shreds. Ralph Cooper admonished him: "Man! As
long as you hang out with me, don't you ever be caught with
a damn one dollar bill!"

But, it was Sunday afternoon in Harlem that offered the week's most exciting times. Seventh Avenue, then a fashionable tree-lined, swank boulevard, was kept immaculate by community pride and by city authorities who fined building superintendents two dollars for allowing rubbish on sidewalks. No one dared to be caught dressed sloppily on Seventh Avenue—colored folks' Broadway. Residents would stare at you, and then you got a long lecture at home about "shaming" the family name. Besides, the existence of Negro policemen—Brisbane, Brown, Pendleton, and Lacey—assured the community that Seventh Avenue would remain impeccable and orderly. Seventh Avenue on Sunday afternoon was where you strolled. No one who knew Harlem from the nineteen-twenties through the nineteen-forties can forget "strolling." We youngsters had suits issued by the WPA (Works Progress Administration). We had tailors "drape" these, put on shirts and ties, wide snap-brimmed hats, then called on our young ladies.

Strolling was seemingly casual, but it was exacting. It had a plan and a purpose. You had to walk with your right leg dipping a bit, resembling a limp. You and your young lady started just below 116th Street, moving north on the west side of the avenue. In front of the Regent Theatre you met a couple. The male tipped his hat to your young lady and you responded, smartly, in an almost military manner. Invariably, the couple invited you to a "function" or a party. You told them: "Lay the pad number on us and we'll pick up that action later. You dug your stroll. We got to dig ours."

On you moved, meeting and greeting folks. You reached 125th Street one hour and a half later. At the Theresa you saw Bill Robinson, George Wiltshire, Ralph Cooper, Pigmeat Markham, Canada Lee, Dick Campbell, or Joe Louis, waving at you, acting like they knew you even if they didn't. They had less ego than many of our present-day celebrities.

Scores of other strollers brought news from all parts of Harlem to 125th Street. Then—replenished and recognized—you strolled north again, knowing you had the "sharpest chick" in the world and that you were the "sharpest cat" that ever strolled!

Three hours after the start of your stroll, you "fell" into Henry's Sugar Bowl at 134th Street and Seventh Avenue. You had a malted, met other friends, then started downtown again. You told the world: "This is black me, in my Harlem. I belong here and I'm somebody!"

Man, we strolled!

We celebrated, too—for any and every reason. The first solo flight to Paris caused a dance to be named the "Lindy Hop." We stood on street corners and cried when Florence Mills died and we sang *Memories of You* with profound respect. We listened, eagerly, to Jack Johnson or any other Negro who had beaten the "system" as he reported to us from the Lincoln Theatre stage. And we loved the New York Yankees. They were our ball club. . . .

Our biggest celebrations were on nights when Joe Louis fought. The Brown Bomber, appearing in the darkness when Italy invaded Ethiopia and the Scottsboro Boys faced lynching, became a black hero the history books could not ignore. It is for sociologists and psychologists to define what Joe meant to Negroes. Writers certainly have failed to do it. But, he was there, and I knew he was there, and he knew I was there. When he won a fight I went into the streets with other Negroes and I hollered until I was hoarse. Then, Joe would come to Harlem, to the Theresa, and he couldn't say what he felt when he saw us hollering at him. And he didn't have to. To paraphrase that old Negro expression: He didn't have to say a mumbling word!

We had culture, too. The Schomburg Collection, a mighty fortress, fed us materials withheld from white history books. Three theatres—the Lincoln, Lafayette, and the Alhambra— housed stock companies, then later became movie and vaudeville houses. In these houses Louis Armstrong's trumpet blared, defiantly, at the world. Cab Calloway hi-de-hoed, Bill "Bojangles" Robinson tap-danced up staircases, and Bessie Smith sang the blues from the soul of a black woman. Here, too, Langston Hughes, Countee Cullen, Arna Bontemps, and others wrote magnificent lines about us. Romare Bearden, Charles Alston, Ernest Crichlow, Charles White, Augusta Savage, and Jacob Lawrence created wonderful works of art about me. The *Amsterdam News* and the *Courier* and the *Age* and the *People's Voice* roared for me.

Much of this Harlem exists today. Interested television and movie cameras, journalists and writers can find numerous art centers, galleries, writers, painters, sculptors, and other cultural forces thriving here. And they could find people, real people, alive, aware. But, a hostile white world is unwilling to see all of Harlem. The community's false friends paint it a jungle or slum, a land of dark terror where "beasts" are created. This is the voice that, allied with other virulent forces, cannot afford to recognize Harlem's humanity and that of black people. Much of the anxiety of modern times has been created because white America has been unable and unwilling to recognize Negroes as people on any basis.

The first generation Harlemites, now past sixty, remain here. Their children—denied the opportunity of buying homes in Harlem by the Mortgage Conference—live in far-flung places. The absentee landlord owns the area and he is not interested in clean streets nor in pressuring indifferent city authorities to enforce health regulations. Newly arrived southerners live beside the first generation Harlemites. These newcomers may be attempting to adjust to urban life, but their children are impatient, angry. They see this violent land of church bombings, firehoses, crooked politicians and policemen, Indian-killers and home-run hitters. They see recklessness and lawlessness in a time when man can hit the moon, but fail to claim his identity here in this large world. . . .

From *Freedomways*, Fall, 1964.

Just Hanging On

The crash of the stock market in 1929 signaled the coming of the Great Depression. But for most Blacks hard times were just like old times. Since slavery, poverty had been general on the Southern countryside. Farm laborer and sharecropper never made a decent living. Early in the twenties soil erosion, the boll weevil, and foreign competition in cotton turned bad living into worse. The gay times of the years of the Charleston craze were unknown in farm cabins.

Nor were boom times universally enjoyed in the city tenements. American prosperity was not something parceled out equally to all. Those working in the shipyards, in the coal fields, in the shoe and textile mills, were scraping along. As the first flutters of alarm were felt even before the crash of '29, thousands of Blacks were laid off. When disaster became widespread, with businesses collapsing and banks failing, proportionately more black workers than white lost their jobs. In 1931, about one out of three Blacks was jobless, and one out of four whites.

With little or no savings to fall back on, what would happen to the unemployed? It was the National Urban League's job to find out. In 1931, while the Depression was still shooting down to greater depths, out of New York and Pittsburgh came these firsthand reports of the hardships Blacks were facing.

New York

. . . THE R. FAMILY came to New York thirty years ago. Eddie, the oldest son, who is twenty-three, was employed in a paint and supply store up to June, when he was laid off. Margaret, age twenty, lost her job in a hat factory that closed down in September. Two children are in high school and two in elementary school. The rent, $65 per month, is four months in arrears, with eviction threatened. When visited the children had been out of school, as they were without shoes and suitable clothing.

The Fords have seven children and expect another in March. Since eviction in October they have occupied one room in a cold water flat, depending wholly on the generosity of neighbors for support. When visited they were without food or fuel. Mr. F. wept like a child when he told the visitor that Mrs. Ford with the baby was at a neighbor's house to keep warm. The entire family invariably slept with their clothes on as there was little or no bedding. Newspapers were frequently placed over the children at night. Two of the children have been given away and the rest have been "farmed" out to neighbors.

T.J. had resolved to "end the whole damned business." And so when he arrived at the investigator's desk, it wasn't a job he wanted, but a loan of fifty cents. With difficulty the interviewer drew out of him that this was to be spent for a bottle of bi-chloride of mercury. Finally, after being supplied with clothing and a job, a clipping was revealed which gave account of a suicide on the preceding day, the victim being the applicant's room-mate who, being out of work for ten months and in despondency, had dressed himself in his evening suit, leaving a note saying, "Death can't be any worse than what I have suffered."

But the silent sufferers who, like the Aspinards from Louisiana, are "too proud to beg," never find their way into a relief agency. Shivering about an oil stove, with five children sick, they had never accepted charity and had never heard of the relief agencies.

Faith may remove mountains, but it is still "the substance of things hoped for," at least in so far as job seeking goes in the Jenks family. J. has lived with his wife and six children, paying $62 per month rent until May, 1929, when he lost his regular job. The family lived for fourteen years at the same address. When they moved to the present basement, the radio and other furniture were forfeited for back rent. Mr. J., thrifty and righteous, had a substantial savings account which has now been used up. Insurance policies have lapsed. Being a "God fearing" man, he finds it hard to explain his present predicament, having always been taught at church to which he has been a regular contributor, to "trust in the Lord." He is still praying that he may yet find a job.

G.S., now twenty-two, left college at the age of nineteen because his father was ill, and there being five smaller children, he became the main support. Since coming from Georgia ten years ago, with the mother working, they had saved about $2,000 which was invested in a suburban home in Jamaica, but unemployment hit them almost a year ago. Foreclosure proceedings followed. Not being the "head of the family," he could not qualify for an emergency work job.

Hundreds of persons have during the past few months experienced similar hardships. From ten to twenty eviction cases per day are reported at the Urban League. Fully seventy-five percent of the persons applying for relief are unknown to relief agencies, and up to the past year have never before requested aid. Many have voluntarily given up their homes, pawned their clothes, sold their furniture and are persistently hanging on by the barest thread. . . .

Pittsburgh

We visit the more or less temporary quarters provided by a group of socially-minded business men as a refuge for men rendered homeless by unemployment. There it stands, a broad, massive five-storied brick structure, overlooking the river. Inside, one feels immediately the impact of an impression of tragedy. . . .

Two thousand souls! Men casually referred to by the comfortably clothed, well-fed man as derelicts—flotsam and jetsam—bums—work dodgers. Two thousand men who roam the streets by day in search of work and return to this haven at night for a cup of stew or soup, and a "flop." White men and Negroes; swarthy Italians and Mexicans, stolid Poles, florid Irishmen and blond Swedes; milling about the spacious lobby of the great building. The newcomers among them distinguishable by their tatters and rags; one or two on crutches; many bearded and grimy, eyes bloodshot from loss of sleep or exposure to the unsympathetic elements. . . .

We manage to squeeze through the crowd that is assembled before the huge stage, the drabness of their existence being temporarily submerged by the flood of music being produced on the borrowed piano by a Negro player. We enter the combined kitchen and dining room which is the goal toward which is headed the almost endless queue of men which writhes and twists and doubles upon itself interminably. Our conductor pridefully points out his kitchen crew recruited from among his "guests." They are busy ladling out large tins of thick, potent soup which we found to be mighty palatable. But to see the eagerness with which the canisters are grasped, and the chunks of bread seized! Now and then comes the shrinking soul whose averted eyes and shamefaced expression immediately points him out as a new recruit to the army of unemployed; another scrap rejected by an impersonal industry; possibly a man reduced to the breadline who once looked upon charity as the refuge of only the indolent, the careless or the improvident. . . .

And everywhere are Negroes—at times seeming to represent the majority, but in reality constituting about forty percent of the two thousand men. Think of it. In a city where Negroes are but 8 percent of the total population, 40 percent are represented in this group of homeless, unemployed men.

But why so many Negroes? Consider Mr. Jones. He is now out of work, although for six years he has been employed by one concern which has not been greatly affected by the depression. "Why did you leave there?"

"I was just laid off—why? Because I wouldn't pay off the foreman. He knows us colored folks has to put up with everything to keep a job so he asks for two–three dollars anytime an' if you don't pay, you get a poor payin' job or a lay-off." Three fellow-workers support this testimony. "My division foreman charged me $20 one time for taking me back on, after he had laid me off; then asked me for $15 more after I had worked a while. I just got tired of that way of doin' and wouldn't pay him; now I'm out of a job."

And this statement is verified by the increasing number of calls from ambitious housewives who want "a bright, lively housemaid who can cook, do laundry and the regular housework, of course—and she must have the very best of references. How much will I pay? Well, there are so many people out of work that I am sure I can find a girl for $6 a week. Oh yes— and she must stay on the place as I have three children and we go out quite often."

To the desk of a colored worker in the city offices comes a middle-aged Negro woman, intense physical and mental suffering depicted on her face. She is the mother of six children, the oldest of whom is fifteen. She wants food to keep body and soul together, clothing to protect her brood from the chill winds; her gas is turned off because of overdue bills; she is threatened with eviction in five days if something is not done. "Where is your husband?" "He worked in the steel mills for four–five years and was a good man. The mill closed and he was laid off. He went out early every morning and walked the streets until night, looking for work. Day after day he done this ever since last June. Once a man told him that he needn't trouble looking for a job as long as there is so many white men out of work. I guess us colored folks don't get hungry like white folks. He just got discouraged and one day he went out and didn't come back. He told me once that if he wasn't living at home the welfare people would help me and the kids, and maybe he just went away on that account—and—maybe something has happened—" here tears gathered in the harassed eyes. . . .

Take the case of James Brown, who has been a sandblaster in one of the pipe mills for over eight years. Everyone who knows him says that he is honest, reliable and a valuable worker. He has four children who, for the first time in their lives are suffering the pangs of real, stark hunger. Yet his plea is not for food, fuel or clothing, but WORK which this highly organized and efficient society fails to provide. He is given a permit to sell apples on the city streets. . . .

From *Opportunity*, February and March, 1931.

No Rent Money

New York, Pittsburgh, Chicago . . . it was the same everywhere. In the "richest and greatest nation on earth" bank doors closed, farmers were forced off their land, millions were thrown out of work, cities were left without a dime to carry on government. And in those first and worst years of the Depression, it was only the cities that made any attempt to provide public relief. Funds were low and ran out repeatedly. There was no help from the state governments; most of them did not even have welfare departments.

In Washington President Hoover was saying that business conditions would get better by themselves. There was no need to do anything. He refused to permit federal funds to be spent on relief. Relief was the concern of the states and the communities, he said, or private charity.

In New York City families were given $2.39 a week to live on. In Detroit, allowances fell to fifteen cents a day per person and then ran out entirely. Only about one in four of the nation's unemployed could get relief. The pennies were allotted for food and fuel. If you needed shoes or a coat, a bed or medicine, you had to beg or steal them—or go without food to buy them.

But no one was starving, insisted President Hoover. He was wrong. The welfare figures showed they starved in the mountains of Kentucky and on the plains of Kansas. They starved in the cities and in the villages. And they died. Thousands of children died of the Depression disease—not enough to eat.

Eviction became common when people had no money to pay the rent. Those kicked out moved in with relatives or friends when they could. The others roamed the streets or sought shelter in miserable, crowded municipal lodging houses. Hoovervilles— shacks made of castoff tin or boards—sprang up along river- banks and railroad tracks or in vacant lots.

One day in 1931, in a restaurant on Chicago's South Side, Horace Cayton chanced to look up from his meal and saw through the window a long file of Blacks marching by, three abreast. They seemed to be moving in a deadly earnest way to some invisible goal. He went outside and stepped into the ranks. What follows is his account of one of the many attempts to stop the eviction of a Negro family.

Cayton, a journalist and sociologist, was the grandson of Hiram Revels, one of the two Blacks who represented Mississippi in the United States Senate during Reconstruction.

TURNING TO MY marching companion I asked where we were headed for, and what we would do when we got there. He looked surprised, and told me we were marching down to put in a family who had been evicted from a house for not paying their rent. Things were awfully tough down in the Black Belt now, he continued, and jobs were impossible to get. The Negro was the first to be discharged and the last to be hired. Now with unemployment they were hungry, and if they were put out in the street their situation would be a desperate one.

The Negroes of the community had been exploited for years by the unscrupulous landlords who had taken advantage of prejudice compelling the Negroes to live only in that district, and had forced them to pay exorbitant rents. Now, continued my informer, hard times had hit them and they were being turned out into the street. Furthermore, as the Negroes did not know their legal rights, the landlords would simply pitch their few belongings out of the window with no legal procedure at all. . . .

We finally came to a dirty, ill-kept street of houses. The first part of our line had arrived ahead, and had successfully put back into the house the few miserable belongings of the evicted tenants. The woman of the house was standing . . . intermittently crying and thanking God, loudly and dramatically. Her audience was very responsive, and seemed about to break into shouts itself. . . .

Suddenly a shout went around that there was another family in the next street that had been put out, and the procession started in that direction. This time I was far in the front to see the fun. We were met at the street by two squad cars of police who asked us where we were going. The black crowd swarmed around the officers and their cars like a hive of bees around their queen. The officers jumped out of their cars and told the crowd to move on. No one moved. Everyone simply stood and stared at them. One officer lost his head and drew his gun, leveling it at the crowd.

Then a young fellow stepped out of the crowd and said, "You can't shoot all of us and I might as well die now as any time. All we want is to see that these people, our people, get back into their homes. We have no money, no jobs, and sometimes no food. We've got to live some place. We are just acting the way you or anyone else would act."

The officer looked at the boy, at the crowd, and the crowd looked at him. No threats, no murmurs, no disorder; the crowd just looked at him. There the officer stood, surrounded by a crowd of dirty, ragged Negroes with a sea of black eyes on him. The officer replaced his gun in his holster and stood looking.

In the back of the crowd some one got up on a soap box and started to speak. It was an old, wild-eyed hag-like woman. The crowd turned and listened to her. . . . This woman was not talking about any economic principles; she was not talking about any empty theories, nor was she concerned with some abstract utopia to be gained from the movement of the "lower classes." She was talking about bread, and jobs, and places to sleep in. It was the talk of a person who had awakened from a pleasant dream to find that reality was hard, cold, and cruel.

Then I realized that all these people had suddenly found themselves face to face with hard, cold reality. They were the people who a few years ago had migrated from the South, in wagons, in cars, in trains, even walking. They had migrated with songs and hymns on their lips—with prayers to the Almighty for deliverance. They had come to the North and had been welcomed. Ah, America's great pool of unskilled labor was tapped; they had been sent to help win the war. But pretty soon the war was over. And, later still, the good times and prosperity were over. With hard times they had felt the pinch of poverty, and now they were virtually starving to death in the paradise of a few years ago.

The talk went on. The crowd stood and listened. It had grown bigger now and many white faces were seen. The officers stood and listened. I don't believe that there was any one there who was not touched by the talk. I don't believe that there was anybody there, white or black, who did not in some degree face the same situation that she was so vividly describing. Even the officers stood with more or less respectful attention. I spoke to one of the officers and asked if he didn't think it was a shame to put people out of their houses when they were in such desperate circumstances. He answered that it was tough, yet a man didn't build a house for charity—but it didn't make any difference to him as long as they started no trouble.

Just then a siren was heard—the whisper went around—the riot squad was coming!

All of the spectators stepped back, and the active participants formed a small nucleus around the speaker—packed in tight—a solid black lump of people. Two young fellows stood holding the woman up on the soap box in the middle.

Then the riot squad turned into the street, four cars full of blue-coated officers and a patrol wagon. They jumped out before the cars came to a stop and charged down upon the crowd. Night sticks and "billies" played a tattoo on black heads.

"Hold your places!" shouted the woman.

"Act like men!" answered the crowd.

They stood like dumb beasts—no one ran, no one fought or offered resistance, just stood, an immovable black mass. Finally the officers were through, and started to pull down the woman speaker. Clubs came down in a sickening rain of blows on the head of one of the boys who was holding her up. Blood spurted from his mouth and nose. Finally she was pulled down. A tremor of nervousness ran through the crowd. Then someone turned and ran. In a minute the whole group was running like mad for cover. One of the officers shot twice at one of the boys who had been holding up the woman speaker. The boy stumbled, grabbed his thigh, but kept on running. The woman was struggling in the arms of two husky policemen. It was all over in a minute, and all that was left was the soap box and the struggling woman. . . .

From *The Nation*, September 9, 1931.

Ain't Make Nothing, Don't Speck Nothing

Bad as the Depression years were for Blacks in the Northern cities, in the South it was even worse. Life in the 1930's on the farms of the South—perhaps the most stagnant backwater of the economy—was depicted in The Shadow of the Plantation. *It*

was the work of Charles S. Johnson, one of the most productive
of the black social scientists.

The scientific study of black life and history began well before
the Civil War. Such Blacks as William C. Nell, James McCune
Smith, William Wells Brown, Martin Delany, and George Washington Williams were the forerunners of scholars who came on
the scene later. Many of these later contributors to research were
members of the Negro American Academy, founded by Alexander Crummell. Foremost among them was W. E. B. DuBois,
with a great many distinguished and often pioneering studies to
his credit in both history and sociology. He was followed by
Carter G. Woodson, the dean of black historians.

Woodson wrote many histories himself, and in 1915 launched
the Association for the Study of Negro Life and History and, a
year later, its chief publication, the Journal of Negro History.
Both sought to promote race pride by researching and teaching
the facts of Negro history.

Born in Virginia in 1893, Charles Johnson was educated at Virginia Union University and the University of Chicago. While research director for the National Urban League, he founded and edited its publication, Opportunity: Journal of Negro Life. *He had already helped prepare a study of the Black in Chicago, and in 1928, moving to Nashville to become head of the social science department at Fisk University, he entered one of his most fruitful periods.*

Among the studies he prepared was a report on plantation life. It appeared in 1934, in the midst of the Depression. In this passage from the book the black farmers often speak for themselves.

Tenant Farmers

"I AIN'T GOT NO children and me and my husband works a one-horse farm and we got 'bout thirty acres. Last year we made 6 bales of cotton and rented the thirty acres for $60; fifteen acres we used for cotton, the rest for corn. We kept the corn and didn't sell none hardly. At ten cents a pound the six bales would bring $300. We had $10 advanced for four months. We turned it all over, and they took out the $40 advances, $30 for fertilizer, and $60 rent. We got through and then they say we come out $72.43 in the hole. . . ."

In more prosperous times when there is a reasonable assurance of returns, the landowners made advances both to tenants and to sharecroppers. It is a most frequent complaint of the tenants now that they cannot get advances. One said: "I ask Mr. —— to 'vance me jest nuff for a pair of overalls. He tell me he needs overalls hisself." In other cases advances to tenants have merely been reduced.

"Last year I drawed $10 to the plow (meaning $10 a month for from four to six months for each 20 acres cultivated) but I ain't getting but $7 this year. I rents the whole place (400 acres) and then subrents it, and pays four bales of cotton for rent. But I don't never make nothing offen it. Didn't clear nothing last year. I paid out $200 last year. Interest steps on me time I pay me rent (for money borrowed from the bank) and interest cost 15 cents on the dollar. I haven't made nothing since 1927. I clears $210 then and ain't cleared nothing since. I got 21 cents for cotton that year."

Another explained: "They don't give nothing now. Use to 'low us $10 provisions a month, but dey done cut us way down. The white folks say some of these banks done fell in; dere ain't no money to be got. That's all. Said this is the suppression time."

Another type of tenant pays a good rental in cash and receives advances.

"We farms 60 acres and pays $150 for rent. That's $75 to the plow. They 'vances us $15 a month for five months. I come out jest $175 in the hole.

"We run a two-horse farm. We was due to pay $150 rent last year, but I don't know what us is paying this year. We cut down on the land we was using. We made 22 bales of cotton last year, and it was selling at 8, 9, and 10 cents when we turned it in to the man. We didn't git nothing back. You see, the man had been carrying us for two years. I took 'sponsibility for the whole patch and let some of it out to three other parties, and stood for them. Besides the cotton the men took 13 loads of corn, but I saved about 200 bushels for myself to live on, and I sold some peanuts and corn."

The normal earning of a man and wife, if both work as tenants on a one-horse cotton farm, would probably average $260 a year in cash value. However, they pay about half of their cotton in rent, use the corn for their stock, and eat the potatoes, peas, and sorghum which they grow along with the cotton. As a result very little cash is handled. They manage to live on the advances, or by borrowing for food and clothing and permitting their crop to be taken in satisfaction of the debt. It becomes very largely a paper loss or gain. In the case of loss the tenant may move away, leaving his debt. In the latter case he may be conscious of having earned more than he got, or of paying for some other Negro tenant's default.

"We got right 'round sixty acres and one-half of it is cotton. We working on halves. We got a two-horse farm. My daughter got one and I got one. I farmed with Mr. P—— last year. We had thirty acres over there and made 5 bales of cotton and paid $100 for rent. We gits $2 a month in cash and $10 in rations. We came out $200 in the hole last year. I don't have to pay off 'cause I let that went when I come here (he had to give up farm tools, etc.). I been farming all my life 'cept two years when we went to Virginia . . . I worked in the coke field out there. That was the year the war was."

One daughter lived at home. Four boys were away living in cities in Alabama. One grown daughter lived in the county and worked with them. One grown son was dead—"got knocked in the head"; seven little children had died between the ages of two and four.

Sharecroppers

There is another type of farmer, the share-cropper, who, without tools or any form of capital, farms on the condition that he give the landlord one-half of the crop. . . . The arrangement varies with the landlord and the condition of the tenant. When the tenant is furnished tools and work animals in addition to the land, he may get only a third of the cotton raised. Most commonly, however, it is halves, and he may find it necessary to rent a mule for his plowing.

The share-croppers frequently are subtenants for small white and Negro tenant farmers, or for their relatives. It is at least a means of beginning, and a good share-cropper can, with good

fortune, place himself in position to undertake the responsibilities of full tenant later.

"I works a one-horse farm on halves. I get 'bout $12 a month
in rations. Last year I worked for the Tallahassee Mill Company, and made $9.75 a week. My wife was working by the
day for 50 cents a day. We been married 'bout four years now.
I moved here from Tallahassee 'cause I was lacking for sense.
The white folks liked me down there and everything, and I
moved. I called myself liking ter farm best."

Farm Laborers

Farm laborers worked on other people's farms for a stipulated wage. [They] had small patches of their own which they
were permitted to cultivate rent free. The wage usually paid
these laborers was 50–65 cents a day, the women receiving
more often 40 cents. The following statement of a farm laborer
indicates the conditions under which this class works.

"We jest work by the day and pay $1.50 a month for this
house. It's jest a piece of house. I gits 50 cents a day and my
husband and the boy gits 65 cents each. We have to feed ourselves and pay rent out of that. My husband is pretty scheming,
but sometimes he can't git nothing to do. I don't know how
much time we lose, but he works most of the time. Course the
boy stops and goes to school in the winter sometimes, but if
he can git work to do, he works too." . . .

Among these families there were also laborers who were
working on railroads, logging, and on county roads. . . . The
wife of one of these laborers related the following history:

"My husband and me married eight years. He works at the
Hardaway log mill and makes $7 a week. He been working
there four years now. . . . We don't have to pay no rent. The
man he works for pays for hit. I don't do nothing but stay
home. . . . My husband was in debt when we left Millstead but

he ain't much in debt now. He don't owe but 'bout a dollar or two. He don't lack this man he's working for 'cause he don't pay him but $1.10 a day. The man's name is Mr. S—— and he is mean to work for. He got 14 or 15 working for him down there at the log mill 'sides my husband. If we git hard up and want some money, he don't help us. He don't do nothing but run you away from there. . . . My husband goes ter work wid sunrise every morning and works till dark. I git up day and cooks his breakfast. He don't come back home ter dinner cause hit's so far. Hit's 'bout seven miles from here."

Casuals

Probably the lowest class of farm laborers was made up of farm hands who did not receive a stipulated monetary wage, but were to get what was known as a "hand's share." This, seemingly, just amounts to enough to keep them living. One old woman who lives by herself in a one-room shack and works for a hand's share told the following story:

"I works for a hand's share in the crop with the folks cross dere. My husband been dead. I ain't never had but one child and dat's de son what's down there. . . . I been up north in Birmingham with my sister . . . but I come back here, 'cause dese chillun kept worrying me to come on here to live wid them. It's mighty tight on me to have to go working in dese fields half starved, and I ain't had a bit of money to buy a piece of cloth as big as my hand since I been back. I washed fer white people in Birmingham, and dey was good to me. I am jest gitting long by the hardest. I works for dese people for a hand's share in the crop. Dey gives me a load of corn and a load of potatoes. I gits some of all the other stuff what's made, and when selling cotton dey give you a little money out of the seed. I don't see no money on time. Dey gives me a little something to eat 'cause I works wid dem and dey gives me a little groceries.

I never was in this fix before in my life. I had good money when I come from Birmingham. I had two fives and five single dollahs. I sho' gonna git what I works for dis year." . . .

The Dreary Cycle of Life

The weight of generations of habit holds the Negro tenant to his rut. Change is difficult, even in the face of the increasing struggle for survival under the old modes. One intelligent old farmer had sensed an important element of the natural conservatism of these tenants. He said:

"Farming is like gambling. If I get out I ought to get back and work a smaller farm next year. But you take an old farmer and if he ever gets out the hole with a good-size farm, instead of cutting down he'll get him another mule and take on some more. That's what keeps us down."

Such philosophy is for the man who retains some hope for improvement. The most dismal aspect of this situation is the air of resignation everywhere apparent.

"If it wasn't the boll weevil it was the drought; if it wasn't the drought it was the rains.

"One thing, we ain't got proper tools we ought to have. If you git any good land you have to buy things to make it good, and that takes lots of money, and if we had money to buy these things we wouldn't be so hard up

"What kills us here is that we jest can't make it cause they pay us nothing for what we give them, and they charge us double price when they sell it back to us."

Year after year of this experience for many of them and the hopelessness crystallizes itself at times into despair. "Ain't make nothing, don't speck nothing no more till I die. Eleven bales of cotton and man take it all. We jest work for de other man. He git everything." Mysticism and religion come to the rescue of some who add to hopelessness a fear of the future. "I axed Jesus to let me plant a little more. Every time I plant anything I say, 'Jesus, I ain't planting this for myself; I'm planting this for you to increase.' " . . .

Henry Robinson had been living in the same place for nineteen years, paying $105 a year rent for his land. He raises three bales of cotton a year, turns it all over, and continues to go deeper in debt. He said:

"I know we been beat out of money direct and indirect. You see, they got a chance to do it all right, 'cause they can overcharge us and I know it's being done. I made three bales again last year. He said I owed $400 the beginning of the year. Now you can't dispute his word. When I said 'Suh?' he said 'Don't you dispute my word; the book says so.' When the book says so and so you better pay it, or they will say 'So, I'm a liar, eh?' You better take to the bushes too if you dispute him, for he will string you up for that.

"I don't want them to hurt my feelings and I just have to take what they say, 'cause I don't want to go to the mines [convict labor] and I do want to live."

Another man complained:

"I tried keeping books one year, and the man kept worrying me about it, saying his books was the ones he went by anyhow. And nothing you can do but leave. He said he didn't have no time to fool with no books. He don't ever give us no rent notes all the time. They got you 'cause you have to carry your cotton to his mill to gin and you better not carry your cotton nowhere else. I don't care how good your cotton is, a colored man's cotton is always second- or third-grade cotton if a colored man sells it. The only way you can get first prices for it is to get some white man to sell it for you in his name. A white man sold mine once, and got market price for it.

"We haven't paid out to Mr. —— in twelve years. Been in debt that long. See, when a fella's got a gun in your face you gotter take low or die."

To the Negro tenant the white landlord is the system; to the white landlord the capital of the banks is the system. The landlord needs credit by which to advance credit to the tenants. The security of the landlord is in the mortgages on his land; the security of the tenant is the mortgage on the crops which he will raise. Because cotton lends itself best to this arrangement, cotton is overproduced and debts descend to obscure still another year of labor, and the vicious circle continues. In the desperate struggle both may lose, but the advantage is always with the white landlord. He dictates the terms and keeps the books. The demands of the system determine the social and economic relations, the weight of which falls heaviest upon those lowest down. There was a song which old women hummed as they hacked the earth with their hoes. The words were almost always indistinct but the mood of the tune, dreary and listless, fitted as naturally to the movement of their bodies as it did to the slick and swish of the earth under the blows of their hoes. One verse only was remembered by one of them, and it ran so:

> *Trouble comes, trouble goes.*
> *I done had my share of woes.*
> *Times get better by 'n' by,*
> *But then my time will come to die.*

From *The Shadow of the Plantation,* by Charles S. Johnson, The University of Chicago Press, 1934.

We Gonna Make This a Union Town Yet!

The hard work and the dirty work was traditionally the lot of Black Americans. Most black men held unskilled or semiskilled jobs, chiefly in the service or farm occupations. And black women were bunched even more tightly in a few lower-level jobs, especially as domestic workers.

Blacks who came north during the twenties broke into new fields of work—glass, tobacco, paper, clothing, food. But whites did not open the unions to them. Many branches of the American Federation of Labor refused to enroll them or shunted them into Jim Crow locals. The NAACP and the National Urban League made progress in these years, but chiefly among the small black middle class. The millions of Blacks whose problems were largely getting enough to eat and a decent place to live were not reached. Only among the Pullman car porters was a solid union organized—in 1925, under the leadership of A. Philip Randolph.

It was not until the frantic first years of the New Deal that the black labor force began to move into the unions. Many new measures were devised by the Roosevelt regime to combat the Depression. The work week was shortened; children under sixteen were forbidden to work; a minimum wage was set; a federal relief plan created jobs by the millions. A vast public works program built new hospitals, schools, community centers, and playgrounds all over the land. Blacks got jobs in several of the work programs, but not in proportion to their actual need. In the South wages paid Blacks were lower than those paid whites.

By now the basic industries of the country had swelled to gigantic size. Mass production brought thousands of workers into auto and steel plants, into meatpacking, rubber, electrical goods. The intricate machines could be run by unskilled or semiskilled hands. Pay was low, speedup was intense, jobs were insecure. Millions were ripe for organization, but the old unions, formed by crafts, could not take on the mass-production industries. It was then that a new law passed by the Roosevelt Congress gave labor "the right to organize and bargain collectively through representatives of their own choosing."

It was a rebirth for labor. Feeling they had the President's blessing, organizers fanned out over the country, recruiting thousands of new members into the unions. Both the American Federation of Labor and the new Congress of Industrial Organizations grew with tremendous speed. Within a few years the CIO embraced 32 national unions with four million members.

It took great strikes to win recognition of the unions. Picket lines seemed to stretch from one coast to the other. What the new unions meant to black workers in Southern industry is told in two selections. In the first, Ted Poston, one of the first black reporters to break through Jim Crow in journalism, went to Richmond to talk to the tobacco workers. In the second, Henry O. Mayfield of Birmingham tells what it was like to organize in the mines and foundries in the 1930's.

Richmond, Va.

SHE WAS A SCRAWNY hardbitten little woman and she greeted me with that politely blank stare which Negroes often reserve for hostile whites or prying members of their own race.

I had been directed to her tenement in Richmond's ramshackle Negro section by another woman, a gray-haired old grandmother whose gnarled hands had been stemming tobacco for five decades.

"The white folks down at union headquarters is all right," she had said, "and we love 'em—especially Mr. Marks. But if you want to know about us stemmers and the rumpus we raised, you better go see Mamma Harris. She's Missus CIO in Richmond."

The blank look softened on the thin dark face when I mentioned this.

"Must've been Sister Jones," she said, still standing near the door. "They all call me Mamma though. Even if I ain't but forty-nine and most of 'em old enough to be my grandmammy."

I edged toward a rocking chair in the other side of the bed.

"I'm a CIO man myself," I remarked. "Newspaper Guild. Our local boys just fixed up *The Times-Dispatch* this morning."

She yelled so suddenly that I almost missed the rocker.

"Bennie!" she called toward the kitchen, "you hear that, Bennie? CIO's done organized *The Dispatch*. Moved right in this morning. What I tell you? We gonna make this a union town yet!"

A hulking overalled Negro appeared in the kitchen doorway. His booming bass voice heightened his startling resemblance to Paul Robeson.

"Dispatch?" he thundered. "God Amighty, we do come on."

Mrs. Harris nodded in my direction.

"He's a CIO man from up New York. Wants to know about our rumpus out at Export. He's a Guilder too, just like the white 'uns."

Benny limped toward the other chair.

"They give us hell," he said, "but we give it right back to 'em. And it was we'uns who come out on top. The cops was salty. Wouldn't even let us set down and rest. But I told the women, I told 'em 'Sit down' and they did. Right in front of the cops too. Didn't I, Louise?"

Mrs. Harris nodded energetically from her perch on the bed.

"You dead did. And they didn't do nothing neither. They 'fraid of the women. You can outtalk the men. But us women don't take no tea for the fever."

Bennie boomed agreement. "There was five hundred of the women on the picket line and only twenty of us mens. But we sure give 'em hell. I talked right up to them cops, didn't I, Louise? Didn't I?"

Finally Mrs. Harris got around to the beginning.

"I wasn't no regular stemmer at first," she said, "but I been bringing a shift somewhere or other since I was eight. I was took out of school then and give a job minding chillun. By the time I was ten I was cooking for a family of six. And I been scuffling ever since.

"But I don't work in no factory till eight years ago. Then I went out to Export. Well, it took me just one day to find out that preachers don't know nothing about hell. They ain't worked in no tobacco factory."

Bennie was smiling to himself and gazing at the ceiling.

"Them cops beat up them strikers something awful out at Vaughn's," he said. "They even kicked the women around. But they didn't do it to us, huh, Louise? We stood up to 'em."

Mrs. Harris waved aside the interruption.

"Then there was this scab," she went on, "only he ain't no scab then, cause we don't have no union. We ain't even heerd of no union nowhere but I knew something was bound to happen. Even a dog couldn't keep on like we was. You know what I make then? Two dollars and eighty cents a week. Five dollars was a too bad week."

"I put in eighty-two and a half hours one week," Bennie said, "and they only give me $18.25. I think about this one day when one of them cops . . ."

Mrs. Harris shushed him.

"Now this scab—only he ain't no scab then—he rides me from the minute I get to Export. He's in solid with the man and he always brag he's the ringtail monkey in this circus. He's a stemmer like the rest of us but he stools for the white folks.

"There's two hundred of us on our floor alone and they only give us four and a half and five cents a pound. We don't get paid for the tobacco leaf, you know. You only get paid for the stems. And some of them stems is so puny they look like horse hair."

Bennie was chuckling softly to himself but a glance from Mrs. Harris held the cops at bay for the moment.

"And as if everything else wasn't bad enough, there was this scab. We's cramped up on them benches from kin to can't, and he's always snooping around to see nobody don't pull the stem out the center instead of pulling the leaf down both sides separate. This dust just eats your lungs right out you. You start dying the day you go in."

She coughed automatically and continued.

"Well, I keep this up for six long years. And this scab is

riding me ever' single day. He's always riding everybody and snitching on them what don't take it. He jump me one day about singing. Course, a stemmer's bench ain't no place for singing and I ain't got no voice nohow. But I like a song and I gotta do something to ease my mind or else I go crazy.

"But he jump me this morning and tell me to shut up. Well, that's my cup. Six years is six years, but this once is too often. So I'm all over him like gravy over rice. I give him a tongue-lashing what curled every nap on his head."

For a moment she had the same beaming look which Bennie displayed when he spoke of the cops.

"I sass him deaf, dumb and blind, and he takes it. But all the time he's looking at me kinder queer. And all at once he says 'You mighty salty all of a sudden, you must be joining up with this union foolishness going on around here.'

"You coulda knocked me over with a Export stem. I ain't even heard nothing about no union. But as soon as he cuts out, I start asking around. And bless my soul if they ain't been organizing for a whole full week. And I ain't heerd a peep."

"I ain't heerd nothing neither then," Benny put, "and I been there fifteen years."

Mrs. Harris caught another breath.

"Well, I don't only go to the next meeting downtown, but I carries sixty of the girls from our floor. They remember how I sass this scab and they're all with me. We plopped right down in the first row of the gallery. And when they asked for volunteers to organize Export, I can't get to my feet quick enough."

"I come in right after," Bennie remarked.

"And it ain't no time," Mrs. Harris continued, "before we got seven hundred out of the thousand what works in Export. The man is going crazy mad and the scab is snooping overtime. But they can't fire us. The boom time is on and the warehouse is loaded to the gills."

She paused dramatically.

"And then on the first of August, 1938, we let 'em have it. We called our strike and closed up Export tight as a brass drum."

Bennie couldn't be shushed this time.

"The cops swooped down like ducks on a June bug," he said, "but we was ready for 'em. I was picket captain and there was five hundred on the line. And all five hundred was black and evil."

Mrs. Harris was beaming again.

"Then this scab came up with a couple hundred others and tried to break our line," she recalled, "but we wasn't giving a crip a crutch or a dog a bone. I made for that head scab personal—but the cops wouldn't let me at 'em."

"I stayed on the line for twenty-four hours running," Bennie chuckled, "and I didn't take a inch from none of them cops."

"And we wasn't by ourselves neither," Mrs. Harris went on. "The preachers, Dr. Jackson, the Southern Aid Society and all the other union people help us. GWU and them garment ladies give us a hundred dollars right off the bat. Malgamate sent fifty. The ship folks down in Norfolk come through, and your white Guild boys here give ten dollars too."

"It was them white garment ladies what sent the cops," Bennie cut in. "They come out five hundred strong and parade around the factory. They got signs saying 'GWU Supports Export Tobacco workers.'

"Them cops jump salty as hell. 'White women,' they say, 'white women out here parading for niggers.' But they don't do nothing. Because we ain't taking no stuff from nobody."

"We was out eighteen days," Mrs. Harris said, "and the boss was losing money hand over fist. But you know how much we spend in them eighteen days? Over seven hundred dollars."

Her awed tones made it sound like seven thousand.

"But it was worth it. We win out and go back getting ten, eleven and twelve cents a pound. And better still we can wear our union buttons right out open. We might even have got them scabs fired if we wanted, but we didn't want to keep nobody out of work."

Bennie stopped smiling for the first time.

"We might be better off if we did," he said soberly. "I bet we do next time."

Mrs. Harris explained.

"They been sniping away at us ever since we win. They give the scabs all the breaks and lay off us union people first whenever they can. They give all the overtime to the scabs and even let 'em get away with stripping the stem down the center. But we ain't licked yet. We still got two hundred members left and we still got union conditions."

Her face brightened again.

"And we fixed that old scab—even if he is been there nineteen years. We moved him off our floor completely, and he ain't allowed to ride nobody.

"We got a good set of people downtown now and we're reorganizing right along. By the time our new contract comes up in June, we'll probably have the whole thousand."

"And if we strike again, and them cops jump salty—" Bennie began.

And this time Mamma Harris let him pursue the subject to his heart's content.

From *New Republic*, November 4, 1940.

Birmingham, Ala.

I worked seven years in the biggest foundry in Birmingham, the Stockham Pipe and Fitting Company. Many of us worked twelve to fourteen hours daily. One worker drove a mule hauling fresh sand into the foundry and cleaned up scrap metal. After the mule worked nine hours the worker had to take the mule to the stable and get a wheelbarrow and finish the work.

I remember one afternoon about 4:30 P.M. the foundry superintendent told the mule driver, "You can work all the overtime
you want to but I don't want the mule working one damn
minute overtime." The mule driver, Nash, said, "O.K. Mr.
Lynn." Nash pushed a wheelbarrow until about 9:30 that
night. . . .

The conditions in the mines were very bad. Back in the early
thirties we were loading coal by the ton. The company had
handpicked men and gave them the contract which we had to
work for the contractors. From week to week, or day to day,
you never knew how much money you were going to make.
Many days we stayed in the mines nine and ten hours and made
only four or five dollars, sometimes less or nothing, because
when you loaded a car you had no way of knowing how many
tons of coal were in the car. You had to take the word of the
company and the contractor. Many of the miners lived in the
company's houses and had to trade at the company's stores
because they seldom had any cash to trade at other stores.
Clothes for the family were out of the question. The iron ore
miners had to work under the same conditions as the coal
miners.

The working conditions in steel and foundry were just as
bad. But there was a difference in pay from the point of knowing how much you made at the end of the week. In steel and
foundry the average hourly pay for Negro workers was about
fifty cents an hour and you had to work from "can see to can't
see . . ." (as long as the boss wanted you to work). If you
asked the boss for pay for overtime, he would say that if you
didn't like your pay, there were others willing to take it, or if
you were a very good worker and the boss liked you, he would
give you a few hours overtime and tell you not to tell the other
workers.

In 1932 the United Mine Workers of America (headed by
John L. Lewis), and the Mine, Mill and Smelter Workers Union,
started an organizing drive to organize coal and ore min-

ers. . . . The bloody battle was on. We had to get a small group of workers together, sometimes meeting in the woods. The companies organized armed thugs to track us down and they would shoot to kill. The ore miners had shooting battles with the company thugs and men were shot on both sides.

The workers rallied to the union around the following demands: eight-hour day and five-day week, higher pay for tonnage or day labor, to do away with contractors, two paydays a month (instead of one pay monthly), upgrading of Negroes as motormen, machine operators and crew leaders, union members to watch the weight of the company scale for those workers loading coal or ore by the ton and, last but not least, recognition of the union.

The company countered with a "company union" which appealed in the main to the white workers. . . . We called the company union a "popsicle union" because when they started the organizing, they told the Birmingham families they would be served popsicles and watermelon. . . . We kept on fighting. . . . Many Negro workers were fired because they were leaders in the union. After the company saw we were going to win, they wanted to make a deal with some of the Negro leadership. I worked in the largest coal mine of U.S. Steel in Birmingham. I took up grievances which cost the company thousands of dollars. The superintendent called me into the office and told me if I dropped the grievances, he would see that I made all the money I wanted. I told them I will starve with the other men until this condition is corrected. . . .

Some of the men serving on grievance committees could not read or write; but they knew what to talk about when they met with the boss, and they were "tough" and would never back down. During contract time the Negro workers took the lead in working out the contracts. The few white workers in the locals were afraid to attend meetings or serve on committees. . . .

We organized women's auxiliaries in the coal and ore mines.

When we were on strike the women would organize into groups and take baskets and go into stores asking for food for needy families and when they asked a storekeeper for help he knew not to say "no." . . . The young boys would be on the picket lines while the girls went out asking for food for the families. . . .

From *Freedomways*, Winter, 1964.

March on Washington

In the same year that Franklin D. Roosevelt entered the White House, Adolf Hitler became the dictator of Germany. Mussolini had been in power in Italy for a decade, and Japan had already seized Manchuria. In 1935 Mussolini invaded Ethiopia, and

Blacks were among the first Americans to protest and to call for international action to halt aggression by the fascist power. Blacks knew what the doctrine of racial supremacy meant; they did not have to wait for Hitler to murder millions to find out. But the democracies took no concerted action to halt the rise of fascism, and Hitler easily annexed Austria and took over Czechoslovakia. In 1939 he rolled over Poland, and Europe was pitched into another world war. America soon began to prepare for what seemed inevitable involvement, building up a large fighting force and making the guns and ships and planes and tanks and ammunition that would be needed.

The armed forces were segregated at that time, and discrimination was common. In the war industries, too, the barriers were up. Blacks had great trouble getting jobs. Federal officials spoke out against discrimination but industry was deaf. Janitors? Sweepers? Yes, those jobs were available. But aircraft mechanics? Welders? No, the corporations said, not for black labor.

What have we to fight for? asked many Blacks. Even black leaders known to be conservative, those who thought things were gradually changing for the better, showed open rebellion. Many Americans, they pointed out, were acting as though the war against Hitlerism were not nearly so important as preventing Blacks from winning some democracy for themselves.

Private pleas and peaceful petitions for equality changed nobody's mind. The industrialists, the generals, and the politicians went on doing their Jim Crow dance. Black leaders saw that powerful, mass action was needed. In January 1941 A. Philip Randolph, the head of the Brotherhood of Sleeping Car Porters, proposed a March on Washington to demand that the government do something. Soon all the heads of the major black organizations had joined in; the movement had the mass support of Blacks everywhere. Washington was alarmed at signs of revolt in time of crisis. The President and others tried to have the march called off, but the leaders refused. As the planned day came in sight and marchers were preparing to board trains for the capital, President Roosevelt told Randolph that it was not necessary to march; he would take the action desired.

On June 25, 1941, the President issued Executive Order 8802, banning discrimination in defense industries or in government "because of race, creed, color, or national origin." A Fair Employment Practices Commission was set up to carry out the order, and the government began its first programs to better the economic position of Blacks.

It was a great beginning, but only that. There was much more to be done, and the need for continuous pressure was great. The tactic of nonviolent, mass resistance to injustice had proved its value, and in the years to come it would be used far more widely, from the little towns of the South to the giant cities of the North. In 1942 Randolph spelled out the program of the March on Washington movement to continue the fight against Hitlerism abroad and for full democracy at home.

1. WE DEMAND, in the interest of national unity, the abrogation of every law which makes a distinction in treatment between citizens based on religion, creed, color or national origin. This means an end to Jim Crow in education, in housing, in transportation and in every other social, economic and political privilege; and especially, we demand, in the capital of the nation, an end to all segregation in public places and in public institutions.

2. We demand legislation to enforce the Fifth and Fourteenth Amendments guaranteeing that no person shall be deprived of life, liberty or property without due process of law, so that the full weight of the national government may be used for the protection of life and thereby may end the disgrace of lynching.

3. We demand the enforcement of the Fourteenth and Fifteenth Amendments and the enactment of the Pepper Poll-Tax

---

bill so that all barriers in the exercise of the suffrage are eliminated.

4. We demand the abolition of segregation and discrimination in the Army, Navy, Marine Corps, Air Corps and all other branches of national defense.

5. We demand an end to discrimination in jobs and job training. Further, we demand that the FEPC be made a permanent administrative agency of the U.S. Government and that it be given power to enforce its decisions based on its findings.

6. We demand that federal funds be withheld from any agency which practices discrimination in the use of such funds.

7. We demand colored and minority group representation on all administrative agencies so that these groups may have recognition of their democratic right to participate in formulating policies.

8. We demand representation for the colored and minority racial groups on all missions, political and technical, which will be sent to the peace conference so that the interests of all people everywhere may be fully recognized and justly provided for in the postwar settlement.

From *Survey*, November, 1942.

Bus Boycott

A "good" Southern town was a peaceful town, peaceful because no Black challenged the system of segregation and discrimination. The peace—never universal, always only on the surface—was soon broken. Step by step through the 1930's and 1940's the NAACP had carried the fight for the franchise and for equal educational opportunities through the courts. On May 17, 1954,

Martin Luther King, Jr.

came the sweeping decision by the U.S. Supreme Court that persons "required on the basis of race to attend separate schools were deprived of the equal protection of the laws guaranteed by the Fourteenth Amendment." Racial segregation in the public schools was outlawed. The "separate but equal" doctrine, which the Court had upheld in 1896, was set aside.

There was jubilation at first. Millions of Blacks rejoiced that at last—over 90 years after Emancipation—the basic rights of democracy for all were recognized. But soon resistance to the Court's ruling developed. The battle for school desegregation became international news. Clinton, Nashville, Atlanta, Little Rock, Oxford—the names flashed across the world's front pages.

Refusal to comply with the law ranged from simple inaction or token integration to riots and bombings.

The pace of school desegregation was agonizingly slow. Ten years after the Court's decision only 9.2 percent of the black public school students in the Southern and border states were attending desegregated classes. (Thirty years later, in 1984, pressed hard by the courts, black citizens, and world opinion, the South had dismantled its dual public school system. But many whites were sending their children to private segregated schools to avoid the law. And in the North, there was now more *segregation in the schools than in the once solidly segregated South. The old pattern of segregated housing and gerrymandered school districts managed to keep black children confined to all-black ghetto schools in many big cities.) Wherever Blacks sought to exercise the basic right of the ballot, or the right to live in homes in whatever neighborhood they chose, intimidation and violence met them. In the realms of law and morality victories had been won, but everyday life had become a battleground of gunpowder and dynamite, cross burnings and beatings, arson and murder.*

Against the violent direct action of the white citizens' councils and the Ku Klux Klan, a new technique came into being. Blacks decided to take matters into their own hands. Nonviolent direct action, a form of mass, passive resistance, emerged as the means of advancing the struggle for civil rights. Montgomery, Alabama, the cradle of the Confederacy, was the scene. The rulers of that city of "genteel" segregation, with a population almost equally divided between white and Black, had long believed in the right of whites to be master and Blacks to be servant. Their contentment with things as they were was shattered the day that courageous Mrs. Rosa Parks refused to move to the Jim Crow section of the bus. The story of Mrs. Parks and the great Montgomery bus boycott of 1955–1956 is told by the Rev. Martin Luther King, Jr., who led the protest movement. Here he not only describes what happened but explains how, during the long

siege, his own thinking was shaped along a path marked out by
Thoreau.

In the end, the Montgomery Blacks won their battle, and the
boycott was picked up throughout the country as the weapon
that could force change. In 1964 Dr. King was awarded the
Nobel Prize for peace in recognition of his championship of the
nonviolence precept.

ON DECEMBER 1, 1955, an attractive Negro seamstress,
Mrs. Rosa Parks, boarded the Cleveland Avenue bus in downtown Montgomery. She was returning home after her regular
day's work in Montgomery Fair—a leading department store.
Tired from long hours on her feet, Mrs. Parks sat down in the
first seat behind the section reserved for whites. Not long after
she took her seat, the bus operator ordered her, along with
three other Negro passengers, to move back in order to accommodate boarding white passengers. By this time every seat
in the bus was taken. This meant that if Mrs. Parks followed
the driver's command she would have to stand while a white
male passenger, who had just boarded the bus, would sit. The
other three Negro passengers immediately complied with the
driver's request. But Mrs. Parks quietly refused. The result was
her arrest.

There was to be much speculation about why Mrs. Parks did
not obey the driver. Many people in the white community
argued that she had been "planted" by the NAACP in order
to lay the groundwork for a test case. . . .

But the accusation was totally unwarranted, as the testimony
of both Mrs. Parks and the officials of the NAACP revealed. . . . Mrs. Parks's refusal to move back was her intrepid
affirmation that she had had enough. It was an individual
expression of a timeless longing for human dignity and freedom. She was not "planted" there by the NAACP, or any

other organization; she was planted there by her personal sense of dignity and self-respect. . . .

Only E. D. Nixon—the signer of Mrs. Parks's bond—and one or two other persons were aware of the arrest when it occurred early Thursday evening. Later in the evening the word got around to a few influential women of the community, mostly members of the Women's Political Council. After a series of telephone calls back and forth they agreed that the Negroes should boycott the buses. They immediately suggested the idea to Nixon, and he readily concurred. In his usual courageous manner he agreed to spearhead the idea.

Early Friday morning, December 2, Nixon called me. He was so caught up in what he was about to say that he forgot to greet me with the usual "hello" but plunged immediately into the story of what had happened to Mrs. Parks the night before. I listened, deeply shocked, as he described the humiliating incident. "We have taken this type of thing too long already," Nixon concluded, his voice trembling. "I feel that the time has come to boycott the buses. Only through a boycott can we make it clear to the white folks that we will not accept this type of treatment any longer."

I agreed at once that some protest was necessary, and that the boycott method would be an effective one.

Just before calling me Nixon had discussed the idea with Rev. Ralph Abernathy, the young minister of Montgomery's First Baptist Church, who was to become one of the central figures in the protest, and one of my closest associates. Abernathy also felt a bus boycott was our best course of action. So for thirty or forty minutes the three of us telephoned back and forth concerning plans and strategy. Nixon suggested that we call a meeting of all the ministers and civic leaders the same evening in order to get their thinking on the proposal, and I offered my church as the meeting place. The three of us got busy immediately. With the sanction of Rev. H. H. Hubbard—

president of the Baptist Ministerial Alliance—Abernathy and I began calling all of the Baptist ministers. Since most of the Methodist ministers were attending a denominational meeting in one of the local churches that afternoon, it was possible for Abernathy to get the announcement to all of them simultaneously. . . .

By early afternoon the arrest of Mrs. Parks was becoming public knowledge. Word of it spread around the community like uncontrolled fire. Telephones began to ring in almost rhythmic succession. By two o'clock an enthusiastic group had mimeographed leaflets concerning the arrest and the proposed boycott, and by evening these had been widely circulated.

As the hour for the evening meeting arrived, I approached the doors of the church with some apprehension, wondering how many of the leaders would respond to our call. Fortunately, it was one of those pleasant winter nights of unseasonable warmth, and to our relief, almost everybody who had been invited was on hand. More than forty people, from every segment of Negro life, were crowded into the large church meeting room. I saw physicians, schoolteachers, lawyers, businessmen, postal workers, union leaders, and clergymen. Virtually every organization of the Negro community was represented. . . .

Bennett moved into action, explaining the purpose of the gathering. With excited gestures he reported on Mrs. Parks's resistance and her arrest. He presented the proposal that the Negro citizens of Montgomery should boycott the buses on Monday in protest. "Now is the time to move," he concluded. "This is no time to talk; it is time to act." . . .

Immediately questions began to spring up from the floor. . . . How long would the protest last? How would the idea be further disseminated throughout the community? How would the people be transported to and from their jobs? . . .

Not once did anyone question the validity or desirability of the boycott itself. It seemed to be the unanimous sense of the group that the boycott should take place.

The ministers endorsed the plan with enthusiasm, and promised to go to their congregations on Sunday morning and drive home their approval of the projected one-day protest. Their cooperation was significant, since virtually all of the influential Negro ministers of the city were present. It was decided that we should hold a citywide mass meeting on Monday night, December 5, to determine how long we would abstain from riding the buses. . . .

The group agreed that additional leaflets should be distributed on Saturday, and the chairman appointed a committee, including myself, to prepare the statement. . . . It read as follows:

> Don't ride the bus to work, to town, to school, or any place Monday, December 5.
>
> Another Negro woman has been arrested and put in jail because she refused to give up her bus seat.
>
> Don't ride the buses to work, to town, to school, or anywhere on Monday. If you work, take a cab, or share a ride, or walk.
>
> Come to a mass meeting, Monday at 7:00 P.M., at the Holt Street Baptist Church for further instruction.

The final question before the meeting concerned transportation. It was agreed that we should try to get the Negro taxi companies of the city—eighteen in number, with approximately 210 taxis—to transport the people for the same price that they were currently paying on the bus.

With these responsibilities before us the meeting closed. We left with our hearts caught up in a great idea. The hours were moving fast. The clock on the wall read almost midnight, but the clock in our souls revealed that it was daybreak.

I was so excited that I slept very little that night, and early next morning I was on my way to the church to get the leaflets out. By nine o'clock the church secretary had finished mimeographing the 7,000 leaflets and by eleven o'clock an army of women and young people had taken them off to distribute by hand.

Those on the committee that was to contact the taxi companies got to work early Saturday afternoon. They worked assiduously, and by evening they had reached practically all of the companies, and triumphantly reported that every one of them so far had agreed to cooperate with the proposed boycott by transporting the passengers to and from work for the regular ten-cent bus fare.

Meanwhile our efforts to get the word across to the Negro community were abetted in an unexpected way. A maid who could not read very well came into possession of one of the unsigned appeals that had been distributed Friday afternoon. Apparently not knowing what the leaflet said, she gave it to her employer. As soon as the white employer received the notice she turned it over to the local newspaper, and the Montgomery *Advertiser* made the contents of the leaflet a front-page story on Saturday morning. It appears that the *Advertiser* printed the story in order to let the white community know what the Negroes were up to; but the whole thing turned out to the Negroes' advantage, since it served to bring the information to hundreds who had not previously heard of the plan. By Sunday afternoon word had spread to practically every Negro citizen of Montgomery. Only a few people who lived in remote areas had not heard of it.

After a heavy day of work, I went home late Sunday afternoon and sat down to read the morning paper. There was a long article on the proposed boycott. Implicit throughout the article, I noticed, was the idea that the Negroes were preparing to use the same approach to their problem as the White Citizens Councils used. This suggested parallel had serious implications. The White Citizens Councils had had their birth in Mississippi a few months after the Supreme Court's school decision had come into being to preserve segregation. The Councils had multiplied rapidly throughout the South, purporting to achieve their ends by the legal maneuvers of "interposition" and "nullification." Unfortunately, however, the actions of some of these Councils extended far beyond the bounds of the law. Their methods were the methods of open and covert terror, brutal intimidation, and threats of starvation to Negro men, women, and children. They took open economic reprisals against whites who dared to protest their defiance of the law, and the aim of their boycotts was not merely to impress their victims but to destroy them if possible.

Disturbed by the fact that our pending action was being equated with the boycott methods of the White Citizens Councils, I was forced for the first time to think seriously on the nature of the boycott. Up to this time I had uncritically accepted this method as our best course of action. Now certain doubts began to bother me. Were we following an ethical course of action? Is the boycott method basically unchristian? Isn't it a negative approach to the solution of a problem? Is it true that we would be following the course of some of the White Citizens Councils? Even if lasting practical results came from such a boycott, would immoral means justify moral ends? Each of these questions demanded honest answers.

I had to recognize that the boycott method could be used to unethical and unchristian ends. I had to concede, further, that this was the method used so often by the White Citizens Councils to deprive many Negroes, as well as white persons of good will, of the basic necessities of life. But certainly, I said to myself, our pending actions could not be interpreted in this light. Our purposes were altogether different. We would use this method to give birth to justice and freedom, and also to urge men to comply with the law of the land; the White Citizens Councils used it to perpetuate the reign of injustice and human servitude, and urged men to defy the law of the land. I rea-

soned, therefore, that the word "boycott" was really a mis-
nomer for our proposed action. A boycott suggests an economic
squeeze, leaving one bogged down in a negative. But we were
concerned with the positive. Our concern would not be to put
the bus company out of business, but to put justice in business.

As I thought further I came to see that what we were really
doing was withdrawing our cooperation from an evil system,
rather than merely withdrawing our economic support from the
bus company. The bus company, being an external expression
of the system, would naturally suffer, but the basic aim was to
refuse to cooperate with evil. At this point I began to think
about Thoreau's Essay on Civil Disobedience. I remembered
how, as a college student, I had been moved when I first read
this work. I became convinced that what we were preparing to
do in Montgomery was related to what Thoreau had expressed.
We were simply saying to the white community, "We can no
longer lend our cooperation to an evil system."

Something began to say to me, "He who passively accepts
evil is as much involved in it as he who helps to perpetrate it.
He who accepts evil without protesting against it is really co-
operating with it." When oppressed people willingly accept
their oppression they only serve to give the oppressor a con-
venient justification for his acts. Often the oppressor goes along
unaware of the evil involved in his oppression so long as the
oppressed accepts it. So in order to be true to one's conscience
and true to God, a righteous man has no alternative but to
refuse to cooperate with an evil system. This I felt was the
nature of our action. From this moment on I conceived of our
movement as an act of massive noncooperation. . . .

From *Stride Toward Freedom*,
by Martin Luther King, Jr., Harper, 1958.

Oh Brothers, If You Only Knew

Three times Martin Luther King's home was shot up or bombed during the Montgomery bus boycott, but in the end the city's Blacks carried the banner of nonviolence to victory. Montgom-

ery was a turning point. It meant new times had come. New leaders came out of that long trial, young men and women native to the South, helped by but not dependent upon remote Northern friends. As the U.S. Supreme Court ruled against segregated buses, and went on with ban after ban against Jim Crow, Blacks were affirmed in their deep feeling that they were right in their protest, that direct action could produce the social change justice demanded. They had won strength through struggle.

Another chapter opened early in 1960, when black college students in Greensboro, N.C., sat down at a "Whites Only" lunch counter in Woolworth's and vowed that they and others would stay there until Blacks were served. The sit-ins won national attention, and swiftly other students were sitting at other lunch counters, risking everything to show they wanted to be treated as human beings.

In six months that first Woolworth's was open to all races. By the year's end Blacks were being served at hundreds of other stores, and in the years that followed sit-ins brought desegregation to movie theaters, amusement parks, beaches, swimming pools, hotels. In the spring of 1961 the movement spread to transportation. Freedom riders attacked segregation in buses and waiting rooms and met savage resistance that ended only when federal marshals by the hundreds appeared. The disorders brought the Interstate Commerce Commission to outlaw segregation in all trains and buses and terminals.

The tactics of white Southern resistance changed. Instead of arresting demonstrators for violating segregation ordinances, the local officials flung them into jail for disorderly conduct or for creating disturbances. The cases had to go to the courts, taking years on appeal and costing heavily for bonds.

But direct action continued. It won victories in some places; it failed in others; but it succeeded in applying the vast pressure needed to obtain the passage of a new federal Civil Rights Act, which put the immediate goals of the movement into law.

What the bus boycotters and the students had begun proved the Blacks' courage. They risked their jobs, their educations, and their lives in the fight for first-class citizenship. They learned as they struggled, and the struggle renewed their will to struggle. They saw themselves in a new light, and they made millions of whites the world over open their eyes to the new reality.

The document that follows is testimony from one young Black on the Southern battle lines. It is from Terrell County in Georgia, where Sheriff Zeke Mathews said in 1962, "We want our colored people to go on living like they have for the last hundred years." The sheriff, twenty years in office without opposition, liked things the way they were. Although the county population consisted of 8,209 Blacks and only 4,553 whites, the voter-registration rolls showed only 51 Blacks as against 2,894 whites. The Student Nonviolent Coordinating Committee (SNCC) put field secretaries in the county to work on a voter registration drive. Charlie H. Wingfield, Jr., was one of the local Blacks who wanted to register to vote.

THERE WAS NINE of us kids in the family and we all had to work a lot. I flunked two grades in school because of the unjust system we had to live under. I stayed out of school a lot of days because I couldn't let my mother go to the cotton field and try to support all of us. I had to decide which was more important, getting an education or letting my mother suffer along. When my father stopped working I had to stay out of school more than ever before. I picked cotton and pecans for two cents a pound. I went to the fields six in the morning and worked until seven in the afternoon. When it came time to weigh up so to speak, my heart, body and bones would be aching, burning and trembling. I stood there and stared the white men right in their eyes while they cheated me, other members of my family, and the rest of the Negroes that were working. They had their weighing scales loaded with lead and the rod would always be pointing toward the sky. There were times when I wanted to speak but my fearful mother would always tell me to keep silent. The sun was awful hot and the days were long. It was like being baked in an oven. When I went to bed at night I could see bolls of cotton staring me right in the face.

I would look at my sisters and my heart would say . . . dear sisters, I wish you could have and enjoy some of the finer things that life has to offer. I would look at my brothers and my heart would cry . . . oh brothers, if you only knew what it's like to live and enjoy life, instead of working like bees all the time to stay alive. Then I would look at my parents and my heart would utter . . . some day I'll build you a castle and you never have to bend your backs in another field. Last and least I would think to myself. I wished I had enough money to help the poor, build a playing center and a new church for our community. All these wonderful thoughts made me forget about my sorrow troubles but as I stop day dreaming I would be the saddest guy in the whole world.

My hands are like a history book. They tell a countless number of sad sad stories. Like a flowing river they seem to have no end. The cost of survival was high. Why I paid it I will never know.

I got expelled from the Lee County Training School for asking for some equipment for our school. All of the facilities that I asked was necessary for the proper kind of education a student needs. The officials of the city refused to let me register to vote. They also notified the surrounding schools not to let me enroll. I went to Shreveport, La., the 29th of September. I attended the Wash. High School there for two weeks. I was really enjoying myself and I was learning an awful lot of things that I had never heard of before. The standards of the school is one of the higher that can be found in the U.S. I talked with the F.B.I.'s and shortly afterward white people started riding by the house. They started calling the lady that I was living with hanging the phone up once she answered it. She told me that she didn't want her home bombed and I had to leave.

Statement to Student Nonviolent Coordinating Committee, by Charlie H. Wingfield, Jr., Terrell County, Ga.

Tell About Mississippi

Mrs. Fannie Lou Hamer
at the Democratic National Convention, 1964

"The right of citizens of the United States to vote shall not be denied or abridged by the United States or by any State on account of race, color, or previous condition of servitude."

So runs the Fifteenth Amendment, written into the United States Constitution in the year 1870. The words are simple and direct, but they were not understood or respected in the South for over a hundred years. When Reconstruction was overthrown, the right to vote was gradually cut down until by the last years of the nineteenth century the Fifteenth Amendment was only a paper promise. First there was the poll tax, pioneered by Mississippi. It made citizens pay a sum of money before they could vote. The result was to deprive most Blacks of the ballot. Then there was the requirement that voters be able to understand and interpret the state constitution, again a Mississippi innovation; and then the grandfather clause, which let only those vote without tests who had a forebear who had voted in 1866 or earlier. Everyone else—meaning all Blacks—had to submit to stiff educational tests.

Some Blacks did vote in the South, even in Mississippi, for several decades after the Civil War. (Around 1900 about 9 percent of the state's voting-age Blacks were still on Mississippi's rolls.) In the next decades the Supreme Court struck down one after another of the unconstitutional barriers to the ballot, but in a large part of the South it made no difference. Blacks still were not allowed to vote. In 1964 only 5 percent of the Blacks in Mississippi were registered. In many counties almost every white was on the voting rolls but not one Black. White supremacy had ruled for generations, and it did not mean to give up or share its power. The methods used to keep Blacks from voting were not subtle. They were crude and trivial at one end, but brutal, inhuman, even murderous, at the other end.

Trying hard on their own to win the ballot, Southern Blacks could make little progress against the economic and political power of the white supremacists. The Civil Rights Act of 1957 allowed the Justice Department to challenge voting discrimination. Now the federal government could no longer say it was without power to enforce respect for the right to vote. But the years that followed saw only the smallest change. The national government did not succeed in establishing the rule of the Constitution in the deep South. Some said it was because Washington was not really trying. The Southern police and local and state officials made their own law, with no regard for the Constitution, and the federal government too often continued to act as though it were powerless.

The record is full of crimes of violence, committed by Southern police against United States citizens. The times when citizens have been denied equal protection of the laws and of freedom of speech and assembly are innumerable. Every such instance was a violation of the Civil Rights Enforcement Act of 1870, but in only a few cases did the Justice Department intervene.

In 1960 Mississippi began to move toward a new day. It started with a meeting between Robert Parris Moses, a young Harlem Black with a master's degree from Harvard, and Alonzo Moore, a farmer from Cleveland, Mississippi, who was head of the local NAACP. They planned a campaign to register Blacks to vote. The first voter registration school—or freedom school—opened in one county the next summer, staffed by SNCC workers. Blacks went down to the county seat to register, and some of them passed the test. The news raced to other counties, and there too schools soon opened. Beatings, arrests, jailings, heavy bail bonds were used to halt the movement. One black farmer was murdered the next month, and a black witness to the killing was later shot to death. But the voter registration drive went on, side by side with sit-ins, marches, and freedom rides. In 1962 a bigger plan was drawn for a unified voter registration program. The NAACP, Congress of Racial Equality (CORE), Southern Christian Leadership Conference (SCLC), and SNCC shared the funds contributed by foundations for the new Voter Education Project (VEP).

Thousands of Blacks in Mississippi were reached by the movement. In 1964 it expanded to a special civil rights program un-

*dertaken for the summer months. Its aim was a massive edu-
cation, community improvement, and voter registration drive.
Under the leadership of several groups combined in a Council
of Federated Organizations (COFO), students, lawyers, doc-
tors, teachers, and clergymen volunteered their time and talents
for a peaceful, nonviolent campaign.*

*Mississippi officials instantly countered the announcement with
plans for resistance. New local and state laws were adopted to
further limit peaceful assembly and free speech, and to hamper
the work of the freedom schools and community centers.*

*To call public attention to the Mississippi summer project, a
group of private citizens concerned with civil rights held unofficial hearings on Mississippi in Washington on June 8, 1964.
The panel took the testimony of many witnesses from the state,
testimony later entered in the* Congressional Record. *Among
the witnesses was Fannie Lou Hamer. Mrs. Hamer, then 47,
was one of a family of 20 children. Married, she was herself the
mother of two, and had worked all her life as a sharecropper
in Ruleville. She went down to register after she heard SNCC
workers talk at a mass meeting in her church. Later, when she
was evicted from the plantation where she had worked as a
timekeeper and sharecropper for eighteen years, she became a
field secretary for SNCC. She also became one of the three Blacks
to run for Congress in 1964 on the Mississippi Freedom Democratic Party ticket.*

Q. WOULD YOU STATE your name and address, please?

A. My name is Fannie Lou Hamer, and I exist at 626 East
Lafayette Street in Ruleville, Miss.

Q. Mrs. Hamer, what is it that brings you before the panel
today?

A. To tell about some of the brutality in the State of Mississippi. I will begin from the first beginning, August 31, in
1962.

I traveled 26 miles to the county courthouse to try to register to become a first-class citizen. I was fired the 31st of August in 1962 from a plantation where I had worked as a timekeeper and a sharecropper for 18 years. My husband had worked there 30 years.

I was met by my children when I returned from the courthouse, and my girl and my husband's cousin told me that this man my husband worked for was raising a lot of Cain. I went on in the house, and it wasn't too long before my husband came and said this plantation owner said I would have to leave if I didn't go down and withdraw.

About that time, the man walked up, Mr. Marlow, and he said, "Is Fannie Lou back yet?"

My husband said, "She is."

I walked out of the house at this time. He said, "Fannie Lou, you have been to the courthouse to try to register," and he said, "We are not ready for this in Mississippi."

I said, "I didn't register for you, I tried to register for myself."

He said, "We are not going to have this in Mississippi, and you will have to withdraw. I am looking for your answer, yea or nay."

I just looked. He said, "I will give you until tomorrow morning. And if you don't withdraw, you will have to leave." . . . So I left that same night.

On the 10th of September, they fired into the home of Mr. and Mrs. Robert Tucker 16 times for me. That same night, two girls were shot at Mr. Herman Sissel's. Also, they shot Mr. Joe Maglon's house. I was fired that day and haven't had a job since.

In 1963, I attended a voter registration workshop and was returning back to Mississippi. At Winona, Miss., I was arrested there. Some folk had got off the bus . . . to go into the restaurant to get food. Two of the people decided to use the restroom. I saw them come right straight out of the restaurant.

I got off the bus to see what had happened. Miss Ponder said, "They won't let us eat." She said, "There was a chief of police and a highway patrolman inside, and they ordered us out." I said, "Well, this is Mississippi."

I got back on the bus, and about the time I just got sat down good, I looked out the window, and they were getting Miss Ponder and the others into the highway patrolman's car.

I stepped off the bus to see what was happening, and one screamed, "Get that one there." I was picked up, the police, Earl Wane Patric (sic), told me I was under arrest. He opened the door, and as I started to get in, he kicked me. They carried me to town to this county jail.

I was in the car with Earl Wane Patric and one plain clothes-man. I don't know whether he was a policeman or not. He didn't have on police clothes, had a crew haircut. They would ask me questions going on to jail, and as I would go on to answer, they would curse me and tell me to hush.

I was carried on to the booking room and carried from the booking room to a cell. After I was locked up in a cell with Miss Euvester Simpson, I began to hear the sounds of licks, and I could hear people screaming. I don't know how long it lasted before I saw Miss Ponder, the southside supervisor for SCLC, pass the cell with both her hands up. Her eyes looked like blood, and her mouth was swollen. She passed my cell. Her clothes was torn. She backed and they carried her again out of my sight.

After then, the State highway patrolman walked into my cell with two other white men. He asked where I was from, and I told him. He said, "I am going to check."

They left my cell, and it wasn't too long before they returned, and he said, "You damn right, you are from Ruleville," and he called me a bad name. He said they would make me wish I was dead.

I was carried out of the cell into another cell where there

were two Negro prisoners. The State highway patrolman gave the first Negro a long blackjack that was heavy. It was loaded with something, and they had me lay down on the bunk with my face down, and I was beat, I was beat by the first Negro until I was exhausted.

After I was beaten by the first Negro, the State highway patrolman ordered the other Negro to take the blackjack. The second Negro, he began to beat. The State highway patrolman ordered the first Negro that had beat me to sit on my feet. One of the white men that was in the room, my dress would work up because it had a large skirt, but I was trying to keep it down and trying to shield the licks from the left side, because I had polio when I was a child. During the time that I was trying to work my dress down and keep the licks off my left side, one of the white men walked over and pulled my dress up.

At this time I had to hug around the mattress to keep the sound from coming out. . . .

Q. Mrs. Hamer, what was the charge on which you were arrested on the bus incident?

A. Well . . . I asked the jailer, "Would you leave the door open so I could catch air." During the time the door was open, I heard discussion: "Now, what is we going to charge them with?" Somebody said something. He said, "Well, you are going to have to get up something better than that. Man, that is the end of the wire."

So I actually didn't know what we were charged with until they got ready to have our trial, and we were charged with resisting arrest and disorderly conduct. . . .

My husband was fired the day after I qualified to run as Congresswoman in the Second Congressional District. Last week he had gotten a second job. The mayor went out on this job on which he was working, so he will probably be fired by the time I get back home.

From *Congressional Record*, June 16, 1964.

*

Less than four years after Fannie Lou Hamer failed that first literacy test, Mississippi magazine named her as one of six "Women of Influence" in the state. And in 1970 Ruleville held a Fannie Lou Hamer Day attended by white and black, young and old, from all over the state. The white mayor, who had once jailed her husband and who wouldn't speak to her two years before, hailed her as a champion of her people. Talking to reporters, Fannie Lou Hamer said:

IF YOU JUST stand there and don't lash back, you can find a real human being in a lot of people. I don't never write nobody off. All this time I've been part of a nonviolent revolution. My policy is to do unto others as you would have them do unto you. I'd tell the white powers that I ain't trying to take nothing from them. I'm trying to make Mississippi a better place for all of us. And I'd say, "What you don't understand is that as long as you stand with your feet on my neck, you got to stand in a ditch, too. But if you move, I'm coming out. I want to get us both out of the ditch." I'm not saying that I can't get angry sometimes. Oh, yes, I do. And when I do, I'll walk up to any of these folks and say: "Look, now we are going to do something about this. Number one, you can write your dates on the calendar because you ain't getting back in office because we'll vote you out!" And they know we mean it.

I've always believed that one day, even if I didn't live to see it, this country would be different. It would be a place for all people to live, where they could be without the hangings and the lynchings and the killings and the bombings. We are our brother's keeper whether he is black, white, brown, red or yellow. As the Bible tells us, God has made of one blood all nations.

In 1977, at the age of 60, she died of cancer. A few weeks later the Mississippi legislature unanimously passed a resolution praising her service to the state.

Ain't Gonna Let Nobody Turn Me 'Round

Fannie Lou Hamer testified in Washington as the Freedom Summer of 1964 began. Hundreds of volunteers arrived in Mississippi to work in the Summer Project organized by civil rights groups. On July 2 President Lyndon B. Johnson signed the Civil Rights Act outlawing segregation in public accommodations. One month later the bodies of three missing Summer Project workers were found buried beneath an earthen dam.

Alabama became another front line in the battle for freedom. "Progress came through agony," as one black Alabaman said. There were over fifty racial bombings in Birmingham alone, with four black girls killed in an explosion at a Baptist church one Sunday morning. Dozens, hundreds, and then thousands of Blacks marched to the courthouses to insist upon their right to register and vote. Police, sheriffs' posses, and state troopers met the nonviolent demonstrators in bloody confrontation. In Marion a black woodcutter, Jimmie Lee Jackson, was shot in the stomach by a state trooper; he died a week later.

In Selma a march was called for Sunday, March 7, 1965, to protest police brutality as well as denial of voting rights throughout the Black Belt. Sheyann Webb, an eight-year-old, was the first child to attend the freedom rallies in her church. She led the singing of the movement songs—"Ain't Gonna Let Nobody Turn Me 'Round," "O Freedom," "This Little Light of Mine."

On what would become known worldwide as "Bloody Sunday," her mother brushed her hair, hugged her, and let her go out to join the proposed march from Selma to the state capital in Montgomery. The marchers, 600 strong, moved through downtown, turned south, and headed for Pettus Bridge arching over the Alabama River. At the bridge troopers ordered the marchers to disperse. When they pressed on, they were attacked. Years later, while in college, Sheyann recalled what happened next.

ALL I KNEW is I heard all this screaming and the people were turning and I saw this first part of the line running and stumbling back toward us. At that point, I was just off the bridge and on the side of the highway. And they came running and some of them were crying out and somebody yelled, "Oh, God, they're killing us!" I think I just froze then. There were people everywhere, jamming against me, pushing against me. Then, all of a sudden, it stopped and everyone got down on their knees, and I did too, and somebody was saying for us to pray. But there was so much excitement it never got started, because everybody was talking and they were scared and we didn't know what was happening or was going to happen. I remember looking toward the troopers and they were backing up, but some of them were standing over some of our people who had been knocked down or had fallen. It seemed like just a few seconds went by and I heard a shout. "Gas! Gas!" And everybody started screaming again. And I looked and I saw the troopers charging us again and some of them were swinging their arms and throwing canisters of tear gas. And beyond them I saw the horsemen starting their charge toward us. I was terrified. What happened then is something I'll never forget as long as I live. Never. In fact, I still dream about it sometimes.

I saw those horsemen coming toward me and they had those awful masks on; they rode right through the cloud of tear gas.

Some of them had clubs, others had ropes or whips, which they swung about them like they were driving cattle.

I'll tell you, I forgot about praying, and I just turned and ran. And just as I was turning the tear gas got me; it burned my nose first and then got my eyes. I was blinded by the tears. So I began running and not seeing where I was going. I remember being scared that I might fall over the railing and into the water. I don't know if I was screaming or not, but everyone else was. People were running and falling and ducking and you could hear the horses' hooves on the pavement and you'd hear people scream and hear the whips swishing and you'd hear them striking the people. They'd cry out; some moaned. Women as well as men were getting hit. I never got hit, but one of the horses went right by me and I heard the swish sound as the whip went over my head and cracked some man across the back. It seemed to take forever to get across the bridge. It seemed I was running uphill for an awfully long time. They kept rolling canisters of tear gas on the ground, so it would rise up quickly. It was making me sick. I heard more horses and I turned back and saw two of them and the riders were leaning over to one side. It was like a nightmare seeing it through the tears. I just knew then that I was going to die, that those horses were going to trample me. So I kind of knelt down and held my hands and arms up over my head, and I must have been screaming—I don't really remember.

All of a sudden somebody was grabbing me under the arms and lifting me up and running. The horses went by and I kept waiting to get trampled on or hit, but they went on by and I guess they were hitting at somebody else. And I looked up and saw it was Hosea Williams who had me and he was running but we didn't seem to be moving, and I kept kicking my legs in the air, trying to speed up, and I shouted at him, "Put me down! You can't run fast enough with me!"

But he held on until we were off the bridge and down on

Broad Street and he let me go. I didn't stop running until I got
home. All along the way there were people running in small
groups; I saw people jumping over cars and being chased by
the horsemen who kept hitting them. When I got to the apartments there were horsemen in the yards, galloping up and
down, and one of them reared his horse up in the air as I went
by, and he had his mask off and was shouting something at
me.

When I got into the house my momma and daddy were there
and they had this shocked look on their faces and I ran in and
tried to tell them what had happened. I was maybe a little
hysterical because I kept repeating over and over, "I can't stop
shaking, Momma, I can't stop shaking," and finally she grabbed
me and sat down with me on her lap. But my daddy was like
I'd never seen him before. He had a shotgun and he yelled,
"By God, if they want it this way, I'll give it to them!" And
he started out the door. Momma jumped up and got in front
of him shouting at him. And he said, "I'm ready to die; I mean
it! I'm ready to die!" I was crying there on the couch, I was
so scared. But finally he put the gun aside and sat down. I
remember just laying there on the couch, crying and feeling so
disgusted. They had beaten us like we were slaves.

*In the evening the people gathered in church. Everyone was
quiet, stunned. Nobody was praying, nobody was singing. Was
the will to go on lost? Sheyann wondered if there would ever be
another march. "It was like we were at our own funeral," she
said.*

BUT THEN LATER in the night, maybe nine-thirty or ten,
I don't know for sure, all of a sudden somebody there started
humming. I think they were moaning and it just went into the
humming of a freedom song. It was real low, but some of us

children began humming along, slow and soft. At first I didn't even know what it was, what song, I mean. It was like a funeral sound, a dirge. Then I recognized it—*Ain't Gonna Let Nobody Turn Me 'Round.* I'd never heard it or hummed it that way before. But it just started to catch on, and the people began to pick it up. It started to swell, the humming. Then we began singing the words. We sang, "Ain't gonna let George Wallace [the Governor of Alabama] turn me 'round." And, "Ain't gonna let Jim Clark turn me 'round." "Ain't gonna let no state trooper turn me 'round."

Ain't gonna let no horses . . . ain't gonna let no tear gas—ain't gonna let nobody turn me 'round. *Nobody!*

And everybody's singing now, and some of them are clapping their hands, and they're still crying, but it's a different kind of crying. It's the kind of crying that's got spirit, not the weeping they had been doing.

And me and Rachel are crying and singing and it just gets louder and louder. I know the state troopers outside the church heard it. Everybody heard it. Because more people were coming in then, leaving their apartments and coming to the church—because something was happening.

We was singing and telling the world that we hadn't been whipped, that we had won.

Just all of a sudden something happened that night and we knew in that church that—Lord Almighty—we had really won, after all. We had won!

From *Selma, Lord, Selma,* by Frank Sikora, 1980.

And they had. For the whole country—the whole world!—saw what had happened that day in Selma. The television cameras had captured the terrible beating the peaceful marchers had taken on the bridge. And the next day people from all over America began arriving to help the cause of civil rights.

Don't Nobody Tell Me to Keep Quiet

On November 5, 1973, Nate Shaw, 88 years old, died; he was buried at Pottstown Baptist Church, Tukabahchee County, Alabama. In his last few years he spent some 120 hours recording on tape his recollections of life as an illiterate black tenant farmer. He had endured nearly a century of the twin bondage of race oppression and economic peonage. A Northern scholar shaped a book that speaks for both Nate Shaw and the nameless black masses whose silence historians lament.

"Don't nobody try to tell me to keep quiet and undo my history," the old farmer says, and out of him poured a passionate flood of memories rich in sensuous detail, acute in characterization of both Black and white, penetrating in analysis of socioeconomic relationships, and loving in its concern for men and women.

Shaw respects labor—"the backbone of the world," he calls it—but bitterly resents that "too many takin' the other fellow's labor." In childhood he realized that though his father was nominally free, "in his acts he was a slave." Determined to overturn this way of life, Nate Shaw joined the Sharecroppers Union in the hard thirties and spent twelve years in prison for this "crime." Coming out at 59, he was a mule farmer lost in a tractor world. But he never lost his dignity, his humor, his readiness to fight for his rights. These words of Nate Shaw are a kind of summing up near the end of his oral history, All God's Dangers, *edited by Theodore Rosengarten.*

*

My boyhood days was my hidin place. I didn't have no right to no education whatever. I was handicapped and handicapped like a dog. When I was deprived of book learnin, right there they had me dead by the throat. I was deaf and dumb, didn't know nothin and weren't given no chance to my rights enough to come in the knowledge of what was right and what was wrong. When I was a little boy comin along—and that runned until way up here when this equal rights movement taken place; that begin to bust these conditions wide open, and many eyes flew open to a great excitement. It's brought light out of darkness. I can just spy the good every day of my life that it's doin—to my first remembrance, here's what was runnin: I was born in 1885. From my birth and I reckon it was before my birth, just as such conditions as I've explained was going on and went on up until recent days. That's well above a hundred years from time to time of the change, well above a hundred years—this is the truth I'm givin; I've kept a record of a heap of things and it gives me a right to speak it. . . .

I didn't like conditions but what could I do? I had no voice, had no political pull whatever. They sang that song stoutly to me, too, let me know that the very best that I could do was *labor* and try to labor to a success under their rulins. I done it. You couldn't count no slackness on Nate Shaw about labor.

I worked all that I had to—as far as I can say, the Lord speaks somethin like this: if a thing is necessary to do on a Sunday, do it. Help the ox out of the mire as well on a Sunday as on a Monday. And that very thing have caused me to do a little work on a Sunday. If I was pullin fodder, in fall of the year in gatherin time, I'd pull it to beat the weather, come Sunday or Monday. But I never did go out and pick no cotton on a Sunday. But, pull some fodder on Friday and Saturday and it cured out; well, if I estimated that the rain liable to come, I scurried out there to get that fodder and carry it to the barn. I've done that on a Sunday. That was necessary. It was no harm—

And in all, I had a hard way to go. I had men to turn me down, wouldn't let me have the land I needed to work, wouldn't sell me guano, didn't want to see me with anything. Soon as I got to where I could have somethin for sure and was makin somethin of myself, then they commenced a runnin at me, wantin to make trades with me.

I had business with many a white man and I come out of the little end of the horn with too many of em. When I got in Mr. Watson's hands, he thought he just goin to drive me to what he wanted, which was my destruction. He was goin to take what I had if I owed him; if I didn't owe him he was going to take it. I'd a died and went home to my Savior before I'd a suffered him to do it. . . .

I never tried to beat nobody out of nothin since I been in this world, never has, but I understands that there's a whole class of people tries to beat the other class of people out of what they has. I've had it put on me; I've seen it put on others, with these eyes. O, it's plain: if every man thoroughly got his rights, there wouldn't be so many rich people in the world—I spied that a long time ago. And I've looked deep in that angle. How can one man get out there and labor for his own way of life and get to be a rich man? Where is his earnins comin from that he's palmin off and stickin it behind? It come out of the poor little farmers and other laborin men. O, it's desperately wrong. There's many a man today aint able to support his family. There's many a man aint able to wear the clothes that he should wear and accumulate nothin that he should have, and accomplish nothin that he should do. And who is the backbone of the world? It's the laborin man, it's the laborin man. My God, the big man been on him with both foots all these years and now don't want to get off him. I found out all of that because they tried to take I don't know what all away from me.

I've gotten along in this world by studyin the races and knowin that I was one of the underdogs. I was under many rulins, just like the other Negro, that I knowed was injurious to man and displeasin to God and still I had to fall back. I got tired of it but no help did I know; weren't nobody to back me up. I've taken every kind of insult and went on. In my years past, I'd accommodate anybody; but I didn't believe in this way of bowin to my knees and doin what *any* white man said do. Still, I always knowed to give the white man his time of day or else he's ready to knock me in the head. I just aint goin to go nobody's way against my own self. First thing of all—I care for myself and respect myself.

I've joked with white people, in a nice way. I've had to play dumb sometimes—I knowed not to go too far and let them know what I knowed, because they taken exception of it too quick. I had to humble down and play shut-mouthed in many cases to get along. I've done it all—they didn't know what it was all about, it's just a plain fact. I've played dumb—maybe a heap of times I knowed just how come they done such-and-such a trick, but I wouldn't say. And I would go to em a heap of times for a favor and get it. I could go to em, even the heavy-pocketed white man, if I couldn't get what I wanted out of one, I could get it out the other one. They'd have dealins with you, furnish you what you needed to make a crop, but you had to come under their rulins. They'd give you a good name if you was obedient to em, acted nice when you met em and didn't question em bout what they said they had against you. You begin to cry about our rights and the mistreatin of you and they'd murder you.

When I jumped up and fought the laws, that ruint me with the white people in this country. They gived me just as bad a name as they could give me; talked it around that I was quick-tempered, I was quick-tempered. The devil you better get quick-tempered or get some sort of temper when you know you livin in a bad country. . . .

I come into the world with this against me: that if a man comes to take away what I have and he don't have a fair claim against me, I'll die before I stand quiet as a fence post and let him do it. If I die tryin to defend myself, why, let me go. I'm going to try, definitely. . . .

But if you don't like what I have done, then you are against the man I am today. I aint going to take no backwater about it. If you don't like me for the way I have lived, get on off in the woods and bushes and shut your mouth and let me go for what I'm worth. And if I come out of my scrapes, all right; if I don't come out, don't let it worry *you*, this is *me*. Don't nobody try to tell me to keep quiet and undo my history. There aint no get-back in me as far as I can reach my arm. And if anything comes up and favors me to knock down and drag out this old "ism" that's been plunderin me and plunderin the colored race of people ever since I got big enough to know, and before that, before that—old mothers and fathers before I come into this world was treated the same, knuckled under. Well, I'm tired of it, I don't want to bear all that. Anything tries to master me I wish to remove it. And I'm willin to slap my shoulder to the wheel if it's ary a pound I can push. And for God's sake don't come up messin with me. If there's any better life for me to live, any more rights that I can enjoy, get out the way and let me enjoy em or let me go down. And if I go down, in the name of the Lord, I'm done with it. Them all that has a mind to stop the wheel rollin by droppin their heads and hidin their faces, that's them. I can't help it but it stirs me from the bottom. I'd fight this mornin for my rights. I'd do it—and for other folks' rights if they'll push along.

I don't call for nobody to run their heads up under a gun,

but if you don't rise up in defense of your portion, what good
are you?

From *All God's Dangers: The Life of
Nate Shaw*, edited by Theodore Rosengarten,
Alfred E. Knopf, 1974.

That Is All There Is,
It's the Work!

Maya Angelou

*Blacks increasingly share the honor and glory that is the proper
recognition of inherent talent and superb performance in sports,
entertainment, the sciences, and arts and letters. They have won*

*many distinctions for themselves and their country, from the
Sports Halls of Fame to Oscars, Emmys, Tonys in entertain-
ment, and from poet laureate to the Pulitzer Prize, The American
Book Award, and the Nobel Prize.*

*When contributions of Blacks to American cultural life were
cited in the not-distant past, it used to be limited to sports and
entertainment. Most Americans have heard of Louis Armstrong,
Willie Mays, Muhammad Ali, Lena Horne. Not so many could
identify Romare Bearden, John Hope Franklin, or Ralph El-
lison.*

*For America did not know much about the black contingent
in the world of arts and letters. Their names usually made the
news not because of their artistic and scholarly accomplishments
but because of their politics.*

*The black-consciousness movement of the sixties did much to
make their names and their achievements visible. It also encouraged exciting new expressions of black life. In the sixties
and seventies new black novelists, poets, painters, playwrights,
composers, choreographers captured public attention as they
enriched American culture.*

*One of them was Maya Angelou, a many-sided talent whose
creativity flowed into many media—fiction, poetry, theater, music,
film, television. She is perhaps best known for her multivolume
autobiography, the first part of which is called* I Know Why the
Caged Bird Sings. *In these passages from an interview with her
conducted by Robert Chrisman of* Black Scholar, *Angelou talks
about what it takes for an artist who is black and a woman to
make her mark.*

Q: CAN YOU COMMENT a bit on the importance of endurance in black writers?

Angelou: Endurance is one thing. I think endurance with
productivity is the issue. If one has the fortune, good or bad,

to stay alive one endures, but to continue to write the books and get them out—that's the productivity and I think that is important to link with the endurance. . . . It is important to get the work done, seen, read, published and *given* to an audience. One has enjoyed oneself, one has done what one has been put here to do, to write. Another thing is that one has given a legacy of some quantity to generations to come. Whether they like it or not, whether the writer values the next generation, or values the work or not, there is something, there is a body of work to examine and to respond to, react to. . . .

Q: I want to talk to you about that. I think any artist in this society is inhibited in many ways because it is not an esthetic society.

Angelou: Materialistic.

Q: I think the black writer has even more difficulty because his vision is antagonistic, it's a racist society, his stuff is different. Do you think the masterpiece syndrome further inhibits output of black writers?

Angelou: To me that inhibits *all* artists. Every artist in this society is affected by it. I don't say he or she is inhibited, he or she might work against it and make that work for them, as I hope I have, but we are affected by it.

It is reaction to that dictate from a larger society that spurs my output, makes me do all sorts of things, write movies and direct them, write plays, write music and write articles. That's because I don't believe in the inhibition of my work; I am obliged, I am compulsive. I will work against it. If necessary I will go to work on a dictionary. . . .

So every artist in the society has to deal with that dictate. Some are crippled by it; others, I believe, are made more healthy, because they are made more strong, and become more ready to struggle against it.

Q: More vigilant.

Angelou: Absolutely. But the black writer or black artist—

I include every type, from graphics to entertainment—has generally further to come from than his or her white counterpart unless the artist is an entertainer. Often this black artist is the first in his family and possibly in his environment to strive to write a book, to strive to paint a painting, to sculpt, to make being an artist a life work. So the black writer, the black artist probably has to convince family and friends that what he or she is about is worthwhile.

Now that is damned difficult when one comes from a family, an environment, a neighborhood or group of friends who have never met a writer, who have only heard of writers, maybe read some poetry in school.

But to try to explain to a middle-aged black that the life of art one wants to lead is a worthwhile one and can hopefully improve life, the quality of life for all people, that's already a chore.

Because, like most people anywhere, the middle-aged black American who comes from a poor background for the most part wants to see concrete evidence of success. So they want things. If you are really going to be a success go and become a nurse, be a doctor, be a mortician, but a *writer*? So there are obstacles to overcome, to be either done or else just given up on.

Q: Or the relationships suspended?

Angelou: Right. Then the work still has to be done in the artist's psyche, because he has to keep dealing with the issue that every artist, from the beginning of time, has to deal with, and that is, "Am I an artist?" That public display of ego on the part of artists, 99 times out of 100, only tells of the doubt he has in private, especially when one has no precedent in one's personal family history. My grandfather Jason did not know anybody who was an artist or sculptor or composer, certainly not a writer. . . . There have not been that many black artists that visible for black youth. There was Langston Hughes, but he was the only one and that was 35 to 40 years ago. . . .

Q: That's true. And Langston Hughes had a very public philosophy of art.

Angelou: That's right. He was one of the rare ones. So I am saying that all of the problems of artists in a mechanistic, materialistic society, all those problems are heightened, if not doubled, for the black American artist.

So as usual the black writer—I can only speak for the writer—the black writer in particular should throw out all of that propaganda and pressure, disbelieve everything one is told to believe and believe everything one is told *not* to believe. Start with a completely clean slate and decide, "I will put it out."

. . . Now my problem is I love life, love living life and I love the art of living so I try to live my life as a poem, an adventure, everything I do from the way I keep my house, cook, make my husband happy, or welcome my friends, raise my son; everything is a part of a large canvas I am creating.

Now there is a very fine line between loving life and being greedy for it. And I refuse to be greedy, I want to walk away from it with as much flair and grace and humor as I have had living it. Okay, I am saying all this to say that when I write, it would seem I am greedy to get the book done, I pray I am just this side of being greedy, on the safe side. But that determination and delight I have in working, in getting a piece done, in the achievement, is delicious. . . .

Q: One of the things I sensed in your autobiographies, is that you have a very definite point of view about work. In a lot of ways not only work as an artist but in the general effort of life. Would you discuss that?

Angelou: I believe my feeling for work is something other than the puritan ethic of work. I do believe that a person, a human being without his or her work, is like a peapod where the peas have shrivelled before they have come to full growth. I have very little to say to people who don't work. I don't know what to say, I mean not that I want to discuss sewing dresses with a seamstress but if she or he respects his or her work we have a jumping-off place because we at least separately know something about respect and respect for something outside our own selves. Something made greater by ourselves and in turn that makes us greater. And that's pretty fantastic, so that I honor the people who do what they do well, whatever it is. I feel that I am a part of that.

Q: Black people are a working people and the sense of work pervades your autobiographies, your mother's rooming house, your own growth as a child; you were always around a working situation. One of your primary motivations for work in your autobiographies seems to be caring for your child.

Angelou: Yes, that's right. Well I can't imagine what life would be like for me without having work that I cared about. I suspect that I have been a "liberated" woman, in the sense that term is now used, most of my life. There may have been a couple of years in my life when I did not choose how I would live my life, who would pay my bills, who would raise my son, where we would live and so forth, but only for a few years.

I am so "liberated" that except on rare occasions my husband does not walk into the house without seeing his dinner prepared. He does not have to concern himself about a dirty house. I do that, for myself, but also for my husband. I think it is important to make that very clear.

I think there is something rather gracious and graceful about serving. Now, unfortunately, or rather the truth is, our history in this country has been the history of the servers and because we were forced to serve and because dignity was absolutely drained from the servant. For anyone who serves in this country, black or white, is held in such contempt, while that is not true in other parts of the world. In Africa it is a great honor to serve, to be allowed to serve somebody is a great honor. You can insult a person by not accepting something from him. In Europe from the great family traditions, work patterns are the patterns of the waiters and the maitre d's and the chefs and so forth. Generation after generation of servanthood. I don't mean to say that class issues are not at issue here too, but there is something beyond that, when people have been made to serve or because of their economic circumstances they have found within that some grace, some style, some marvelous flair.

Well, I refuse, simply because I happen to be born in this country, to take on the coloration of the larger society which says to serve, to take off your sister's shoes when she walks into the house, is really belittling yourself. I don't see that. . . .

There is something about the way people look at work that I think is completely off. I believe I know why there are the negatives about work, especially in the black community, but I refuse to get out of one trick bag and get caught in another. Now that I know what it means, I don't have to fall into that.

Q: Yes, while there is that element of the disdain for work, there is at the same time the mystification of excellence so that people will talk about the inspired genius of John Coltrane while they forget he ran scales—

Angelou: —for five hours a day.

Q: Right. Hard work was at the base of Trane's revolutionary music—and the courage to be audacious.

Angelou: Audacity is fine, it's splendid. . . . Again we come back to your earlier question about work. When Louis Armstrong came to Chicage he was wearing a suit, the pants of which were about three inches too short, his white socks showed, he had those brogans on and he wore a derby hat. He got up on the stage and all the musicians laughed until he started to play. When he finished playing, the next day the musicians went out and bought some pants three inches too short, some white socks and some brogan shoes and a derby hat. Louis Armstrong was on J—and never got off his J—never, never stopped. I mean for all intents and purposes, died with his trumpet in his hand. So did Duke Ellington, all those people who inspire one, who inspire me.

I appreciate that, I respect it and I am grateful for it. I am grateful, in the name of my grandson I am grateful.

Q: Has the example of these men influenced your own development as a writer?

Angelou: Well, certainly. I tell you one of the most aggravating things of all is to pick up a review of a work of mine and have a reviewer say, "She is a natural writer." That sometimes will make me so angry I will cry, really, because my intent is to write so it seems to flow. Alexander Pope says, "Easy writing is damn hard reading," and vice versa, easy reading is damn hard writing. Sometimes, I will stay up in my room for a day, trying to get two sentences that will flow, that will just seem as if they were always there. And many times I come home unable to get it so I go back the next day, 6:30 in the morning, every morning, 6:30 I go to work. I work till 2:00 alone in this tiny little room, 7x10 feet. I write in longhand. If it is going well I might go to 3 but then I pull myself out, come home, take a shower, start dinner, check my house, so that when Paul comes in at 5:30 I have had a little time out of that, although my heart and my mind are there, I still try to live an honest life. Then when you go back it looks different to you. I think that a number of artists again, or people who have pretensions that in order to be an artist you must have the back of your hand glued to your forehead, you know, and walk around and be "terribly, terribly—" all the time, thinking great thoughts of pith and moment. That's bullshit. In order to get the work done *and really that is all there is*, it's the *work!* all the posturing, all the lack of posturing, none of that matters, it is finally the work. You don't really get away from it when you try. . . .

Q: You mentioned some of the attitudes toward life that one gets in this society. When you were abroad did you get a different perspective on being a black American?

Angelou: Well, I came to, if possible, regard my people, black Americans, ever more affectionately. Once out from the daily pressure of oppression, hate and ridicule and all, the negatives that permeate this whole air we breathe, just being out from under that, not having to use 30 to 40 percent of my energy just kicking that crap out of my doorway before I can even get out and go to work, it was amazing. First off I didn't know what to do with myself. I was so geared to struggle, when I was living in Ghana, for the first year I had my fist balled up for nothing, it was like tilting at windmills. I was absolutely so highly sensitive as to be paranoid. Any time anything happened I would say, "Oh yes, I see. I understand why you are saying this; you are saying it because I am black."

Well, of course, everybody around me was black, so for the first time in my life, my defenses not only did not work, they were not necessary, not those particular ones.

Then I began to examine my people and I thought, my God! How did we survive this! Good Lord! It's like growing up with a terrible sound in your ears day and night. Terrible, a kind of sound that is unrelenting, that pulls your hairs up on your body. And then to be away from it. At first you miss it, naturally, but then you get used to the peace, the quietude, the lack of pressure, then you begin to think, my God, how have my people survived that crap and still to survive it with some style, some passion, some humor; so living in Africa made me even more respectful of black Americans.

I suppose too my family directly and my people indirectly have given me the kind of strength that enables me to go anywhere. I can't think where I would be afraid, apprehensive, about going in the world, on this planet. I have had some very rough times in my life . . . so what else is new?

From *The Black Scholar*, Vol. 8, No. 4, January–February 1977.

Troubled on Every Side

John E. Jacob

In spite of much violent opposition, progress in the exercise of the right to vote was made. By 1962, aided by a reapportionment of voting districts ordered by the Supreme Court, black voters in Georgia elected Leroy Johnson to the state senate, the first such victory in more than 50 years. By 1965 there were 5 black representatives in Congress; by 1984, there were 22. As the sixties ended, other Blacks were serving in elective and appointive posts in counties, cities, states, around the country, helped mightily by the passage of the 1965 Voting Rights Act.

Early in the 1970's Georgia had 13 Black state representatives, and several other states North and South could count as many. As the black population continued to shift from the South to the North and West, and from the farms and small towns to the big cities, black mayors became no longer a rarity. In 1970 there were 50 of them; in 1984 there were more than 200, and scores of them were women. Los Angeles, Chicago, Philadelphia, Cleveland, Atlanta, Detroit, Washington, Newark, Gary, chose Blacks to hold their highest offices and reelected many of them.

Nevertheless, the 1980's appeared to many social observers to be a decade of retreat. The gains made in the sixties and seventies were being eroded. The dream of black equality was giving way to the intense pressure simply to survive. What facts documented this picture of black people in trouble? And what could be done about it? John E. Jacob, President of the National Urban League, sketched how America looked from the point of view of the Black and the poor in a speech made in New Orleans on July 31, 1983.

BLACK PEOPLE are in trouble today.

America is in trouble today.

Look at what has happened in America in the past three years: Five million more people are poor. A third of all blacks are poor. Half of all black children are growing up in poverty. The black infant mortality rate in the United States is worse than the national rate of Bulgaria—that's right, Bulgaria!

This is an America in which a black child born today has a fifty percent chance of growing up underprivileged, undereducated, and underemployed.

We read about an economic recovery in the newspapers. Where is it? It's the best-kept secret in history for black people.

In this so-called economic recovery the official black unemployment rate is frozen at more than twenty percent. A third of blacks who want work can't find it. Two out of three black teenagers who want to work are unemployed.

Hunger and want stalk this land. Hundreds of thousands of homeless people search for shelter and for a scrap of food. Here in New Orleans the number of people in need of emergency food aid doubled last year. In Detroit, 50,000 people a month exist on surplus cheese handouts.

A lot of very nice people are upset about famine in Ethiopia, about refugees in Afghanistan, about suppression of workers in Poland. They're worried about the arms race. They're concerned about war in El Salvador.

But where is the concern about suffering right here in the U.S.A.? What about the millions of Americans, black and white, who go to bed hungry and thank the Lord for having a roof over their heads, knowing full well how many don't even have that.

Where is the concern for the millions of poor children, who face a bleak future, condemned to lives of desperation?

Where is the concern about the dangerous drift toward a divided nation, one part largely white and employed, the other largely minority and poor?

We ask these questions to wake the sleeping conscience of a nation that was once proud of its commitment to equality and to racial progresss. And we ask these questions because the future of black Americans is at stake.

Black people are being driven to the margins of our economy by their worst depression in fifty years. They are being driven to the margins of despair by the most hostile administration in fifty years.

Black people looked to Washington for fair play and for protection of our civil rights. Instead, we got Pac-Man social policies and cave man civil rights policies.

As black people view this Administration, we are reminded of the grim words of Isaiah:

"None calleth for justice, nor any pleadeth for truth; they trust in vanity and speak lies; they conceive mischief and bring forth iniquity."

This Administration knows it is feared and mistrusted by the overwhelming majority of black Americans. It knows it has alienated black and brown people. But it claims they've got it all wrong. The administration says it just has a "perception" problem.

But the perceptions of black and poor people conform to reality. When people lose their jobs—that's reality. When hungry people lose food stamps and poor children lose school lunches—that's reality. When the Administration tries to override the Constitution and the will of Congress to give tax exemptions to segregated private schools—that's reality.

This Administration demonstrates a startling ability to refuse to admit facts. It's a fact that its policies have widened racial and class divisions in our torn society. It's a fact that it has slashed the safety net and violated the unwritten social contract that mandates decency and fairness. It's a fact that those policies have dealt permanent blows to black and poor people.

The legacy of this Administration's policies is a bitter one: closed day care centers, less help for pregnant women and their infants, fewer legal and health services for the poor. The only thing we have more of is poverty, unemployment, and hopelessness. . . .

I want to talk a little about affirmative action. It is an issue of primary importance. Too many people, including many of our friends, have been brainwashed into thinking it amounts to harmful reverse discrimination. Too many agree with the Administration when it says it wants color-blind policies that are racially neutral.

Well, black people too, want a society that is color-blind and racially neutral. Our four hundred year history of protest and struggle has tried to move society to treat the races equally. If there were parity in the distribution of society's rewards and responsibilities there would be no need for affirmative action; for numerical goals, for compliance timetables.

But there is no parity. We have a racial spoils system, but it is a spoils system that favors white males and excludes blacks, other minorities and women. We face not only the results of historic discrimination, but the effects of persistent present discrimination. That discrimination exists despite the laws forbidding it—laws the Justice Department is not enforcing.

We are a nation still gripped by racial and group prejudices. It is a fantasy to suppose we can act as if race were not a factor. The only way we can create a truly color-blind society in the long run is by positive, race-conscious affirmative action policies in the short run.

Affirmative action is not a preference system or a reparations system. It is a sensible tool to bring into the mainstream groups that have always been excluded from it and who are today relegated to the margins of our society. As Justice Blackmun wrote in the *Bakke* decision: "In order to get beyond racism, we must first take account of race. There is no other way."

Affirmative action programs go beyond racism to create opportunities for those who would otherwise be denied them. Companies with affirmative action programs hire far more blacks and women and have far more black and women managers than other companies. . . .

Black politics in 1983 is a politics of frustration.

But frustration can be a positive tool. Anger can be liberating. Black people know that if we just sit on the sidelines we'll get nowhere. We know we have to have political clout if we want economic empowerment. And we have that clout if we mobilize the black vote. . . . There are 17 million blacks of voting age: but only ten million are registered and only seven million vote.

Massive black voter registration can make both parties more responsive to our needs. And coalitions of blacks, Hispanics and poor whites, who share our suffering, can move America toward justice and fairness. . . . We do have power—the power of the ballot. But it is up to us to use it. It's up to us to accept our responsibilities and get out the black vote. . . .

There is another dimension to the realities of decision-making. And it is a dimension that transcends the purely political. . . . Our economy has been undergoing vast structural changes. The Steel Belt has become the Rust Belt. The Cotton Belt has become the Growth Belt. There's a massive shift of jobs and more important, a massive shift in the kind of jobs our economy creates.

We are entering a High Tech era. The good news is that entire new industries are emerging: industries that will create new opportunities for people with skills in computers, advanced electronics, and financial services. The bad news is that there won't be very many of those jobs. Most of the new jobs will be in low-paying service areas. The middle is dropping out. Well-paid, unionized manufacturing jobs are shrinking. The labor market is polarizing. There will be a few good jobs at the top, many bad jobs at the bottom, and fewer decent jobs in the middle. . . .

What happens to displaced workers and to new entrants in the labor force? Service jobs are growing, but most are menial, dead-end, minimum wage and part-time. There will be jobs processing information and manufacturing High Tech products. But those are low skill, low pay jobs that are moving offshore fast. . . .

So High Tech is no salvation for blacks. And it is no salvation for whites, either. If America loses its industrial base, many of those High Tech, information jobs must ultimately go down the drain. Our economy is based on mass consumerism; on the premise that most people work, earn and spend. But if they are not working or if they aren't earning enough, who will buy those goods? Robots don't buy autos. And the producers of imported goods spend their money at home, not in the U.S.A.

Sooner or later, America must develop policies for a new era. Black people have to be at the table when those policies are negotiated. We have to insist on a balanced economy, with opportunities for all. We have to insist on black parity in employment—with our fair share of the good jobs as well as the bad ones. And we have to insist on policies that ensure that every American who wants to work has a decent job at a liveable wage.

We need to build coalitions around those policies. We need to work with other minorities, with women's groups, and with labor. We need to build coalitions with government and with business to ensure that the needs of the American people are met in the future economy. We need to build coalitions to ensure that the choices America makes are democratically arrived at and the benefits of technology democratically distributed.

And one place to begin building those coalitions is around the issue of public education. High Tech means high skills and higher educational levels. Even service jobs will demand basic skills levels, and some will demand computer literacy. Black economic survival is directly linked to quality education.

Even small amounts of federal aid to poverty area schools have raised achievement levels among inner city youngsters. More resources are needed to attract better teachers and to provide more specialized and personalized help for schoolchildren. More resources are needed so poverty area schools have the computer terminals the rich schools are getting. We want our kids to help run the computerized society of the future, not to sweep up after it.

The schools need better human resources too—teachers and administrators capable of teaching our children, who believe they can learn, and who insist that they learn. We must demand that the highest standards apply to our children's schools—not only to the children themselves, but also to the teachers and managers responsible for their education.

There is no short-cut to improving our schools. The black community itself must take the lead in insisting on quality education. It is self-destructive to get hung up on wanting jive courses, lower standards, and no tests. Our children have to function in a fast-changing society. They have enough cards stacked against them without further handicapping them.

I'm talking about responsibility—accepting responsibility for our own fate. We have to make demands on a society that wants to ignore us and our needs. We have to keep up the pressure to get the resources and the programs we need. But at the same time we have to do on our own what we can do on our own. . . .

We call on America to sow the seeds of social justice and racial equality that it may reap a harvest of righteousness and freedom for all.

We call on Americans to work together to cast out racism and injustice and to raise up fairness and equality; to root out the effects of discrimination and nurture the blessings of justice.

We call on this nation that has prospered with the blood and sweat of its black people to share the bounties of this land we worked so hard for; to act right and do right to all of its children.

From a speech by John E. Jacob, President, National Urban League, New Orleans, July 31, 1983.

Notes
Acknowledgments
Index

A Note on Sources

For readers who want to look further into documents of Black American history and culture, there are many useful collections. The unearthing of primary sources began late—one mark of the oppression of Blacks in a racist society. But now that neglect is being remedied steadily as the records of black life are recovered, published, and interpreted.

Perhaps the most helpful single source to start with is *Blacks in America: Bibliographic Essays*, by James M. McPherson and others, Doubleday, 1971. This book is a superb guide for anyone doing research in black history, for it provides annotated references to the best and most useful literature. (As an example, for documentary collections see the dozens of volumes listed on pages 12–17.)

Some collections concentrate on a particular period, place, theme, or form of expression. For the decade after the Civil War, for instance, see Dorothy Sterling's *The Trouble They Seen: Black People Tell the Story of Reconstruction*, Doubleday, 1976. There are several anthologies on black women, among them *We Are Your Sisters: Black Women in the Nineteenth Century*, edited by Dorothy Sterling, Norton, 1984; *Black Women in Nineteenth Century American Life: Their Words, Their Thoughts, Their Feelings*, edited by Bert J. Loewenberg and Ruth Bogins, Pennsylvania State University, 1976; and Gerda Lerner's *Black Women in White America: A Documentary History*, Pantheon, 1972.

You can find anthologies of speeches, of letters, of religious literature, of poems, of spirituals, of slave autobiographies. During the 1930's members of the WPA Federal Writers Project collected some 2,300 interviews with ex-slaves in seventeen states. Most of the Blacks were eighty or older, and the slave experience they talked about was mainly that of childhood. Selections from this material were published by Benjamin Botkin in *Lay My Burden Down*, University of Chicago, 1945, and all of it by George P. Rawick in his multivolume *The American Slave: A Composite Autobiography*, Greenwood, 1970.

Former slaves such as Frederick Douglass, Solomon Northup, Harriet Brent Jacobs, William Wells Brown wrote their autobiographies, and in more recent times many political and cultural leaders such as W. E. B. DuBois, Mary Church Terrell, James Weldon Johnson, Malcolm X, Langston Hughes, Zora Neale Hurston have left us their life stories.

Taking the tape recorder into the field, oral historians are collecting the voice of contemporary Black Americans. One of the first to do it was Robert Penn Warren, in *Who Speaks for the Negro?*, Random House, 1966. Warren interviewed on tape many Blacks who were helping to make the civil rights revolution. Examples of more recent work of this kind include *All God's Dangers: The Life of Nate Shaw*, edited by Theodore Rosengarten, Alfred E. Knopf, 1974, and *When I Was Comin' Up: An Oral History of Aged Blacks*, by Audrey Faulkner and others, Archon, 1983.

Acknowledgments

Grateful acknowledgment is made for permission to reprint the material on the following pages: pages 28–36, originally published in *The Negro in Virginia*, copyright 1940 by The Hampton Institute; pages 87–89 and 108–9, first appeared in *Lay My Burden Down*, edited by Benjamin A. Botkin, copyright 1945 by the University of Chicago Press; pages 142–43, from *The Story of John Hope* by Ridgely Torrence, copyright 1948 by Ridgely Torrence, used by permission of The Macmillan Company; pages 161–67, excerpt from "Central High" from *The Big Sea* by Langston Hughes, copyright 1940 by Langston Hughes. Copyright renewed © 1968 by Arna Bontemps and George Houston Bass. Reprinted by permission of Hill and Wang (now a division of Farrar, Straus and Giroux, Inc.); pages 169–71, letters used by permission of the *Journal of Negro History*; pages 172–78, from *Uncle Tom's Children* by Richard Wright, copyright 1937 by Richard Wright, renewed 1965 by Ellen Wright, used by permission of Harper & Row, Publishers, Inc.; pages 179–85, from *12 Million Black Voices* by Richard Wright, copyright 1941 by Richard Wright, used by permission of Paul R. Reynolds, Inc.; pages 186–88, 195–98, excerpts from *The Crisis* used by permission of the National Association for the Advancement of Colored People; pages 203–9, excerpt from "Harlem Reconsidered" originally appeared in *Freedomways*, used by permission of Loften Mitchell; pages 211–15, excerpt from *Opportunity* used by permission of the National Urban League, Inc.; pages 222–29, from *The Shadow of the Plantation* by Charles S. Johnson, copyright 1934 by The University of Chicago Press; pages 232–37, copyright © 1940–1941, Harrison-Blaine of New Jersey, Inc., used by permission of the *New Republic*; pages 237–40, used by permission of *Freedomways*; pages 246–52, from *Stride Toward Freedom* by Martin Luther King, Jr., copyright © 1958 by

Martin Luther King, Jr., used by permission of Harper & Row, Publishers, Inc.; pages 255–57, used by permission of Howard Zinn; pages 266–69, from *Selma, Lord, Selma: Girlhood Memories of the Civil Rights Days*, as told to Frank Sikora by Sheyann Webb and Rachel West Nelson, copyright © 1980 The University of Alabama Press, used by permission; pages 271–75, from *All God's Dangers: The Life of Nate Shaw* by Theodore Rosengarten, copyright © 1974 by Theodore Rosengarten, used by permission of Alfred A. Knopf, Inc.; pages 276–83, used by permission of *The Black Scholar*; pages 285–91, used by permission of the National Urban League, Inc.

Thanks are due the following for permission to reproduce the illustrations on the pages indicated (all other illustrations are in the editor's collection): Picture Collection of the New York Public Library, pages 3, 11, 107; The Bettman Archive, page 27; Culver Pictures, Inc., pages 90, 103, 114, 125, 135, 144; The Schomberg Center for Research in Black Culture, pages 98, 154, 172, 179, 189, 199, 203, 210, 221, 230, 240, 253, 257; the National Urban League, Inc., page 284; Langston Hughes, 160.

Index